THE CROSS AND THE CRESCENT

Understanding the Muslim Heart & Mind

Phil Parshall

Gabriel
Publishing

PO Box 1047
129 Mobilization Dr.
Waynesboro, GA 30830, U.S.A.
Tel.: (706) 554-1594
E-mail: gabriel@omlit.om.org

Other books by Phil Parshall:
The Fortress and the Fire
New Paths in Muslim Evangelism
Bridges to Islam
Beyond the Mosque
Inside the Community
The Last Great Frontier
Divine Threads Within a Human Tapestry

Copyright 2002 by Phil Parshall
Fifth printing.

ISBN: 1-884543-68-5

Scripture quotations are from the *New American Standard Bible*. Copyright 1960, 1962, 1971, 1973, The Lockman Foundation.

Quaranic quotations are from *The Meaning of the Glorious Koran*, translated by Mohammed Marmaduke Pickthall (New York: New American Library, 1953).

Cover design: Paul Lewis

In appreciation to those who have been my spiritual guides

Lee Robertson
Chancellor, Tennessee Temple University, a man of God who modeled Christ before me in my early years as a believer

George Verwer
Founder-director, Operation Mobilization, a revolutionary for Christ and close friend

Calvin Olson
A godly missionary who incarnates intimacy with Christ

Art and Ruth Payne, Jim and Jean Root
Special friends who have endured adversity with exemplary grace and dignity

International Christian Fellowship
Now merged with SIM International, my tolerant and ever forgiving mission

Highland Park Baptist Church, Southfield, Michigan
My home church, which has given me twenty-seven years of love and faithful support

Julie
One who has consistently lived the Christian life before me, my best friend, my wife

Contents

THE CROSS AND THE CRESCENT

Foreword

Is this fascinating book designed to help us understand Islam in the light of Christian thinking or to understand our own faith at a deeper level against the backdrop of Muslim thinking? Or is it designed to lift me personally out of misperceptions and complacency?

Perhaps it is not aimed at enlightenment at all, but feeling – feeling my own insensitivities and hypocrisies, feeling the heartbeat of people controlled by the Quranic view of life. Or experience – perhaps the author wants me to be a more authentic follower of Christ.

If any of these is the purpose of the book, it was achieved in me. You will find here a kaleidoscope of Christian and Muslim thinking compared and contrasted – not exhaustive, but extraordinarily diverse. Though factually accurate, it is far from being a theological treatise or a study in comparative religions. Through scores of autobiographical vignettes the author draws us into feeling with him the glory and pathos of both authentic and hypocritical Islam and authentic and hypocritical Christianity, portrayed in the experiences of living examples.

But enough of describing what the book is like – plunge in and open up for an exciting mental, emotional, and spiritual experience.

Robertson McQuilkin,
Former President
Columbia International University

Acknowledgments

In seeking to explore the subject of spirituality, I have relied on research, observation, and experience. Research is the most straightforward. Quotes from books and articles require only time, a discerning eye, and a photocopier. However, I sought to move into new areas through the distribution of a specially prepared questionnaire (see Appendix). 390 evangelical missionaries ministering in 32 countries with 37 mission societies returned the completed form. I am particularly grateful to those respondents who took time from busy schedules to fill in a questionnaire that was both personal and probing. Also helpful was studying the results of a congregational survey conducted by Elmbrook Church, pastored by Stuart Briscoe. The survey was taken following a Sunday morning church service where 2,972 parishioners participated. Both of these computer-compiled reports are cited in appropriate contexts throughout this book.

Is it possible to evaluate spirituality by observing? This is not an easy question to answer, particularly because of the abstract and subjective nature of spirituality. But throughout this book I will refer to that which I have seen. It will be the task of the discerning reader to pass judgment on these observations. A word of caution needs to be said in regard to the confining influence of our rigid presuppositions. The more neutral we can be in approaching new data, the greater the potential for an expanding and enlightening learning encounter.

Lastly, I have made many references to actual spiritual experiences. Without this personal dimension, we would be left aloft in an ethereal world of theory and conjecture. Spirituality must be applied to be genuine.

It would be impossible to cite all of the positive spiritual contributions that various people have made to my life. In a representative manner, I have dedicated this book to eight individuals and two institutions that mean more to me than I can possibly express. My special thanks to Robertson McQuilkin for graciously sharing his thoughts in the foreword. At certain places in the book I have used pseudonyms in order to protect the identity of individuals living in sensitive situations.

Stephen Lang, book editor at Tyndale House Publishers, has graciously and perceptively interacted with me. I am grateful for his editorial insights.

Introduction

An instrument of punishment and torture, the cross has, because of its association with the sacrificial love of Jesus, come to be a symbol of ultimate love. Christians also regard it as an emblem not of tragedy, but of triumph. For on the cross Jesus Christ brought holy God and sinful man together. No wonder the cross has become the symbol of Christian spirituality.

At certain times of the month the moon appears as an arc of light defying the darkness of the cosmos. Such a sliver of reflected glory is commonly referred to by Muslims as the "crescent" of Islam. As the moon gives witness to the sun, so Islam bears testimony to the radiance and glory of the sovereign Allah. As the Christians revere the cross – or, better, what it symbolizes – so Muslims revere the image of the crescent. Both symbols speak of the relation of the one God to human beings.

Christianity and Islam are similar in many ways. The unity of God is a foundational truth discernible within both. Allah, like the Christian God, is a deity of mercy, truth, and judgment. The ninety-nine names ascribed to Allah are, for the most part, in harmony with the biblical description of God. In Islam, Jesus is described as virgin-born and a performer of miracles. He is alive in heaven today and will return to earth in the end times. Muslim ethics, with few exceptions, parallel those of Christianity. The ethical distinctives of Islam that are in conflict with the New Testament are generally in harmony with those of the Old Testament.

Yet much separates the world's two largest monotheistic religions. Sin, to Muslims, is a choice, not an inheritance, whereas in Christianity it is both. For Muslims, God is a force, not a friend. The Quran, not the Bible, is the in errant, syllable-by-syllable, dictated word of Allah. Jesus Christ was not crucified. And most importantly, Christ is neither Savior nor Son of God. With such obvious divergence, how is it possible to use the word *spirituality* to describe the central dynamic within the two religions? Is it even possible to think of Islam in terms of spirituality? Would Muslims be agreeable to such a designation for describing their allegiance to God?

Technically the word *spirituality* is inadequate when applied to Islam. There is not an equivalent word for spirituality in the Arabic language. Muslims focus more on *submission* than spirituality. Submitting to the revealed word of Allah is, to the Muslim, a more concrete and objective task than interaction with a more subjective "spirit force." The word spirit is largely ignored in the Quran. Having made this distinction, I am still proceeding to use the concept of spirituality in a general sense to describe the quest for God as experienced by followers of Islam and Christianity.

I am encouraged and reinforced in my decision to write in these terms by the publication of the 1987 book titled *Islamic Spirituality: Foundations,* a compilation of articles by leading Muslim academicians. The editors felt free to use *spirituality* as a descriptive term for *godliness* within Islam.

A desire for God, however, is far from the end of the story. Many questions remain. What are the motivations behind one's spiritual quest? Are the sacred writings upon which the experience is based reliable and authoritative? What are the practices and behavioral norms of such a spiritual encounter? How does one view people of other religious persuasions? This book is an attempt to deal with these questions and to compare spiritual perceptions and realities within Islam and Christianity.

Not too many years ago this book would have been of interest only for missionaries or students of comparative religions. Few people in the U.S. or in Western Europe knew any Muslims personally. But the situation has changed radically. Immigration has brought many Muslims to Europe and North America. Mosques have appeared in many cities in the U.S., and Muslims have applied for chaplaincy positions in the U.S. military. For the first time in history, Americans must deal with the presence of Islam, which, like Christianity, is a missionary faith. To deal with this presence we must understand Islam.

Comparing and contrasting Christianity and Islam is not easy. Understandably, some readers will feel I have been soft on Islam. My attempts to be fair may well be misunderstood by some evangelicals. Yet I must take the risk of erring on the side of love rather than contribute to a type of medieval crusader mentality that only serves to alienate the very people we are seeking to win to Christ. I do this without in any way straying from my firm belief in the uniqueness of salvation as found only through the merit and blood sacrifice of Christ. Likewise, I affirm my conviction that Muslims are spiritually lost unless they place their faith in Jesus Christ. This conviction is my whole motivation as I serve my risen Lord among Muslim people.

Expressions of belief and practice vary immensely within Christendom. Even by limiting my observations to evangelical Christians, I am still confronted with a bewildering array of distinctives. The reader should bear this in mind. Islam, too, ranges from the strict orthodoxy of Saudi Arabia to the free-wheeling mystic Sufi orders of Pakistan, India, and Bangladesh. The common perception of Islam as monolithic is more a myth than a reality. Throughout this book I will be describing both traditional and nontraditional facets of Islam. And I will be looking at both Christianity and Islam as they are actually practiced, not as ideals on paper.

The Christian and Spirituality

The *Evangelical Dictionary of Theology* describes spirituality as "the state of a deep relationship to God" (Houston 1984, 1046). This "deep relationship" can be facilitated by a quiet time of isolated, reflective meditation or by an emotional hand-clapping, foot-stomping act of community worship. Personal and temperamental preferences account for a great deal of this variety in expression.

The world today seems uncomfortable with spiritual realities. Modern man is bombarded constantly with materialistic, narcissistic values. Political and technological advances are presented as the saviors of society. Alexander Solzhenitsyn's famous 1978 commencement address at Harvard University decried such a secular orientation to life.

> *We have placed too much hope in politics and social reforms, only to find out that we were being deprived of our most precious possession: our spiritual life. It is trampled by the party mob in the East, by the commercial one in the West. . . . No one on earth has any other way left but upward. (Solzhenitsyn 1978, 59, 61)*

Alexander Solzhenitsyn was analyzing and pleading on the macro level. Societal reform was his primary concern. But actually, reform commences on the micro plane of life – that is, with the individual. Spiritual attainment involves personal conflict, struggle, pain, and even failure.

In my early days as a Christian, I became deeply discouraged about my inability to break free from a sin-confession-forgiveness-sin cycle of behavior. Where, I wondered, was the reality of Romans 8 to be found? I only knew the defeat of a Romans 7 experience of frequently doing that which was spiritually debilitating. During this time I came into contact with the "deeper life" movement. Its teaching concerning the wretchedness of self and the total adequacy of Christ sent a piercing ray of hope into my battle-fatigued soul. Quickly I stretched forth my open hands of supplication. How I hungered for a higher level of consistent spiritual experience. In a dramatic manner, I was filled to overflowing. For three months my wearied heart found rest. What a blissful and enriching experience it was.

Prayer was as real as conversing with my best friend. The Bible came alive with pulsating vitality. Witnessing was a joy.

But slowly the emotions ebbed. Evil thoughts once more began their assault. A chill wind began to blow across my innermost being. Inwardly I cringed. It seemed I had stepped on an express elevator that moved rapidly and relentlessly between the roof of victory and the basement of defeat. Why was there not a gradual climb to spiritual victory? What did Scripture mean when it spoke of a Christian life that is always triumphant? How does one appropriate the abundant life of John 10:10? Are the gushing springs from within bringing forth cool, fresh, cleansing water, or is the flow often adulterated and polluted?

Is spiritual victory only an elusive phantom, much like the phenomenon I observed while on an overnight safari in Kenya? In the dust and heat of our van, how refreshing it was to look off in the distance across the miles of bushland and fix my eyes on a beautiful lake. The sun's rays danced across the tranquil surface of this great body of water. Soon it became obvious we had only seen a mirage. Is spiritual victory no more than a desert illusion?

Christians, like people of all religions, have difficulty viewing themselves objectively. Non-Christian critiques of our words and behavior are often helpful. I am an admirer of Mohandas K. Gandhi, of whom I have read ten biographies. I sat through the film *Gandhi* four times. Without a doubt, this man of little stature was mighty in spirit. In his autobiography, Gandhi recalls an encounter he had with an evangelical whose argument for the Christian faith was framed in these words:

You cannot understand the beauty of our religion. From what you say it appears that you must be brooding over your transgressions every moment of your life, always mending them and atoning for them. How can this ceaseless cycle of action bring you redemption? You can never have peace. You admit that we are all sinners. Now look at the perfection of our belief. Our attempts at improvement and atonement are futile. And yet redemption we must have. How can we bear the burden of sin? We can but throw it on Jesus. He is the only sinless Son of God. It is His word that those who believe in Him shall have everlasting life. Therein lies God's infinite mercy. And as we believe in the atonement of Jesus, our own sins do not bind us. Sin we must. It is impossible to live in this world sinless. (Gandhi 1957,124)

Has this been a fair presentation of God's plan of salvation? Consider Gandhi's reply:

The argument utterly failed to convince me. I humbly replied: "If this be the Christianity acknowledged by all Christians, I cannot accept it. I do not seek redemption from the consequences of my sin. I seek to be redeemed from sin itself, or rather from the very thought of sin. Until I have attained that end, I shall be content to be restless. To which the brother rejoined: "I assure you, your attempt is fruitless. Think again over what I have said." And the brother proved as good as his word. He knowingly committed transgressions, and showed me that he was undisturbed by the thought of them. (Gandhi 1957, 124-125)

I am not sure Gandhi was fair in his evaluation of the Christian's response to evil. But the important point is to consider how Gandhi, as a Hindu, was protesting the continuing bondage to sin. He wanted not only freedom from evil but also deliverance from even the thought of sin. A lofty goal indeed!

The Muslim and Spirituality

Seyyed Hossein Nasr is an Iranian Muslim with academic credentials that qualify him to lecture at Harvard University. Nasr is orthodox in his belief but at the same time has a more mystical emphasis in his writings. His insight into the very ethos of Islam is perceptive.

Islam, in fact, being the religion of Unity has never distinguished between the spiritual and temporal or religious and profane in any domain. The very fact that there is not even a suitable word in Arabic, Persian or other Islamic languages for temporal or secular is the best indication that the corresponding concepts have not existed in Islam. Such a division does not exist because the kingdom of Caesar was never given unto Caesar in Islam. Being based on Unity, Islam has envisaged a total way of life which excludes nothing. (Nasr 1966,30)

The "total way of life" is strongly emphasized in Islam. The Muslim worldview is integrated and cohesive. Segmentation of life into categories is resisted. One's activities are to be governed by the realization that Allah is involved in every aspect of being and doing. Nothing is external to the concern of God. Constant repetition of the word *Allah* by Muslims is a personal reinforcement and affirmation of the theocratic rule of God, both in one's life and in society in general.

A friend of mine who is a missionary among Muslims recently made this statement:

An orthodox Muslim who is unaffected by Sufi mysticism or other Islamic aberrations will be rigid, intolerant, unloving, and basically in a posture of jihad [holy war] against those outside the household of Islam. This behavior will be the natural result of following the teaching of the Quran and the example of Prophet Muhammad. Such attitudes and actions are endorsed by the Muslim community. True Islam is more accurately represented by the revolutionary guards of Iran than by the Muslim mystics of the Indian subcontinent. In contrast, the true follower of Jesus Christ will be loving, humble, patient, and gracious to others, even to those outside the Christian faith.

If this mind-stretching observation is true, it is a powerful condemnation of the millions of Muslims who are dedicated to the task of following each "jot and tittle" of Islam. If it is false, we can declare Khomeini and Muslims of his type to be Islamic heretics. In the chapters that follow, I trust the reader can grapple more deeply with the vital question of the meaning and multifaceted nature of Muslim spirituality.

Confusion or Conclusion?

So much is unclear about Christian spirituality. I can illustrate this with the story of the man who was instrumental in my turning to Christ.

One Thursday evening in March 1955, I drove up to a businessman's home in the suburbs of Miami, Florida. I was there in response to a high school classmate's invitation. After playing basketball and eating hot dogs in the backyard, I was preparing to leave when the teenagers began pushing their way toward the living room of the lovely home. I joined the crowd, thinking there would be a time of dancing and flirting with the girls. To my great surprise, all of the teenagers began to sing spirited gospel songs. They then began to give sincere testimony to the reality of Jesus Christ in their lives. This was a totally new experience to me. I only knew Christ as a curse word, not as a Savior.

Ray, the businessman, then stood and gave a simple exposition of God's wonderful provision for sinful mankind. The message of John 3 and Ephesians 2 drove deeply into my raw, heathen heart. That evening I walked out of Ray's home as a new creature in Christ. My life had made a dramatic turn toward God.

Ray soon left the business world and was ordained. He became a pastor and then the founder-president of Florida Bible College, which soon became the Bible college with the largest enrollment in North America. Ray's church supported Julie and me as we went to East Pakistan (now Bangladesh) in

1962. During our first furlough Ray, along with the deacons of his church, laid hands on me in a moving service of ordination.

A few years later, one terribly bleak day in Bangladesh, I received a letter chronicling the downfall of my spiritual father. Ray, the letter said, had been committing adultery with his secretary for many years. All of this time he had been an effective personal soul-winner. Ray's wife and three lovely grown children had all been at his side in the ministry. And then suddenly came the revelation of deceit and hypocrisy. Ray subsequently divorced his wife, walked away from his ministry, and married a girl thirty years his junior.

My wife grew up in a stable Christian home in rural Ohio. Her pastor was a dynamic, personable man of God. Through his influence, Julie went to Tennessee Temple University, where we met. It was our mutual desire for Jim to perform our wedding in 1961. Following this, we sought to keep in contact with him.

On our first furlough we visited Jim and his family. He was then associate pastor of a large church. One evening Jim and his wife took us to the home of a church family for a backyard barbecue. During the time of fellowship I had an uncomfortable feeling about Jim and the hostess of the home we were visiting.

Another terribly bleak day in Bangladesh, Julie and I received a letter telling of Jim's spiritual defeat. As suspected, it was the young, beautiful mother of several children whom we had visited who was the object of Jim's affection. The church became suspicious and had hired a detective to confirm their doubts. Upon confrontation, Jim admitted the affair, left the church, divorced his wife, and later married another woman. Today he is far from God. He has abandoned the ministry and the faith.

I have described an important component of the spiritual

heritage of Julie and myself. The very men God used to lead us in paths of righteousness were themselves used as instruments of Satan to break up homes and bring terrible disrepute to the church of Jesus Christ.

It is obvious that the subject of spirituality is extremely complex. Are climactic sanctification experiences legitimate? Can they be sustained? How are we to deal with the emotional highs and lows of our Christian lives? Can the dry periods of life be times of spiritual growth? Do we take our stand with Gandhi and insist on a release, not only from the bondage of sin, but even from the thought of sin? Then what do we say about the fall of the spiritual giants? If our spiritual guides fall into the grossest sins, what chance is there for the rest of us?

And what about Islam? Can Muslim spirituality be defined and evaluated? Are orthodox sons of Ishmael crude, unloving, and violent? What about Sufi influence in Islam? Are Muslim mystics a counterpart to the more mystical type of Christian? How do we explain a Muslim who professes to have found a deep, abiding peace within his Islamic faith and then backs, up such a statement by a consistent pattern of exemplary behavior?

Are we destined to sink in a morass of confusion? Or can we carefully work our way toward conclusions that will somewhat satisfy us spiritually and intellectually? It is my hope that these chapters will indeed elucidate us and strengthen us in the Spirit. I have written quite personally and emotionally. Thus the book is, in a true sense, a "reflection" and not to be considered an academic treatise. In contrast to my earlier prescriptive missiological works, this book is more descriptive.

It is my earnest hope that this book will lead to a deeper

understanding between Muslims and Christians. Is it too much also to pray that these considerations will lead us as Christians to hunger more for holiness and, therefore, cause us to become more powerful witnesses to Muslims on behalf of Christ, who is the only Way, Truth, and Life?

THE CROSS AND THE CRESCENT

1

The Christian's God,
The Muslim's Allah

For both Islam and Christianity, belief in one God is foundational. This common focus of faith has been the subject of much debate. Almost all of the names of Allah as affirmed by Islam are in keeping with the attributes of the God of the Bible. Many scholars, stressing these similarities, propose an evangelistic cease-fire between the world's two largest propagating religions. Common ground, they say, should be emphasized. Both Jesus and Muhammad should be highly esteemed as bearers of light. They each should be recognized for their successful mission of pointing people toward the one and only true God.

Is this fair? I have asked many Muslim converts to Christianity this question: "When you became a Christian, did you, cognitively or emotionally, think of yourself as commencing worship of a different God from that whom you worshiped as a Muslim?" This question put to converts has, without exception, been answered with a strong no. H. B. Dehqani-Tafti, esteemed bishop of the Iranian Anglican

Church, has given his perspective as a Muslim convert on this vital issue.

> *Some people tend to think that Muslims have one God and Christians another. While I agree that the two concepts are very different indeed from each other, I cannot agree that they really worship two utterly different gods. At least, the way it happened with me was that my faith in a Christian God was related to my early childhood's faith in a Muslim God. When through the Book of Psalms and the Book of Job I learnt anew the meaning of trust in God, and came to worship Him at the foot of the Cross, the basis of it all was the same God my brother was trying to teach me about with the help of the simile of the big basket of light, and my father through the Muslim philosophical terms. I never had a sort of complete "brainwash," as it were, of my past faith in God; neither did I think it was necessary to do so. It was when I really put my trust in God that I started to stud and experience the different conceptions of Him in the two religions. I knew that a God whom I could define with human knowledge, reason and logic would not be enough. Nevertheless my spiritual pilgrimage in the faith in the Christian God was not absolutely disconnected with what was already in me. (Dehqani-Tafti 1959, 66-67)*

These Muslim converts are, in my view, not compromising their unique faith in the biblical God. From childhood they have been taught an ongoing continuity of God's being and acts as presented in the *Torah* (Law), *Zabur*

(Psalms), *Injil* (Gospel), and Quran. Conflict arises because Islamic theology teaches that Christians have perverted pure monotheism by elevating Jesus to a position of deity. Christians then respond by asserting that Islam has undercut God's central message of redemption by denying the saving work of Christ.

Without being dogmatic on the subject, I lean toward Dehqani-Tafti's position. Islam presents an inadequate and incomplete – but not totally misguided – view of God. It seems to be unfair to declare the God of Islam to be absolutely distinct from the God of the Bible. But more crucial is the clear biblical teaching that God is only to be known and experienced through his Son, Jesus Christ. Over this issue Islam and Christianity come into irreconcilable conflict.

Still, it is essential that Christians and Muslims attempt to understand each other at the deepest possible level. This takes us, as Christians, to the mosque, but also beyond the mosque. We are obligated to scrutinize the Muslim rituals of prayer, fasting, and pilgrimage. But we must probe deeper and enter into the *meaning* of each external observance. The Muslim constantly verbalizes the word *Allah*. What, if anything, is going on in the deeper level of the psyche as the precious name is articulated incessantly day and night? It is not particularly easy to identify an ethos for Islam and Christianity. But, after due reflection, I have chosen to highlight the concept of God-awareness in Islam. For Christianity, it seems that faith is the focal point in the religious outworking of belief and practice.

Islamic God-Awareness

"Your God is One God; there is no God save Him" (the Quran, Sura 2:163) combines with "Muhammad is the messenger of Allah" (Sura 48:29) to make the key confession (*Shahadah*) of Islam. These two quranic verses are probably repeated more often by more people than any other phrase in any language in the world. The confession is even found prominently displayed in the flag of Saudi Arabia. These words are sweeter than honey and more precious than gold to the average Muslim. They are his inner rest, harmony, and tranquility. The confession is his entree into the world's second-largest religious fraternity and also his passport into the eternal delights of paradise.

In chapter 7 I discuss the latter half of the *Shahadah*. Prophet Muhammad's exalted position in Islam is highlighted by his inclusion in this central confession of faith. His name is to be uttered repeatedly just after that of Allah. In this chapter, however, I want to focus on the Islamic conception of God.

Linguistically, Allah is a contraction of *al-ilah*. It is important to note that this Arabic word is not just ilah (a god) but *al-ilah* (the god). The exclusiveness of this term is foundational to Islamic theology. There never was, nor can there ever be, a god equal to Allah. Consider this description of Allah by Muslim author F. R. Ansari:

He is the Possessor of all the dimensions of Highest Excellence indeed, of Absolute Perfection. He is the Fountainhead of all Values and Ideals. He is the Omnipotent, the Omniscient, the Omnipresent, the

Infinite, the Absolute, the One and the Indivisible God, Who neither incarnates nor has any Partner or Son or Compeer. He is Transcendent in His Being and Immanent in the cosmos through His Love, Knowledge and Power. He is the Creator, the Sustainer, the Nourisher and the Evolver of everything that constitutes the cosmos. (Ansari 1944, 212-213)

Allah's Presence

The Quran declares God to be omnipresent. "Unto Allah belong the East and the West, and whithersoever ye turn, there is Allah's countenance. Lo! Allah is All-Embracing" (Sura 2:115). God is spoken of as being nearer to the believer than his jugular vein (Sura 50:16). This acknowledged presence of Allah in the life of a Muslim is a counterpart to the Christian being indwelt by the Holy Spirit. Orthodox Islam, however, seems more comfortable with the concept of Allah being *near* rather than having residence *within*. The mystical Muslim, as will be seen in chapter 6, tends to come closer to the Christian position of God (as the Spirit) indwelling the believer. But to all Muslims, accessibility to a very near God provides a reinforcing framework to their spiritual lives. As one author states, "The believer has to feel that he stands every moment in the presence of God, that he has to behave with awe and respect, and must never fall back into the 'sleep of heedlessness,' never forget the all-embracing divine presence" (Schimmel 1975, 29).

Shibi, the Baghdad mystic, meditates on God-awareness in his thoughtful poem.

Never are my limbs empty of you – they are occupied
*   with carrying my passion for you.*
God knows: Never runs over my tongue anything
but mention of you.
You assumed a form while you were in my eye –
*   whether you are present or absent, it sees you!*
*   (Gramlich 1979, 138)*

Shibi is having a vision of an actual form which depicts God. It could be asked if this is not borderline idolatry, particularly in view of Islam's insistence that God is totally spirit. But Shibi is reflecting on the mystical experience of the psyche encountering the incomprehensible Allah of the Quran. How can such a meeting ever be described within the inadequacies of human language? He is moved toward what some would call a pictorial theophany. Mystical Muslims are comfortable with such symbolism. The more orthodox ones react in protest.

Another Baghdad mystic of old puts forth a poem of powerful imagery.

I have diverted my heart from tile world and its
*   pleasures,*
You and my heart are nothing separate,
And never are my eyelids pressed together by
*   slumber*
But I find you between the eye and the lid.
*   (Schimmel 1982, 27)*

A person of no poetic inclination may find it difficult to imagine finding God pressed between one's eye and eyelid. To a mystic this is a deep expression of soul-language. How close and intimate Allah is to the seeker. Jalal al-Din Rumi is one of the greatest of all Muslim writers who sought to express the concept of the God who is forever near. These words were written around A.D. 1260:

When I start from the beginning, He is my leader;
  when I seek my heart, He is its ravisher.
When I strive for peace, He intercedes for me; when
  I go to war, He is my dagger.
When I come to the gathering, He is the wine and
  the sweetmeats; when I enter the garden, He is
  the narcissus.
When I go down to the mine, He is the ruby and
  carnelian; when I dive into the sea, He is the
  pearl.
When I cross the desert, He is the oasis; when I
  ascend the spheres, He is the star.
When I show my fortitude, He is my breast, when I
  burn from heartache, He is the censer.
When I enter battle at the time of war, He keeps the
  ranks and leads the army.
When I go to a banquet at the time of joy, He is the
  saki, minstrel, and cup.
When I write letters to my friends, He is paper, pen,
  and inkwell.
When I awaken, He is my new awareness; when I
  go to bed, He enters my dreams.
When I seek a rhyme for my poetry, He eases the
  way for my mind.
He stands above whatever form you can picture,
  like painter and pen.

No matter how much higher you look, He is still
higher than that "higher" of yours.
Go abandon speaking and books – much better it is
to let Him be your book.
Be silent! for all six directions are His Light; and
when you pass beyond the directions, He Himself
is the Ruler (Chittick 1983, 234)

Remembering God

The Quran has several explicit exhortations regarding the believer's duty to keep Allah within the higher level of consciousness. "Remember Allah, standing, sitting and reclining" (Sura 3:191) is one of these all-embracing commands. Another is, "Therefore remember Me, I will remember you" (Sura 2:152). One other citation is, "Think of Allah much, that ye may be successful" (Sura 8:45). (The latter verse sounds a bit like an exhortation from a positive-thinking manual.)

The most authoritative of the Traditions (Hadith) of Islam are those compiled in the *Sahih* of al-Bukhari (A.D. 810-870). It was his task to bring together the recollections of the words and deeds of the Prophet Muhammad. (Most of the Hadith citations in this book will be excerpted from Bukhari's English-Arabic nine-volume, 4,705-page diglot.) His collection contains comments on almost every conceivable subject.

In regard to the believer's duty to remember Allah, one such citation relates to the time when one partakes of food. "You should mention Allah's Name and eat" (Bukhari [Vol. 9], 366). The normal formula for the Muslim is, prior to eating, to say, *Bismillahr Rahmaner Rahim* ("In the Name of God the Merciful, the Compassionate"). The so-called

Bismillah along with *Al-Hamdu-li-llah* ("praise to God") are among the most common religious phrases of Islam.
The invocation of God's name extends even to the act of love-making. "If anyone of you, when intending to have a sexual relation (sleep) with his wife, says: 'In the Name of Allah. O Allah! Protect us from Satan and keep Satan away from what you will give us,' Satan would never harm that child, should it be ordained that they will have one" (Bukhari [Vol. 9], 365). This command highlights the outworking of the integrated worldview of Islam. The devout Muslim is happy to call upon God, even in the most intimate of human acts.

Lost in antiquity is the origin of the rosary. Current usage, however, is widespread among Roman Catholics and Muslims. Walking the streets of Manila are hundreds of Filipino Muslims quietly working thrice through a rosary of thirty-three beads. (Use of rosary beads among Muslims is known as *tasbih*.) Millions of Christians and Muslims will testify that their devotional life is enhanced by this act of mental concentration. The onlooker is struck by the apparent ease with which the devotee performs a mental ritual while at the same time carrying on a normal conversation. (It is interesting to note that many Arab Christians living among Muslims in the Middle East have also adopted the use of prayer beads. The difference is these Christians call them "worry beads" and use them as an outlet for their nervous energy!)

In the Hadith it is stated, "Allah has ninety-nine names, one-hundred less one; and he who memorized them all by heart will enter Paradise" (Bukhari [Vol. 9], 363). Folklore declares that the only one who knows the hundredth name of Allah is the camel, and thus he struts about in a most proud and domineering manner. Some mystics have also declared themselves as the sole possessors of the greatest and final name of Allah. To be privy to such a mystery of God almost assures one of a devoted following.

Annemarie Schimmel has commented on the categories of the ninety-nine names. "These are divided into *lutfiyya*, connected with God's beauty and lovingkindness, and *qahriyya*, connected with His wrath and majesty. These two categories constantly work together to produce the whole fabric of the world and are mysteriously connected with human beings" (Schimmel 1975, 177). In Islam and Christianity we see operating the dual forces of God's lovingkindness and wrath. Muslims would prefer the word *mercy* over Schimmel's *lovingkindness*.

Ayesha Bridget Honey, a British university student, tells of how the Muslim's constant remembrance of Allah was one of the things which led her to convert to Islam:

> *A Muslim takes the name of Allah whenever he does anything. And when he remembers Allah he examines his own self and in this he tries to reach a high standard. In this way the gulf between daily life of the world and the demands of religion is bridged and both sides become proportionate, evenly balanced and essential for each other. (Honey n.d., 30)*

To Ms. Honey and other Muslims, constant reference to Allah is reverent. The Jewish people, on the other hand, gave honor to God by regarding His Name as so holy that they refused to pronounce it. Christians are somewhere between these two extremes. (Naturally there are variations within Protestantism. Presbyterians, for example, tend to feel comfortable with using the word God, whereas Pentecostals focus on the name of Jesus.)

Dhikr, which means "recollection" or "remembering," is very important in the worship of Muslims. The name of Allah or, alternatively, a short religious phrase, is repeated with intense concentration. Usually *dhikr* is done communally in the mosque or at a special gathering. This type of repetition of God's attributes can cause the devotees to be swept away in a sea of emotion. The world is forgotten, the pains of the everyday world temporarily fade, and Allah becomes a pulsating, dynamic reality. Such an encounter with God can be emotional and overwhelming. Sufis of old were ordered to drink water after performing *dhikr* in order to cool down the internal heat that had been produced. Other stories of the effects of *dhikr* have found their way into Muslim folklore.

Sahl ibn Abdallah bade one of his disciples endeavor to say "Allah! Allah!" the whole day without intermission. When he had acquired the habit of doing so, Sahl instructed him to repeat the same words during the night, until they came forth from his lips even while he was asleep. "Now," said he, "be silent and occupy yourself with recollecting them." At last the disciple's whole being was absorbed by the thought of Allah. One day a log fell on his head, and the words "Allah, Allah" were seen written in the blood that trickled from the wound. (Nicholson 1975, 45-46)

Any ritual or habit can easily lose its force. Repetition tends to have an anesthetizing effect. The devout Muslim is very aware of this insidious danger to his spiritual life. My Muslim friends have assured me they seek to deeply concentrate on the name of Allah as they repeat it. I must express some reservation in this regard.

Most Muslims utter God's name continually. When they sit, they slowly utter, "Alllaahh." This is repeated when they rise. Interspersed in conversation, "Allah" forms a natural point of exclamation to anything of significance. *Al-Hamdu-Ii-Ilah* ("praise to God") is a joyful expression. *Inshallah* ("if it is the will of God") incorporates a tentative addition to any statement of future intent. (This is a bit unsettling when, on a Muslim-owned airline, the stewardess announces the flight's arrival time *inshallah*. At thirty thousand feet, a more positive affirmation would be appreciated!)

For Muslims, Allah unremembered is not God at all. Salvation as taught by Islam is not only just credal, it is also verbal. The question arises, Does all of this verge on the magical, the superstitious, the manipulative? Muslims respond, "We leave that analysis to the scholars." Meanwhile, "Allah, Allah, Allah, Allah, Allah . . ."

Christian Faith

In the New Testament, one theme presents itself with unrelenting repetitiveness. Faith was, is, and ever shall be the cornerstone of Christianity. Mary expressed it initially in her startling exchange with an angel when she replied with a firm voice, "Be it done to me according to your word."

John the Baptist follows with his cry, "Behold the Lamb of God." The disciples join the chorus by affirming, "Lord, we believe." Paul takes his place in Faith's Hall of Fame by an act of belief that instantaneously transforms him from a zealous persecutor to a zealous believer. Others have marched forth in the train of faith and "conquered kingdoms, performed acts of righteousness, obtained promises.... They have gained approval through their faith" (Heb. 11:33, 39). Then on the Judgment Day the obscurity of faith will unfold into a blazing ray of glorious light.

> *After these things I looked, and behold, a great multitude, which no one could count, from every nation and all tribes and peoples and tongues, standing before the throne and before the Lamb, clothed in white robes, and palm branches were in their hands; and they cry out with a loud voice, saying, "Salvation to our God who sits on the throne, and to the Lamb." (Rev. 7.9-10)*

Faith vindicated!

Doubt

One could wish life's progression was always as glorious as that which has just been described. Instead, there are the moments of deep despair when, like John the Baptist in the dark confines of the dungeon, we too cry out for a glance at Jesus' ID card. Like the early disciples, we also whisper, "We believe, but, Lord, help us in our unbelief." More than one Christian has entered the slough of doubt and questioned not only whether there are white robes and palm branches in their future but whether there is even such a thing as a literal heaven and hell.

I recall my encounter with a handsome, tall, reasonably articulate graduate of a Chinese university. His first proletarian assignment was to serve as a guide to American tourists visiting the Great Wall. Our tour group of ten evangelicals happened to be his initiatory run.

Our group leader had cautioned each of us to refrain from verbal witnessing while in China. I dutifully obliged until I struck up a friendship with this particular guide. On the bus journey back from the Wall to Peking I began to carefully probe into this young man's religious orientation. It was soon evident that he knew nothing about Christianity, had never met a Christian, and had not even seen a Bible in his lifetime. His presuppositions in life were totally materialistic. He was a product of an atheistic state that declared this life as an end in itself. At one point, I asked him what he thought of religion. His answer was as succinct as it was unforgettable. As the bus weaved its way through the roadside markets, this intelligent young man looked directly at me and said with a strong, firm voice, "Imagination."

Imagination! The voice in the Garden of Eden, Noah's response to a command to build an ark, Abraham obeying and moving out into the unknown, Moses coming down from Sinai with two tablets containing the Word of God, Joshua marching around Jericho, and all the prophets speaking and acting in the name of Almighty God – all of this is "imagination?"

Satan subtly carries us further in our anxious inquiry. What about Hinduism and its rich historical heritage of millions of devotees seeking to appease the multitudinous deities of heaven? Traditional religion postulates gods within the forces of nature. Is it possible that all of these religious formulations, along with Christianity and Islam, are mere fabrications of the psyche?

A. W. Tozer wrote penetratingly of the struggle between faith and nonfaith.

> *The world of sense intrudes upon our attention day and night for the whole of our lifetime. It is clamorous, insistent, and self-demonstrating. It does not appeal to our faith; it is here, assaulting our five senses, demanding to be accepted as real and final. But sin has so clouded the lenses of our hearts that we cannot see that other reality, the City of God, shining around us. The world of sense triumphs. The visible becomes the enemy of the invisible; the temporal, of the eternal. That is the curse inherited by every member of Adam's tragic race. (Tozer n.d., 56)*

And so the Christian – seeing the unseeable, feeling the untouchable, hearing the inaudible – at times walks off the beaten path of life and, looking up to a heaven garrisoned with brass, begins to shout, "O God, if you are there, if you do love, if you do know, then please let me see, touch, and hear anew." Faith's embers so easily change from a vibrant red glow to a dull ashen gray. The tangible triumphs. The spirit is broken.

In the questionnaire I sent to missionaries (see this book's Appendix), 40 percent of the respondents acknowledged that they are, at least occasionally, beset by intellectual doubts concerning their Christian faith. Another query was, "Do you ever feel you are preaching a message you don't fully believe?" Fourteen answered that this was a frequent problem to them, while 120 replied that it is an infrequent concern. Christian author Flannery O'Connor comments, "I think there is no suffering greater than what is caused by the doubts of those who want to believe."

Robert is an evangelical missionary possessing what I would consider to be impeccable spiritual credentials. He has endured great hardship in his many years of Christian service. His family is a model of warmth and graciousness. Robert's many friends regard him, his wife, and children as an excellent example of Christian dedication and servanthood. What almost no one knows is that Robert is plagued by an avalanche of doubt that has, at times, become almost overwhelming. He has gone to the very precipice of a deep, dark canyon. Peering into the abyss, he has seen nothingness – no God, no light, no eternity, no salvation, no peace. Recoiling from taking the final leap into the black hole of oblivion, he retreats to the solace of the prayer closet. There he finds temporary respite. But then the questions again come. *Where are you, God? Why don't you speak? How can you be so oblivious to suffering? Are you powerless to overcome evil? Can you not release me from my torment?*

How many "closet agnostics" are there in Christendom? I do not mean those who are agnostics from a desire to be purposely doubtful, but those caught in a conflict between the seen and the unseen, the tangible and the intangible. Further complicating the issue is the problem of degree. Who among us can say he has never doubted? I do not believe Satan is so kind as to never harass believers in this vital area of spirituality.

When do doubts become convictions? At what point is a minister or a missionary compelled to resign his position and walk away from all that is precious and stable in his life? Truly, the torment of undeclared doubts is an overwhelming force for internal destruction, especially in light of the high cost of open declaration. Perhaps more churches should sponsor "Agnostics Anonymous" groups, such as the one that meets at All Soul's Anglican Church in London. Doubts then could be worked through within a support group of informed, sensitive, caring Christians.

Francis A. Schaeffer dealt with these problems in a number of his writings.

> *Little by little, many Christians in this generation find the reality slipping away. The reality tends to get covered by the barnacles of naturalistic thought. Indeed, I suppose this is one of half a dozen questions that are most often presented to me by young people from Christian backgrounds: Where is the reality? "Where has the reality gone? I have heard it spoken in an honest, open desperation, by fine young Christians in many countries. As the ceiling of the naturalistic comes down upon us, as it invades by injection or by connotation, reality gradually slips away. (Schaeffer 1977, 69.)*

Reality dissipates and doubts invade. The "I know whom I have believed" affirmation becomes muted. Witness withers into a feeble fulfilling of job expectations rather than an expression of joyful conviction. Schaeffer consistently held that reason and faith are compatible. But to some, the issues are not so clear. One missionary ministering within evangelicalism decided he had to resign from his mission because of doubts he encountered while translating the Gospel of Mark.

Elisabeth Elliot tells of her crucible experience when she observed the death of an Indian who could have been the key to the whole Quinones tribe coming to Christ:

> *In my heart I could not escape the thought that it was God who had failed. Surely He knew how much was at stake. Surely He could have done better by all of us. To my inner cries of questionings no answer came. There was no explaining any of it. I looked into the abyss . . . there was nothing there but darkness and silence. (Elliot 1975, 82-83)*

Many times I have looked back with a measure of longing to my Christian college days. I was a new believer with an unquestioning faith in Christ – and in my professors. Few biblical issues were dealt with in a critical manner. With amazing naivete I skipped over problem areas in my Bible reading. The unspoken assumption was that only liberals asked the hard questions. Real Christians, I thought, are people of faith who are not sidetracked by higher criticism. However, within a few months of arriving in Bangladesh, I knew I was going to be stretched far beyond anything I had previously imagined. *How can God be one and yet three? Why did God have intercourse with Mary and beget baby Jesus? What about all the other "son of God" passages in Scripture? Why are the genealogies of Jesus contradictory in Matthew 1 and Luke 3? What is the explanation for the obvious errors in the recording of numbers in the Old Testament? Why do the Epistles read like personal letters to churches rather than like the very Word of God?* These and scores of other hard questions have been asked of me by Muslims hundreds of times during the past years.

In a class at Harvard, Wilfred Cantwell Smith, the great scholar of Islam, looked teasingly at his students and said, "The study of comparative religions makes one comparatively religious." Smith was not far off base. Hundreds of students have drifted from evangelicalism to universalism. A strong, exclusive faith has given way to the socially more acceptable affirmation of inclusiveness.

Calvin Miller articulately analyzes the strategy of reason as it launches its attack in the believer.

> *Reason is the cynic for all seasons. Square-jawed and impudent, it has always circled faith in grinning triumph, demanding something exact for its voracious appetite.... After our most profound statements of faith, reason has said with belittling arrogance, "Is that all there is?" (Miller 1973, 6)*

I have never met a deep-thinking Christian who has not been troubled by doubt. Affirmation must encounter opposition before it becomes confirmation. The ongoing process of faith development will be tested and contested at each progressive stage. It is appropriate for believers to be instruments of encouragement to our fellow pilgrims who are being assaulted by one of the most insidious and seductive weapons of Stratagems armory.

Bishop H. B. Dehqani-Tafti has a faith that has survived an assassination attempt on his life and the murder of his only son. He writes of the early days of his Christian life.

My simple faith had already been a little shaken during my last year in the Stuart Memorial College through studying elementary practical psychology, but there I was surrounded by wise Christian teachers. One of these had advised me never to give up prayer and church-going, even if the whole thing seemed meaningless at times; I listened to this sound advice. . . . Surely we do not live only by our feelings! We certainly have to learn to go on with the life of our faith irrespective of how we feel about it. (Dehqani-Tafti 1959, 39)

Faith

The invitation to visit the Turkey Point nuclear plant south of Miami, Florida, was just short of unbelievable. Donald, my brother's son-in-law, who is an instructor at the facility, was able to get me clearance for a tour. On the appointed day we drove through a wooded area alongside a long creek that is used in recycling the plant's water. Our first glimpse of the two containment domes was awe-inspiring. After extensive security checks, we lay down on a conveyor belt that slowly moved us through a facility that checked our internal radiation level. We then put on special hats, overalls, gloves, and boots. Tape was applied to ensure a tight fit. We were given two radiation counters to pin to our clothes.

Our first stop was the room where all of the plant's radioactive wastes are stored under ten feet of water. Donald turned off the light, and suddenly we saw an eerie glow reflecting upward through the water from the canisters. Herein was one of the twentieth century's most perplexing problems: what to do with used but still very active nuclear waste.

The central control room was filled from floor to ceiling with unlit bulbs. As we sat casually talking to the four engineers, suddenly one of the lights began wildly blinking. Quickly, the chief engineer pushed some levers and made an urgent phone call. Soon all became normal once again. From this surrealistically charged room we walked through a five-foot-thick open door into the heart of the containment structure and peered down past the control rods and into the core of the reactor. Needless to say, the reactor was shut down and under repair!

How sobering it was to realize that an operational accident taking place at that precise place could cause enough radiation leakage to kill or injure hundreds of thousands of people, plus curtail the supply of electricity to 40 percent of Florida's residents. Every few minutes we looked at the radiation counters pinned to our clothes. Donald seemed especially concerned and protective of me. Back in the trailer we carefully removed our clothes and again went through the conveyor belt. We were pronounced well within the reasonable bounds of radiation exposure. Donald's count was added to his cumulative record on the nearby computer.

No analogy is perfect, but I did reflect on this experience in relation to faith. I could not see, feel, or taste the radiation that was all around me. It was all totally invisible, tasteless, and impossible to touch. Yet signs within the containment facility warned us not to linger. Even though the reactor was shut down, radiation levels were still high. Our compulsory clothing testified to the reality of danger. The radiation counters and conveyor belt spoke eloquently of the need of extreme caution. Most assuredly there was a reality present that I had to accept by faith. Powerful radiation was all about me. I would ignore the warnings and precautions only at great personal peril.

God is not among us in human form today. We cannot invite Him to our home for a meal and evening of warm fellowship. He is an unseen reality. But, He has graciously incarnated Himself, not only in Christ, but also in His Word. We now have a guidebook that reveals, exhorts, warns, and leads the people of faith. The human race ignores such a heavenly communication at a risk level much greater than that connected with warnings concerning radiation.

"Now faith is the assurance of things hoped for, the conviction of things not seen" (Heb. 11:1). Two strong, stable words are used in this verse to describe faith. *Assurance* is reliance with a built-in guarantee for positive performance. *Conviction* is a strongly held view with substantiating evidence. Are we talking about Christianity in terms of "blind faith" or "reasonable faith?" One doesn't need anything for blind faith except a willingness to take a leap into the dark. Little or no supporting documentation is necessary. Feeling, more than logic, provides the criteria for evaluation. On the other hand, a reasonable faith often becomes more reason than faith. The focus is on scientific investigation and appraisal. Again, Schaeffer postulates,

> *Christian faith is never faith in faith. Christian faith is never without content. Christian faith is never a jump in the dark. Christian faith is always believing what God has said. (Schaeffer 1971, 87)*

We need to think of faith as somewhere between a leap and an analysis. Faith is, at times, rational, and in other instances, nonrational. It is rational to think in terms of first cause, but try to convince a Muslim of the rationality of a triune God! As in many areas of life, the Christian holds a truth in tension. At times we long for God to be as constant and explainable as a mathematical formula. But it is not to be. "Faith and mystery are codependent. Eliminate either one and you have destroyed the other. Faith cannot be faith once it is fully explained and the mystery is gone" (Miller 1973, 73).

An area of study that greatly interests me is the role of temperament in faith development. I have observed that the easygoing, phlegmatic person is hardly touched by controversies created by higher criticism. This person's faith is simple and yet profoundly real. There is no deep-level grappling with complexities and shades of varying interpretation. Next comes the task-oriented Christian. His focus is on action, not reflection. Basically he is moving too fast to be bothered by what he considers a detour from the main issues of life. I well remember trying to get a very successful businessman to think with me about evil and suffering. He was happy to talk about a task-oriented approach toward alleviation of hurting humanity, but he was totally uninterested in a discussion of the more philosophical and theological aspects of the subject.

Lastly comes the temperament I can closely identify with. The reflective Christian is a struggler. Faith must be dissected and analyzed. He is prone toward discouragement and depression when adequate answers are not forthcoming.

He knows the dilemma of suffering that is presented in some detail in chapter four of this book is an intellectual dead end, but he cannot let it go. When he reads of the birth of a deformed baby, he reflects on the agony of the parents. Hearing of a destructive earthquake causes mental distress. Within this interaction with a real world, the melancholic Christian fights constantly for the maintenance of a vibrant faith.

Sheldon Vanauken is an outstanding author. His prize-winning autobiography, *A Severe Mercy*, is the story of the death of his beloved wife, Davy. It is instructive to step into Vanauken's life when he, as a deeply introspective person, told God to go to hell.

One sleepless night, drawing on to morning, I was overwhelmed with a sense of cosmos empty of God as well as Davy. "All right," I uttered to myself. "To hell with God, I'm not going to believe this damned rubbish anymore. Lies, all lies. I've been had." Up I sprang and rushed out to the country. This was the end of God. Ha!

And then I found I could not reject God. I could not. I cannot explain this. One discovers one cannot move a boulder by trying with all one's strength to do it. I discovered – without any sudden influx of love and faith – that I could not reject Christianity. Why I didn't know. There it was. I could not.
(Vanauken 1977, 191)

Even though pushed to the brink, Vanauken pulled back at the crucial moment. He could only go so far toward rejection and no further.

While in Kenya, I observed the powerful Masai tribespeople. As we drove through the bush, within the safety of our van, we saw several lions and cheetahs. But out in the bush were brave Masai walking with only a spear to protect themselves. Vincent J. Donovan tells of a penetrating discussion with a Masai on the subject of how best linguistically to define faith.

> *I was sitting talking with a Masai elder about the agony of belief and unbelief. He used two languages to respond to me – his own and Kiswahili. He pointed out that the word my Masai catechist, Paul, and I had used to convey faith was not a very satisfactory word in their language. It meant literally "to agree to." I, myself, knew the word had that shortcoming. He said "to believe" like that was similar to a white hunter shooting an animal with his gun from a great distance. Only his eyes and his fingers took part in the act. We should find another word. He said for a man really to believe is like a lion going after its prey. His nose and eyes and ears pick up the prey. His legs give him speed to catch it. All the power of his body is involved in the terrible death leap and single blow to the neck with the front paw, the blow that actually kills. And as the animal goes down the lion envelops it in his arms (Africans refer to the front legs of an animal as its arms) pulls it to himself, and makes it part of himself. This is the way a lion kills. This is the way a man believes. This is what faith is. (Donovan 1978, 62-63)*

Faith, then, is not passive agreement. No one who stands afar and professes to believe has really understood the reality of an encounter with "Christ the tiger." When Sheldon and Davy Vanauken were truly converted, their perspective was radically altered. "Now we saw the church, splendid and terrible, sweeping down the centuries with anthems and shining crosses and steady-eyed saints. No longer was the faith something for children: intelligent people held it strongly" (Vanauken 1977, 91).

During my tour of China, I had an unforgettable experience. It was nine-thirty Sunday morning in a hotel room in midwest China. Our tour leader had placed a blaring television set in the bathroom near the door which led into the hall where an informant for the hotel was sitting. Over a period of fifteen minutes the ten members of our group casually walked into the room. At the appointed moment, the door opened and in walked a strong, dynamic Chinese pastor who belongs to the "underground church." For the next thirty minutes I had the unique privilege of sitting at the feet of a great man of God who had spent twenty years in a horrible Chinese prison undergoing terrible deprivation and humiliation because of his faith in Christ. His message, powerful even through interpretation, was interspersed with songs.

In such a humble spirit, the pastor spoke of the intense pressure on him to deny Christ or to come under the direction of the state church. His pungent response to these overtures is etched forever in my heart. He slowly sat upright and with a voice filled with conviction said, "I may be a Peter, but I am not a Judas." At times, perhaps, our brother's faith has wavered.

But he determined to struggle back to belief and not to take the much easier path of permanent denial of his Lord.

Often this humble pastor would point to his knees and exhort us to pray with renewed fervency for a spread of revival in China. He lives in a one-room shack on the outskirts of town and each day works on a construction gang, even though he is about sixty-five years old. At night and on Sundays this man of God is uniquely active for the kingdom. The week before we met him, he had baptized a hundred new believers.

This scarred Chinese pastor humbly shared some of the insights of his life gained while left to rot in a dingy, grimy prison cell:

"This is our Babylon, but our heart is in Jerusalem."

"Satan attacks believers with sweetness and ease as well as with the force of a roaring lion."

"We must walk with Jesus from Bethlehem to Golgotha."

And that is what Christian faith is all about.

Faith is central to orthodox Christianity. For the Muslim, God-awareness is the pulsating spiritual motivation. These two similar religious themes can be explored as bridges for dialogue.

THE CROSS AND THE CRESCENT

2

Sacred Scriptures

How much would be known about Christianity and Jesus Christ if the Bible did not exist? How much would be known about Islam and Prophet Muhammad if the Quran did not exist? These sacred writings are absolutely essential to the historical verification of the world's two largest religions. Academia has spent centuries in intensive investigation of these holy books. Religious mystics have engaged in lofty meditation and speculation centering on the esoteric passages of Holy Writ. The more sensation-oriented interpreters have always focused on the dramatic events of Scripture, such as a river parting or a moon splitting. To all, the foundation of belief is their faith in the revealed "Word of God."

This presents a problem. Advocates of both Christianity and Islam adhere to strict monotheism. But how can this one God speak in contradiction? The conflict in biblical and quranic content forces the God-seeker to be a judge. It is impossible to be, at the same time, a Christian and a

Muslim. The "Battle of the Books" sets the stage for the "Battle of the Believers."

Any exploration of alternative systems demands maximum objectivity and fairness. If Islamic spirituality is deeply rooted in the Quran, then the Christian is obliged to study it. Many Muslims have told me with great conviction that I would accept Islam if I would only read the Quran with an open mind. Their request is legitimate. Likewise, I enjoin my Muslim friends to study the Bible and to pray for a spirit of discernment and guidance. Unfortunately, this ideal of impartial investigation is at an impasse. The only reason most believers read Scriptures other than their own is to arm themselves more effectively for debate. An open mind is perhaps to be wished for, but it is hard to come by among those who already have convictions.

This chapter is designed to place spirituality within the framework of Christian and Muslim beginnings, and the beginnings are, respectively, the Bible and the Quran.

What is the Quran?

The word *Quran* in Arabic means "recitation." It is possible that the root of this word is the Syriac *qeryana*, which carries with it the meaning of giving a scriptural reading or lesson in church. This word was adopted into Arabic as a title for the Muslim compilation of Scriptures (Bell and Watt 1970, 136-137).

Muslims vigorously defend the need for a later and complete record of the revealed word of Allah. They affirm the *Torah*, *Zabur*, and the *Injil* (Law, Psalms, and Gospel). But a compilation became necessary because of biblical revelation being distorted through years of transmission. Also, they contend it is logical to believe in progressive revelation. After all, Christians affirm a later communication from God known as the New Testament, even though Jews protest this belief as religious heresy. Muslims, then, are carrying this process just one step further than Christians. Jews, Christians, and Muslims all claim their Scripture is final and totally authoritative.

The Hadith is blunt and to the point on this subject.

Why do you ask the people of the scripture about anything while your Book (Quran) which has been revealed to Allah's Apostle is newer? You read it pure, undistorted and unchanged, and Allah has told you that the people of the scripture (Jews and Christians) changed their scripture and distorted it, and wrote the scripture with their own hands and said, "It is from Allah," to sell it for a little gain. (Bukhari [Vol. 9], 339)

Muslims claim the Quran to be pure and unchanged. The Bible is charged with distortion and with being used for unethical purposes. I recall a well-dressed young Muslim who came by our display of Christian books on the streets of Manila, picked up a New Testament, and said, "This book is like a newspaper." Seeking to probe further, I said, "Yes, it does convey contemporary information, but it is far more than just a newspaper." Interrupting me, the Muslim youth soberly stated, "No, I mean that your Bible is only worthy of wrapping smelly fish in!" I countered by asking, "What would you say if I declared your Quran to be worthy only for the purpose of wrapping fish? How would that make you feel?" He turned and walked away. I wonder if he was feeling as hurt and alienated as I was.

Consider this Muslim view on the untrustworthiness of the Bible:

> *It is clear, therefore, that the language which Jesus and his disciples spoke was Hebrew, not Latin or Greek. So copies of the New Testament written down in Latin or Greek must have been written down long after the time of Jesus. . . . Books of this kind, composed 100 or 200 years after Jesus by unknown authors and attributed by them to Jesus and his disciples, can be of little use to any believer today. It was necessary, therefore, that we should have another book sent to us from Heaven, free from these defects and one which readers could regard with certainty as the very Word of God. (Ajijola 1975, 87-88)*

It is appropriate, therefore, to examine in greater detail this Quran in which nearly one billion people have placed their total faith and confidence.

Mode of Quranic Inspiration

It is important to understand that Muslims allow for no human contribution to the content of the Quran. In totality the author was Allah. Seyyed Hossein Nasr comments, "The Prophet was purely passive in the face of the revelation he received from God. He added nothing to this revelation himself. He did not write a book but conveyed the Sacred Book to mankind" (Nasr 1966, 44).

One of the controversies surrounding the Prophet Muhammad is his alleged inability to read or write. Illiteracy assured the purity of the revelation. Muhammad could not add anything to that which God had given. He was only a conduit faithfully passing on to others that which he had received. Sura 53:1-4 reinforces this position: "By the Star when it setteth, your comrade erreth not, nor is deceived; Nor doth he speak of (his own) desire. It is naught save an inspiration that is inspired."

A further affirmation of this position is found in Sura 6:50, "Say (O Muhammad, to the disbelievers): I say not unto you (that) I possess the treasures of Allah, nor that I have knowledge of the Unseen; and I say not unto you: Lo! I am an angel. I follow only that which is inspired in me." Muhammad is exhorted to be humble and to point to Allah as the exclusive source of all inspiration and revelation.

Muhammad had to contend with detractors in the early days of Islam. Sura 25:4-6 is an internal apologetic for quranic authenticity:

Those who disbelieve say: This is naught but a lie that he hath invented, and other folk have helped him with it, so that they have produced a slander and a lie. And they say: Fables of the men of old which he hath had written down so that they are dictated to him morn and evening. Say (unto them, O Muhammad): he Who knoweth the secret of the heavens and the earth hath revealed it.

This is a most interesting passage. The Quran is declared to be a lie and a fable. Muhammad is alleged to have invented its content based on stories he has heard from other people. The modern reader is thus given an insight into the allegations of seventh-century opposition as regards quranic authority. This is followed by a strong assertion of the direct authorship of Allah. The Prophet is instructed to boldly proclaim this message to all who will hear.

The "Night of Power" refers to the evening in the month of Ramadan when Muhammad first began to receive quranic revelations. It is described in the five verses of Sura 97. The Sura is simply entitled "Power."

Lo! We revealed it on the Night of Power. Ah, what will convey unto thee what the Night of Power is! The Night of Power is better than a thousand months. The angels and the Spirit descend therein, by the permission of their Lord, with all decrees. (That night is) Peace until the rising of the dawn.

This particular night, during the month of fasting, is one of the most holy and revered of all days in the Muslim calendar. The orthodox gather in mosques throughout the world to pray and chant the Quran until dawn. Muhammad's key role in receiving divine revelation is remembered and appreciated.

Much speculation has been made concerning the Prophet's intellectual, emotional, and spiritual condition at the time of receiving the words of Allah. Muhammad has been pronounced a lunatic, an epileptic, and a saint at various times and by assorted authors. More than one Christian writer has declared Muhammad to have been possessed and controlled by evil spirits. Our most accurate information concerning the moments of actual revelation to Muhammad have been recorded in the Hadith by Bukhari.

*While I was walking, I heard voices from the sky. I
looked up, and behold! I saw the same Angel who
came to me in the cave of Hira sitting on a chair
between the sky and the earth. I was too much afraid
of him. (Bukhari [Vol. 6], 420)*

The angel who mediated God's Word to Muhammad
was Gabriel. This process went on over a period of 22 years.

The most renowned statement the Prophet made concerning
how he received divine inspiration is, "Sometimes it is (revealed)
like the ringing of a bell, this form of Inspiration is the hardest of
all and then this state passes off after I have grasped what is
inspired. Sometimes the Angel comes in the form of a man and
talks to me and I grasp whatever he says" (Bukhari [Vol. 1], 2).
This phrase, "like the ringing of a bell," has been a focus of
some non-Muslims who declare Muhammad to have been in an
unbalanced psychological state at the time of hearing a heavenly
voice.

A famous poem, titled "The Prophet," by Russian poet
Alexander Pushkin recalls, with considerable imaginative
force, Muhammad's encounter with the angel of revelation.

*I dragged my steps across a desert bare,
    My spirit parched with heat,
And lo, a seraph with six wings was there:
    He stood where two roads meet.*

*Soft as the coming of a dream at night
    His fingers touched my head:*

He raised the lids of my prophetic sight,
  An eagle's wide with dread.

He touched my ears, they filled with sound and song.
  I heard the heaven's motion,
The flight of angels, and the reptile throng
  That moves beneath the ocean.

I heard the soundless growth of plant and tree.
  Then, stooping to my face,
With his right hand he tore my tongue from me,
  Vain, sinful tongue and base.

A serpent's fiery fang he thrust instead,
  Through my faint lips apart:
He slit my breast, and with a sword stained red,
  Hewed out my quaking heart.

A coal of living fire his fingers placed
  Deep in my gasping side.
Dead, as I lay upon the desert waste,
  I heard God's voice that cried.

Arise! O prophet, having seen and heard:
  Strong in my spirit, span
The universal earth, and make my word
  Burn in the heart of man.
                    (Cornford 1943, 20-21)

The Attraction of the Quran

Millions of Muslims have testified to the impact of the

Quran on their lives. My intimate Muslim friend, Dr. Ali, about whom I have written in previous books, has testified to a life-changing experience when he began to read the Quran in his own language. Reading and reciting Scripture in Arabic, which he did not understand, made minimal impression on his daily life. But when he was able to comprehend the teachings of Allah, his life was brought to a full point of dedication. Even though he is a busy layman, he still finds time to search the Quran for guidance.

An experience like the following is not at all uncommon in the Muslim world:

They waited now with emotion for that old voice, melodious and worn with age, to utter the opening strophes of the Holy Book, and there was nothing feigned in the adoring attention of the circle of faces. Some licked their lips and leaned forward eagerly, as if to take the phrases upon their lips: others lowered their heads and closed their eyes as if against a new experience in music. The old preacher sat with his waxen hands folded in his lap and uttered the first Sura, full of the soft, warm coloring of a familiar understanding, his voice a little shaky at first, but gathering power and assurance from the silence as he proceeded. His eyes now were as wide and lusterless as a dead hare's. His listeners followed the notation of the verses as they fell from his lips with care and rapture, gradually seeking their way together as they fell from and into the main stream of the poetry like a school of fish following a leader by instinct out into the deep sea. (Durrell 1958, 256)

It may be of interest to note that John 3:16 is not the most frequently quoted Scripture in the world. The above-mentioned first Sura of the Quran holds that distinction. Five times a day Muslims bow in prayer while facing Mecca and recite these first words of the Quran:

Praise be to Allah, Lord of the Worlds,
The Beneficent, the Merciful.
Owner of the Day of Judgment,
Thee (alone) we worship; Thee (alone) we ask for
*   help.*
Show us the straight path,
The path of those whom Thou hast favored; Not
*   (the path) of those who earn Thine anger*
nor of those who go astray.

The Quran has played a significant role in the conversion to Islam of a number of Westerners. Mavis B. Jolly, a British convert, relates the impact of the Quran on her.

Above all I read the Holy Quran. At first it seemed mainly repetition. I was never quite sure if I was taking it in or not, but the Quran, I found, works silently on the spirit. Night after night I could not put it down. (Jolly n.d., 40)

Dr. Ali Selman Benoist, a French medical doctor, writes of the effect of the Quran on his conversion.

The essential and definite element of my conversion to Islam was the Quran. I began to study it, before my conversion, with the critical spirit of a Western intellectual, and I owe much to the magnificent work of Mr. Maled Bennabi, entitled Le Phenomene quran Coranique, which convinced me of its being divinely revealed. There are certain verses of this book, the Quran, revealed more than thirteen centuries ago, which teach exactly the same notions as the most modern scientific researches do. This definitely convinced me, and converted me to the second part of the Kalima, "Muhammad Rasul al-Lah" ("Muhammad is the Messenger of God"). This was my reason for presenting myself on 20 February 1953 at the mosque in Paris, where I declared my faith in Islam and was registered there as a Muslim by the Mufti of the Paris Mosque, and was given the Islamic name of Ali Selman. I am very happy in my new faith. (Benoist n.d., 38)

Such testimonies indicate the subjective and tentative nature of human experience. Over the years I have heard and read of life-changing encounters given by followers of Hare Krishna, Islam, Communism, Children of God, Mormonism, and Jehovah's Witnesses. Chapter 6 will investigate such Muslim claims more thoroughly. One further illustration pungently describes the effect of the Quran on a group of Arabs confined in prison awaiting their execution:

Suddenly I heard a voice singing verses from the Quran. "Who is that?" I said. "Come with me and you can see for yourself." He led me to the end of

*the courtyard, to the cell from which the song came.
I looked in. On the floor were seated six Arabs. They
were in rags and their feet were bare, but they were
unusually handsome and vigorous, appearing to be
in the prime of life. One of them was singing. Their
faces shone with a sublime calm as if they hardly
knew that they were in prison, and their eyes were
set in a fixed gaze as if they hung on every word
that was formed on the lips of the singer. "They are
condemned to death," said the pockmarked Arab,
"and they will probably be shot tomorrow, in the
back like the others because they are rebels." They
continued listening to the heart of the Quran, the
death sura, Ya Sin. (Padwick 1961, 118-119)*

The Quran provides a perceived spiritual reality for the
Muslim. The first sentence chanted in the newborn infant's
ears is the *Shahadah* (Confession). At a very early age the
child sits in a Muslim school and learns the Quran by rote
memory. The Muslim marriage ceremony contains large
sections from the Quran. Throughout life the prayers recited
by Muslims are selections from the Quran. At death the
final remembrance of the devotee is spoken in a service
dominated by the chanting of the Quran. "The Quran is the
tissue out of which the life of a Muslim is woven; its
sentences are like threads from which the substance of his
soul is knit" (Nasr 1966, 42).

It is important to understand the Muslim's theological
view of the Quran. The Quran is unchangeable: "There is
naught that can change His words" (Sura 6:116); "There is
no changing the Words of Allah" (Sura 10: 65). Fazlur
Rahman comments on the style of quranic revelation: "The

voice from the depths of life spoke distinctly, unmistakably and imperiously. Not only does the word Quran, meaning 'recitation,' clearly indicate this, but the text of the Quran itself states in several places that the Quran is *verbally revealed* and not merely in its 'meaning' and ideas" (Rahman 1966, 30-31).

So the Quran is inerrant and a product of what is known in Christian circles as "mechanical dictation." That is, every word and syllable are directly from Allah. There is no room for any human component in the formulation of quranic content. This belief leads naturally to the view that the Quran is uncreated and is coeternal with God. It simply always was. It had no beginning and will come to no end. Its status is equal to God. So in a sense, Islam teaches an incarnation, not an incarnation into a human body, but rather into a voice which then became the written revelation of God. Christian apologists should explore these incarnational concepts as an analogy to assist in explaining to Muslims the biblical teaching of God revealed in Christ.

Muslims also firmly believe in the reliable transmission of the Quran from the time of the Prophet to the present. Though there is no "original manuscript'" of the Quran, the present copies are regarded by scholars to be generally reliable and fair representations of the earliest compilations. All of this leads to a very high level of reverence for the Quran. The holy book is kept wrapped in linen and placed on a high shelf in Muslim homes. It is not to be touched with unclean hands. I have frequently seen Muslims kiss the Arabic Quran while rolling their eyes heavenward with a look of intense piety. This reverence has affected the Christian's use of the Bible in the context of Muslim countries. A preacher visiting in Pakistan was speaking to a large crowd and wished to express his spiritual relationship to the Bible. He placed the Bible on the floor beside the pulpit and then stood on it while proclaiming the Christian is to stand on the promises of the Word of God. Immediately a roar went through the crowd and the preacher was almost mobbed. No one could understand a man of God placing his feet upon, and thus defiling, a holy book.

Popular Islam and the Quran

Orthodox use of the Quran for the purpose of facilitating spirituality is quite straightforward. Islamic scriptures are quoted, recited, chanted, preached, and memorized. Each of these forms are practiced throughout the Muslim world. The Word of Allah is an integral part of communal and personal worship. There is, however, an added dimension of usage that is more mystical and even regarded by some as heretical.

Popular Islam seeks to integrate the Quran into the experiential level of life. Many Muslims are not as interested in traditional worship forms as they are in developing a more intimate relationship with Allah. Their methodology for such a spiritual quest is often controversial. Yet literally millions around the world can accurately be referred to as adherents of popular Islam. Their use of the Quran is as varied as it is unique.

On journeys one may be kept from thirst by writing verse 6 of the second sura on a clean paper or on a glass dish. He should wash the writing with spring water and put it into a glass. After three days he should mix it with attar of roses and the milk of a red goat, and he should boil this mixture until it becomes thick and black. Then if some of this is eaten every morning, the traveler will not thirst. If one is journeying on foot, he should bind verse 25 of sura Ya Sin to his feet, and he can then walk any desired distance and not suffer fatigue. If he journeys by sea, storms may be calmed by using verses 256-260 of the sura "Cow" (2). These verses will also keep away beggars and dervishes on the road (Donaldson 1937, 259).

A large crowd had gathered around two men on a train platform in a remote town of Bangladesh. These middle-aged men were obviously seeking to sell something. I made my way over to the group and looked in utter amazement at what I saw. One of the men held a giant snake up to the extended tongue of the other "salesman." The snake appeared to bite the tongue. Immediately, blood gushed forth while the patient writhed in pain. Putting the snake in a secure box, the assistant then placed a small brass amulet on the tongue of the bitten man. Quickly, his countenance changed from indescribable distress and terror to that of release and joy. Such a terrible ordeal had been aborted by the timely application of an amulet containing a protective verse from the Quran. With gusto, both men began preaching the perils of walking through snake-infested rural pathways where danger lurks behind each blade of grass. For only a reasonable twenty-five cents a Muslim can be assured of healing from the bite of any type of snake, no matter how deadly. A buzz of excitement rippled through the crowd as scores took out their coins to purchase such Allah-sanctioned protection of their lives.

Samuel M. Zwemer tells of a challenge he repeatedly received in eastern Arabia. Muslims firmly believed that if the Quran was wrapped in a fresh sheepskin and thrown into a fire, it would not be burned or even singed. Zwemer was urged to place the Bible in a similar sheepskin and then both holy books would be tested by fire. The one that survived would be authenticated as being truly God's Word (Zwemer 1920c, 26). There is no indication Zwemer ever accepted the challenge.

The Quran is chanted at the time of the death of a Muslim. Zwemer describes one such ceremony:

> *At night, dervishes, sometimes as many as fifty, assemble, and one brings a rosary of 1000 beads, each as large as a pigeon's egg. Then beginning with the 67th chapter of the quran Koran, they say three times, "God is one," then recite the last chapter, and then say three times, "O God, favor the most excellent and most happy of thy creatures, our Lord muhammad Mohammed, and his family, and companions, and preserve them." They next repeat three thousand times, "There is no god but God," one holding the rosary and counting each repetition. After each thousand, they sometimes rest and take coffee. (Zwemer 1920b, 33-34)*

There is a malicious side to the use of the Quran. Sura 3:122-124 can be written on an old water pot or on a piece of horseskin and then placed in an enemy's house. His property will, so some believe, be destroyed within a short time. If someone's death is desired, Sura 2:256-260 should be read twenty-nine times. Alternatively,

> *On Tuesday at sunset a man makes a mask of his enemy's face out of plaster of Paris, writes verses 30-33 of Sura 5 on the face of the image and the enemy's name on the back of it. He sticks a dagger*

into the head where the name is written, at the same
time saying "O angels of God, do this to this
person," and the enemy will be struck dead.
(Donaldson 1937,261)

Lest we become overly critical of the superstitious side of popular Islam, let us recall that Jews utilized amulets stuffed with a paper on which was written a portion of the Old Testament: Genesis 21:1 to ease the pains of childbirth; Genesis 32:31 for protection on a journey; Exodus 33:23 to deflect the danger of witchcraft; and Numbers 11:2 for overcoming the effects of the evil eye (Zwemer 1920c, 23-24). And consider the superstitious use often made of the cross in Christianity. Many believers bow before the cross, wear it around their neck, or frequently make the sign of the cross. Seyyed Hossein Nasr comments that this all looks magical to Muslims. He wonders why Christians criticize Muslims for their use of the Quran in a somewhat similar way (Nasr 1966, 52).

Problems with the Quran

It is important to affirm what millions of Muslims deny: The Quran indeed does have internal problems. Muslims enjoy quoting liberal Christian scholarship in its attacks on biblical authority. But they cannot countenance even the slightest hint that there are academic questions which undercut the Quran as being a reliable basis for spiritual experience.

An overview is as follows: Abu Bakr, after the death of the Prophet, began compiling the Quran "by collecting it from the leafless stalks of the date palm tree and from the pieces of leather and hides and from the stones, and from the chests of men (who had memorized the Quran)" (Bukhari [Vol. 9], 229-230). Somewhere between A.D. 650 and 656, under the rule of Caliph Uthman, the canon of the Quran was formed. Uthman's commission decided what was to be included and excluded. The order of the Suras was fixed. It was then that a radical move was taken to ensure the singularity of an authoritative Quran. "Uthman sent to every Muslim province one copy of what they had copied, and ordered that all the other quranic materials, whether written in fragmentary manuscripts or whole copies, be burnt" (Bukhari [Vol. 6], 479). In one decisive move, some twenty years after Muhammad's death, much potential for a critical analysis of conflicting scriptures was rendered impossible. This Uthman Quran is essentially that which has been preserved and passed down faithfully through the past thirteen centuries.

The Quran is not an easy book to understand. Even Seyyed Hossein Nasr affirms that "many people, especially non-Muslims, who read the Quran for the first time are struck by what appears to be a kind of incoherence from the human point of view" (Nasr 1966, 47). Another scholar has observed that the Quran contains "the intrusion of an extraneous subject into a passage otherwise homogeneous; a differing treatment of the same subject in neighboring verses, often with repetition of words and phrases; breaks in grammatical construction which raise difficulties in exegesis, . . . the juxtaposition of passages of different date, with the intrusion of late phrases into early verses" (Bell and Watt 1970, 93). All of these textual problems seem to indicate rather extreme revision and alteration liberties taken by the earliest redactors.

There are several indications of a low view of quranic

inspiration. The Prophet, on one occasion, heard a reciter reciting the Quran in the mosque and said, "May Allah bestow His Mercy on him, as he has reminded me of such-and-such verses of such-and-such suras, which I missed!" (Bukhari [Vol. 6], 510). The feisty young Aisha, Muhammad's favorite wife, noted the revelation of Sura 33:51, which gave the Prophet permission to receive his wives in any order he desired. This led her to observe, "I said (to the Prophet), 'I feel that your Lord hastens in fulfilling your wishes and desires' " (Bukhari [Vol. 6], 295).

Sura 2:106 reads, "Such of Our revelations as We abrogate or cause to be forgotten, we bring (in place) one better or the like thereof. Knowest thou not that Allah is Able to do all things?" A verse like this explains why the penalty for adultery is, in Sura 24:3, a scourging of one hundred stripes; while Sura 4:15 requires the adulteresses to be confined in their houses until death. The problem is to find out which verse is abrogated and which is relevant for today. An attendant question relates to why God has to abrogate his word when it was all revealed during a short span of twenty-five years.

At the beginning of twenty-nine of the suras is to be found a letter or group of letters which are simply letters of the Arabic alphabet. These are a complete mystery. No reasonable explanation for their existence has ever been given, although Sufis have thoroughly enjoyed some of the most outrageous speculation imaginable.

Dr. Maurice Bucaille, a French physician and convert to Islam, has written a widely circulated book entitled *The Bible, The Quran and Science*. Rather surprisingly, he comments, "Apart from one or two possible mistakes in copying, the oldest documents known to the present day, that are to be found throughout the Islamic world, are identical. . . . The numerous ancient texts that are known to be in existence all agree except for very minor variations which do not change the general meaning of the text at all" (Bucaille 1979, 131). That sounds strangely like an evangelical apologetic for inerrancy!

Bishop Stephen Neill puts the Muslim quandary into perspective:

> *But far more difficult is it for the Muslim even to think of applying criticism to the Quran. For him this is the very word of God, eternal and uncreated; how then subject it to the probe and scalpel of the surgeon? . . . But the Muslim scholar may rest assured that sooner or later he will be driven, by the same irresistible impulse as the Christians, to look on the Quran with the same critical eyes as have been trained in other fields. What the consequences for his faith may be it is not for a Christian even to imagine. (Neill 1970, 229)*

A word needs to be said here about the very important Hadith (Traditions). As important as the various Hadith collections are to Muslims, they are not in the same category as the inerrant word of Allah in the Quran. It is the Quran, the highest level of communication direct from God, that shapes and molds the lives of the vast multitude of humanity known as Muslims. Without a Quran there could be no such thing as spirituality within Islam.

The Bible

We continue the "Battle of the Books" with the obvious statement that Christian spirituality is predicated upon an allegiance to God's Word, the Bible. Without these Scriptures almost nothing would be known of Jesus Christ. This statement highlights the absolute necessity of a high view of biblical authority. Literally millions of people have had their lives revolutionized by an encounter with the Christ of the Bible. The Old and New Testaments are the focus of Christianity and will continue to be so until the consummation of the age.

Truth is a universal quest. From the highest level of Ivy League academia to the simple illiterate farmer, man desires to encounter truth. Caught between academia, philosophy, and religion, modern man cries out, "Where truly is truth?"

Into this confusion the Bible comes, not so much with an apologetic, but rather with an assumption. The internal bias of the Bible is toward affirming what it considers to be obvious, and that is that truth is to be found only in Holy Scripture. It is to be found nowhere else. "O Lord God, Thou art God, and Thy words are truth" (2 Sam. 7:28). Another verse states, "The sum of Thy word is truth" (Ps. 119:160). Personification of the Word of Truth was then revealed in Christ as attested to in His own bold declaration, "I am . . . the truth" (John 14:6).

Two million Hebrew, Aramaic, and Greek words are found in the Bible. More than forty authors over a period of sixteen hundred years placed themselves at God's disposal to compile the modern world's most consistent best-seller. These writers were supernaturally inspired to produce their allotted portion of Scripture. The resulting unity of these sixty-six books is nothing short of a miracle.

Preservation of the Bible in the face of fierce antagonism is equally miraculous. Jealous emperors and angry atheists have sought to effect the demise of Christianity by destroying the Bible. I paused and reflected on the futility of such efforts as I stood by the side of Voltaire's tomb. His printed words of attack on God's Word live on, but they are insignificant compared to the force and authority of the Bible as it penetrates ethnic and linguistic barriers around the world.

It is true that Muslims have given testimony of how the Quran has assisted them in their spiritual pilgrimage. But there is another side to the coin. A Pakistani Muslim relates how reading the Bible brought him to the point of faith:

> *The Bible's message about the love of God revealed in Christ touched me to the core of my being. It was not the kind of book I had previously supposed. In it I found good news – in fact, the most wonderful news a human being could ever receive. My life was radically changed by the power of Jesus Christ who loved me and gave himself for me on the cross. The reading of the Bible led me to surrender myself to him unconditionally. (Hannah 1975, 3)*

Still, Scripture distribution among Muslims can be a very disheartening task. Even as I write this I am feeling the hurt of rejection of God's message. Tonight at our Reading Center in Manila a young Muslim with a goatee stopped by the book table and requested a free booklet. I gave him one which he took and promptly tore into little pieces. For the rest of the evening I watched God's Word fluttering about in the breeze. Muslims like this, in most instances, feel they are sincerely defending the cause of

God by protecting other Muslims from that which could adversely affect their faith.

Therefore, it is all the more exciting to read of a dramatic conversion which came solely from the reading of a Gospel. John A. Subhan was a Sufi mystic who lived in prepartition India. His heart was hungry for God. After a long pilgrimage of exploring options, Subhan encountered Christ and went on to become one of the most influential bishops in all of Asia. His own pungent words describe his moment of enlightenment:

> *In the Injil I found something which spoke to my soul. The gospel spoke to me in my own mother tongue, whispering to me the secrets of God. Its reading was comforting to my soul, every sentence touched it to its very depth, and it roused the slumbering faculties of my soul to a new state of consciousness. If the gospel was not true, the sun was not shining, the moon was not bright and the stars did not illuminate the path of heaven. I find it difficult to describe the experience that I had at the reading of the gospel on that memorable day; words are inadequate to express it. It was something like an object finding its missing complement. My spiritual life was incomplete without it, but as it had never known that which was intended to complete it, it never missed it till it came to it... It was sufficient! I decided to become a Christian. Christianity of which I had not learnt yet anything beside the reading of a single gospel. But this was after all, to me, the only true religion, for it could*

not be otherwise. (Subhan 1950, 22-23)

I read such a testimony with emotions of intermingled joy and sadness. How thrilling to step into Subhan's life and to realize how powerfully and thoroughly this Muslim was affected by the naked power of the Word of God. What a radical transformation! And the experience was maintained throughout Subhan's life. He never looked back. So, then, why sadness? My mind can only respond with the obvious question. Why are not all Muslims gripped in a similar manner by the reading of the Bible? Don't they understand it is indeed the good news which liberates captives? Why does my Muslim acquaintance on the streets of Manila declare that the only practical use of the Bible is for wrapping smelly fish?

Does predestination explain our dilemma? The elect will receive the Word joyfully and the non-elect will constitute the massive majority of the Muslim world who will reject the only message which can grant eternal life to their souls. At times I have leaned heavily in this direction even though I consider myself a "whosoever-will" Calvinist. Hidden in the counsels of God and beyond the reach of human intellect, I am sure there is a definitive answer. But for now I seek to emphasize my personal responsibility in propagation. The actual task of selection and conversion must be left in the competent hands of our sovereign Lord. But I continue to work and pray toward the day when many more Subhans will so demonstrably be apprehended by the living Word of God.

J. B. Phillips, the famous Bible translator, suffered from severe depression most of his adult life. The frank description of his emotional struggles is chronicled in his autobiography, *The Price of Success,* an excellent book for all

Christian leaders to read. In the midst of the "God is dead" controversy in the late 1960s, Phillips wrote his biblical apologetic *Ring of Truth*. His words piercingly highlight the intense spiritual "aliveness" of the Bible.

Although I did my utmost to preserve an emotional detachment, I found again and again that the material under my hands was strangely alive; it spoke to my condition in the most uncanny way. I say "uncanny" for want of a better word, but it was a very strange experience to sense, not occasionally but almost continually, the living quality of those rather strangely assorted books. To me it is the more remarkable because I had no fundamentalist upbringing, and although as a priest of the Anglican Church I had a great respect for Holy Scripture, this very close contact of several years of translation produced an effect of "inspiration" which I have never experienced even in the remotest degree, in any other work. (Phillips 1967, 18)

Bible Difficulties

At this point it would be preferable to affirm that the Bible is in no way vulnerable to the assaults of Muslim critics. It would be comfortable to state an airtight case and then watch the fiery darts of the Wicked One just bounce off our impregnable position. Unfortunately, this is not to be. The Bible has been under perpetual attack, and in recent times Muslims have been particularly active in this area. A key person in this tirade against the Bible's trustworthiness is Ahmed

Deedat, an Indian living in South Africa. His Islamic Propagation Center sends out free literature and inexpensive tapes and videos[1]. This elderly man is well known around the world. He has received a state award from Saudi Arabia for his efforts in propagating Islam. Deedat has debated biblical theology with a number of Christian leaders. He has tried, unsuccessfully thus far, to persuade the pope to debate him. Though Deedat is not always academically credible, he is an orator par excellence. Where he lacks content, he utilizes emotion and ridicule. His small booklet, *Is the Bible the Word of God?* is the mainstay of his attack on Christianity. In this widely circulated booklet Deedat makes the following points:

- He quotes W. Graham Scroggie and Kenneth Cragg to prove the human authorship of the Bible (pages 1-2).
- Bible translations are compared to highlight variations and omitted portions such as Mark 16:9-20 (pages 7-11).
- The Trinity is attacked (pages 15-16).
- In a section entitled "100 Percent Plagiarism," Deedat quotes 2 Kings 19 and Isaiah 37, which are identical in a number of verses (pages 31-33).
- 2 Samuel 24:13 is compared with 1 Chronicles 21:11; 2 Chronicles 36:9 is compared with 2 Kings 24:8; 2 Samuel 10:18 is compared with 1 Chronicles 19:18; 1 Kings 7:26 is compared with 2 Chronicles 4:5; and 2 Chronicles 9:25 is compared with 1 Kings 4:26

  (These verses present conflicts in regard to numbers found in parallel accounts [pages 34-44]).
- The genealogies of Jesus in Matthew 1 and Luke 3 are said to

---

[1]Islamic Propagation Centre International, Box 2439, Durban 4000, South Africa.

be "grossly contradictory" (pages 52-53).
- Luke 1:1-4 proves to Deedat that Luke's authorship was on a very human level (pages 55-56).
Deedat concludes his writing by stating,

If this humble little contribution of mine "Is the Bible God's Word?" finds a place in the Muslim home as a bulwark against the missionary menace my effort would be amply rewarded. A great reward would be if even one sincere disciple of Jesus (on whom be peace) were to be led to the truth and be removed from fabrications and falsehood. (Deedat n.d., 64)

It is fair to say Deedat has impacted some Christians with his arguments. In Africa a large group of evangelical missionaries sat in a small room intently watching a Deedat video. The next morning not a few said they had been disturbed by both content and delivery of what Deedat had shared. Deedat's videos are played in desert towns of Kenya and in small villages in the tropical island of Mindanao in the Philippines. His debates are particularly appreciated in London. So goes the influence of one of Christianity's main Muslim antagonists.

In my survey of missionaries I asked, "Do Bible problems bother you?" Nearly 70 percent indicated that this was a concern to them. Seeking to be more specific, I queried, "Do you fully subscribe to inerrancy?" This question was affirmed by 358 and denied by 15. The most provocative response came from the following question: "If you subscribe to inerrancy and came to doubt it, would you inform your mission leadership and colleagues?" Thirty-five did not answer the question. Fifteen said no. Then a fairly large group of 70 expressed some reservation as to whether they would share this doubt with their fellow missionaries. Comments included, "Not unless asked, I suppose," "I would reveal it only to thinking colleagues," "Yes, but not immediately," "I should," and "If I were to doubt it, what point would there be in living?"

Clark Pinnock has been one of the strongest advocates of inerrancy over the years. His early books and articles were unequivocal in their stand on this important issue. His latest book, *The Scripture Principle*, seems to undercut this clear position.

Why, then, do scholars insist that the Bible does claim total inerrancy? I can only answer for myself, as one who argued in this way a few years ago. I claimed that the Bible taught total inerrancy because I hoped that it did – I wanted it to. How would it be possible to maintain a firm stand against religious liberalism unless one held firmly to total inerrancy? Factors in the contemporary situation accounted for the claim, at least in my case. All I had to do was tighten up the case for inspiration one can find in the Bible and extend it just a little further than it goes itself. The logic of inspiration coupled with the demands of faith today were quite enough to convince me. Looking at the actual biblical evidence today, I have to conclude the case for total inerrancy just isn't there. At the very most, one could say only that it is implicit and could be drawn out by careful argument – but this is disputable and not the basis for the dogmatic claims one hears for inerrancy. In the last analysis, the inerrancy theory is a logical deduction not well supported exegetically. Those who press it hard are elevating reason over Scripture at that point. (Pinnock 1984, 58)

These words represent a rather serious defection from the inerrancy camp and have caused no small ripple among evangelical theologians. It is fair to ask where this progression of thinking is going to lead Pinnock. I, however, applaud him for his honesty. I am not sure all other Christian leaders have equal integrity regarding their position on inerrancy.

Two specific attacks from Muslims as noted by Deedat need a bit more elucidation. One is the human ingredient found in the Bible and the other relates to problems in text transmission. As noted earlier, the Quran is written as though God is dictating every word. Muslims have traditionally held strongly to this doctrine of a mechanical dictation theory of revelation. They simply cannot understand our claiming that the Bible is God's Word when it reads like history, personal letters, recollection, and speculation. Muslims urge us to call our Bible the "Christian Hadith." They feel this is a more accurate designation for biblical content and form.

The Muslim, confronted with the Bible and with modern Christian explanations of it, cannot understand how Christians can possibly regard it as a holy book. Throughout it is the work of men. Even the Gospels are not the word of Jesus Christ but only words about him, with an element of distortion which is evident in the variant forms in which even the words of Christ are put forward. The most rigid Christian fundamentalist admits some human element in Scripture. The Muslim does not admit any human element at all in the Quran; it is the Word of God himself, existent with him from the beginning; it is a word addressed to Muhammad, and in no sense at all a word of Muhammad. (Neill 1970, 52-53)

Muslims ask why there are four Gospels. Isn't there only one Christ? Why are there multiple accounts of his life in four books? One Muslim explanation is that the early church lost the original Gospel which Jesus had dictated. Therefore, some leaders set out to reconstruct the written life of Christ, but they all ended up contradicting each other. These men's names were Matthew, Mark, Luke, and John – and their variant accounts have survived! The Muslim view of the Epistles is that they are horizontal, not vertical in form. "How can correspondence, from here to there, however wise or holy, be authentic 'revelation'? The concept of tanzil by which Islam lives cannot possibly admit of personal letters constituting 'God's word.' *Tanzil* only comes down from heaven" (Cragg 1985, 92).

The other problem area relates to what Deedat describes as obvious errors and contradictions which are found in the Bible. All evangelicals limit the application of the term inerrancy to original manuscripts which, regrettably, we do not possess. John H. Skilton, an evangelical author, writes of the process by which we have ended up with a Bible with a small number of errors in it.

Men make mistakes no matter how high their regard for the text which they are copying. In the case of the New Testament, variations may be attributable also in some measure to such special factors as untrained copyists in the early days, the wide geographical extent of the church, the unavailability or loss of the original manuscripts or the standard copies of them for comparison, attempts at harmonization, including Tatian's Diatessaron, and the survival in early times of authentic information not given in the Scriptures which men might be moved to record in the margins of their manuscripts as glosses and which copyists of those manuscripts might by a very natural misunderstanding include in the text of their new documents. (Skilton 1946, 165-166)

Gleason Archer, professor emeritus of Trinity Evangelical Divinity School, has written the *Encyclopedia of Bible Difficulties,* dedicated to resolving problems encountered in reading and understanding the Bible. In his book Archer admits to the errors Deedat highlights.

Copyists were prone to making two types of scribal errors. One concerned the spelling of proper names (especially unfamiliar proper names), and the other had to do with numbers. Ideally, we might have wished that the Holy Spirit had restrained all copyists of Scripture over the centuries from making mistakes of any kind; but an errorless copy would have required a miracle, and this was not the way it worked out. (Archer 1982, 206)

Are we then destined to sink in defeat at the hands of Muslims who know how to direct their attacks at our most vulnerable points of spirituality?

Resolution of Problems

A statement came from the Council on Inerrancy which puts biblical revelation in proper perspective:

> *We deny that it is proper to evaluate Scripture according to standards of truth and error that are alien to its usage or purpose. We further deny that inerrancy is negated by phenomena such as a lack of modern technical precision, irregularities of grammar or spelling, observational descriptions of nature, the reporting of falsehood, the use of hyperbole and round numbers, the topical arrangement of material, variant selection of material in parallel accounts, or the use of free citations. (Pinnock 1984, 119)*

A succinct definition of inerrancy, and one with which I am in full agreement, is found in the *Evangelical Dictionary of Theology*. "Inerrancy is the view that when all the facts become known, they will demonstrate that the Bible in its original autographs and correctly interpreted is entirely true and never false in all it affirms, whether that relates to doctrine or ethics or to the social, physical, or life sciences" (Feinberg 1984, 142). This statement gives clarity to the view that scriptural authority extends to the sciences as well as to theology. I have never been able to understand the logic of a view that limits inerrancy to theology. If the Bible can err in history and scientific data, how can we be assured of its reliability in theology?

We have in hand many ancient manuscripts which highlight the trustworthiness of the Scriptures currently in circulation. Stephen Neill comments that "for about 98 percent of the text of the New Testament, we have before us exactly the words which the original authors wrote; it is impossible that any extensive corruption can have taken place between their time and ours" (Neill 1984, 82-83). This dogmatic declaration by an outstanding scholar is faith-reinforcing. Even if we place the King James Version under critical scrutiny because of its being based on an inferior Greek text, we would still see that it has been the conduit of salvation and blessing to millions of people in the past three centuries.

It is obvious that there is a very significant human component in the Bible. In the Old Testament we do find the words, "The Lord said, . . . " but these quotes are in the minority. Also, the "red letter" Jesus quotes are a very small part of the New Testament. There is a dual human-divine authorship that must be recognized. But our conviction is that God superintended the human component to the degree that Scripture has come forth as "God-breathed." It is understandable why a Muslim is at a loss to comprehend this process. A Christian, if he is honest, will also confess it is beyond his ability to explain how the Word of God can be framed in such very human terminology. But confess this we must, or we are left with no basis for faith or spirituality.

As mentioned earlier, Islamic apologists certainly have no fewer theological problems than Christians. It is just that they choose to ignore their existence. When Muslims verbally attack me on the subject of biblical authority, I am tempted to offer to debate an imam on the question, "Is the Quran the Word of Allah?" Then I am quietly reminded by our Lord of the scriptural principle of turning the other cheek. Also, I am convinced such a counterdebate would be counterproductive. It would only generate a tremendous lot of heat and little, if any, light.[2]

J. I. Packer writes of the ongoing influence of God's Word:

We can be thankful that there is today a movement of return to the Bible. For too long the Bible has been in the dock, on trial without its own voice ever being heard. In the common mind it has been discredited by the advances of science. In the church it has been too often dismembered by its critical students. Thus its testimony has been silenced by some and mutilated by others. We need again to recognize that the place of the Bible is not in the dock, nor even in the witness stand, but on the judgment seat, on the Throne, as the word of the Eternal. (Packer 1980, 63)

I was a student of Clark Pinnock at Trinity Evangelical Divinity School. He is not only an impressive scholar but also a warmhearted man of God. Therefore I am particularly pleased with these words also found in his book *The Scripture Principle:*

[2]As for Deedat's specific attacks on biblical credibility, I would refere the reader to a Christian attorney in South Africa who has written responses to Deedat. To obtain these well-written booklets write: Mr. John Gilchrist, Box 1804, Benoni 1500, Republic of South Africa.

Notice may as well be served right here that large numbers of us are not going to abandon our belief in the Bible as the written Word of God in favor of some view of it as mere human tradition without a very severe struggle – simply because we know, as our opponents ought to know, that Christianity in any sense deserving of the name stands or falls on that belief. (Pinnock 1984, xi)

THE CROSS AND THE CRESCENT

3

Worship, the Holy Privilege

Ken and I jostled through crowded inner-city Manila and finally arrived at the gate of the Golden Mosque. We were greeted by a sign, which stated that women must wear conservative clothes inside the worship area. The mosque is an awesome structure with a minaret that boldly penetrates the thick smog in a city of smoke-belching buses and industrial complexes spewing forth noxious fumes.

Walking away from the streets filled with the clamor of sidewalk vendors, one is struck by the serenity of the mosque. The old and young pause on the marble steps, take off their shoes, walk over to a small pool, and begin the washing that they believe will make them more acceptable in the sight of Allah. This preparation is followed by the low murmur of a communal chant as individuals merge into a universal *ummah* (community). Bodies bend, kneel, and prostrate in a rhythm of worship that humbles man and exalts God. The concluding ritual synthesizes the vertical with the horizontal as the worshiper bestows his peace upon the person to his left and to his right. As Ken and I discreetly walked away from the curious Muslims, some eagerly inquired if we were converts to Islam.

A few short blocks away, we confronted the famous Roman Catholic church known as "the Church of the Black Nazarene." This house of worship stands guard over a plaza best known as a scene of carnage when, in the early 1970s, unidentified terrorists threw hand grenades at a rally, injuring some of the most powerful political leaders of the Philippines. All across the front of the church were stalls filled with every type of religious relic imaginable. The hawkers gave assurance of immense blessing to be received for only a few pesos. Just before entry, a last line of saleswomen aggressively waved booklets of lottery tickets in our faces, indicating that our chances of winning a million were enhanced by our geographical proximity to divinity. Resisting such a sure bet, we pressed on through the crowd of devotees. Soon we stood before a glass-encased coffin containing a six-foot statue of a black Jesus. A long line of somber Catholics awaited the opportunity to caress and kiss Christ's bare feet, which extended beyond the encasement. Some took small bottles of water and pressed them close to the coffin. Others passed handkerchiefs to nearby attendants who broke the line and quickly passed the cloth over the protruding feet of the crucified Savior.

In the huge sanctuary a few women with black veils over their heads slowly crawled down the central aisle on bended knees. Several couples enjoyed a moment of heavenly rapture, though not exactly in a church-sanctioned form! I gazed at the eyes of the supplicants seated on the wood benches. There I saw hope and despair, longing and fulfillment, peace and fear, joy and depression.

We slowly walked past the bowl of holy water, the row of candles, and a grotesquely deformed beggar. Outside, in the blazing sun, we paused to reflect. Ken, with some obvious discomfort, said, "Phil, I hate to say this, but the mosque was a much more worshipful setting than was the church."

Representatives of the world's two largest religions had been observed at close range in the sacred moment of worship. This chapter will now seek to unfold some of the intricacies and realities of such worship as practiced both in Islam and in Christianity.

Ritual

Ritual is a natural and integral outworking of experience. The rites may be sophisticated and extensive or simple and brief. They may be obligatory or optional. Variety can be a valued or a rejected component. Ritual may be pregnant with meaning and dynamics or deteriorate into lifeless repetition.

Once again, I reiterate the complexity of being selective. The Sufis and the orthodox of Islam differ in ritual as much as Eastern Orthodox Christians and Pentecostals. My goal is to concentrate on the representative, mainstream Muslim.

Muslim Liturgy

Thomas Clayton, an American convert to Islam, recalls his first encounter with Muslim worship:

The sun had just passed the meridian. As we walked along the hot, dusty road, we heard or rather felt a monotonous but strangely beautiful chant fill the air about us. Passing through a group of trees, a strange and wondrous sight befell our unbelieving eyes. There, on a recently improvised high wooden tower, a blind Arab, clad in spotless raiments and white turban, seemed to harangue the very heavens with his fascinating intonation. We sat down with no conscious effort, hypnotized by his weird, spiritlike refrain. The words we did not understand fell fascinatingly upon our ears. (Clayton 1976, 102-103)

Soon a large group of people seemed to appear out of nowhere, and spreading long mats on the ground, they began to pray. Clayton continues,

Almost three years have now passed since that event, two of which I have been a Muslim and I find myself even now awakening in the middle of the night to hear once more that beautiful and plaintive chant, and to see again those men who displayed the true attributes of men who sincerely seek their God. (Clayton 1976, 103)

Clayton has succinctly highlighted the core of Muslim spirituality. Prayer is Islam's closest ritual equivalent to a Christian sacrament. (Muslim circumcision would qualify except for its practice being limited mostly to men.) Muslim prayer actually has more impact in that it is mandated five times daily, whereas baptism is a once-in-a-lifetime experience and the Lord's Supper is observed once a week or less.

The model for prayer involvement was the Prophet himself. His wife Aisha related, "God's Messenger, on him be peace, would talk to us and we to him, but when it was time for prayer it seemed as though he did not know us, nor we him. This was because he was completely in awe of God" (Ghazali 1983, 29). Prayer was very much a life-style to Muhammad.

Salat is the universal Muslim practice of prescribed ritual prayer. The word is probably best translated as "worship," as it carries with it the connotation of supplication with adoration. The Quran does not enjoin the five daily prayers. Rather, it speaks of two morning prayers and one evening prayer. Tradition, however, has made the five-times-a-day prayer cycle absolutely obligatory for devout Muslims.

If at all possible, the prayers should be recited in the mosque. A Hadith (tradition) states, "The prayer in congregation is twenty-seven times superior to the prayer offered by a person alone" (Bukhari [Vol. 1], 351).

Once inside the mosque, the Muslim goes directly to the washing area to perform his ablutions. The washing of the face, hands, arms, and feet is more than a mere physical ritual. There is a deep symbolism in these acts that link the external body to the internal purification of mind and soul. Muslim scholars highlight a spiritual and psychological relationship between the two. "The development of the outward form is, to a certain extent, absolutely essential for the development of the inner self" (Rahman 1979b, 50). I particularly like the prayer of repentance of the more mystical Muslim as he moves slowly through the ceremony of washing the different parts of his body:

Eyes: "Allah, forgive me for any thought of lust which has entered my soul through the eye-gate."

Ears: "Please cleanse my inner soul from defilement caused by that which I have heard which is evil."

Mouth: "I acknowledge my weakness to criticize and speak harshly of others. Keep me from this sin."

Hands: "Allah, with these hands, I have not done good deeds helpful to others. Assist me to be more kind and considerate."

Feet: "I have gone places where you would not want to accompany me. Forgive my urge toward waywardness and help me to walk consistently in the straight path."

A ritual of contrition and remembrance such as this, performed five times a day, could have real spiritual value for any God-seeker, or so it seems to me. One of the greatest deterrents to true spirituality is God-forgetfulness. A thought of crude lust cannot coexist with a mental focus on the beauty and holiness of the Lord. We so easily cast God aside and opt for the sensual. But a meaningful ritual, performed every few hours, that refocuses our attention on holiness could cause a spiritual revolution in our hearts. This, of course, could be done internally as a prayer without the attendant ablutions and physical ritual.

Muslims are particularly proud of the egalitarian nature of the prayer rows.

The prayer in congregation is a training in brotherhood. All Muslims, irrespective of colour, race or nationality, stand in prayer before their Lord as equals.... This is an example of democracy such as no religion or social group other than Islam has successfully established in this world. Human distinctions are levelled down in prayer and the pride of the rich is cut down and the lowness of the poor is raised, so that all feel equal and humble before their Lord. The organization of prayer in rows destroys all class distinctions in society and all narrow class feelings of nationhood, or tribe, or color or race. (Rahman 1979b, 147)

Prostration as a prayer form of humility is commanded in the Quran "But prostrate thyself, and draw near (unto Allah)" (Sura 96:19). Bowing down to the earth is regarded as the highest act of submission. Ghazali likens this to the restoring of the branch to the root (Ghazali 1983, 47).

There are some interesting Hadith relating to prayer. Aisha was not comfortable with being placed in the same category as animals.

Prayer is annulled by a dog, a donkey and a woman (if they pass in front of the praying people). I said, "You have made us (i.e., women) dogs." (Bukhari [Vol. 2], 135)

A person was mentioned before the Prophet and he was told that he had kept on sleeping till morning and had not gotten up for the prayer. The Prophet said, "Satan urinated in his ears" (Bukhari [Vol. 2], 135).

The Prophet said, "If anyone of you rouses from sleep and performs the ablution, he should wash his nose by putting water in it and then blowing it out thrice, because Satan has stayed in the upper part of his nose all the night." (Bukhari [Vol. 4], 328)

Muslims are warned against allowing rites to become an end in themselves. The Quran says, "It is not righteousness that ye turn your faces to the East and the West; but righteous is he who believeth in Allah" (Sura 2:177). The mandated direction of prayer becomes of lesser importance than one's heart condition. Praying to be seen of man is also deplored: "He who does good things in public to show off and win the praise of the people, Allah will disclose his real intention (and humiliate him)" (Bukhari [Vol. 8], 334).

In Muslim worship, as in all worship, form cannot be divorced from content. Spirituality, at its most dynamic point of contact between God and man, is experienced as the worshiper, with an intense level of submission and concentration, bows prostrate before Allah in the company of the faithful in the mosque. God is present in the community as well as in the individual. The devout Muslim can ask for nothing more.

Christian Freedom

When teaching a course on Islam, I often make the following statement to my students: "Muslims are more biblical in their worship forms than are contemporary Christians." Immediately I have the students' attention and curiosity! The following prooftexts are then presented:

• Numbers 16:22: Moses and Aaron fell on their faces and prayed.

- Joshua 5:14: Joshua "fell to the earth and bowed down" and prayed.
- 1 Kings 8:22: Solomon stood before the LORD and spread out his hands.
- 2 Chronicles 6:13: Solomon knelt and spread out his hands toward heaven.
- 2 Chronicles 7:3: The sons of Israel, seeing the glory of the LORD, "bowed down on the pavement with their faces to the ground, and they worshiped and gave praise to the LORD."
- 2 Chronicles 20:18: All the people of Jerusalem fell down before the LORD.
- Psalm 95:6: "Come, let us worship and bow down; let us kneel before the LORD our Maker."
- Daniel 6:10: Daniel knelt on his knees three times a day and prayed and gave thanks to God.
- Matthew 26:39: Jesus "fell on His face and prayed."
- Mark 11:25: Jesus told his followers to stand and pray.
- Luke 22:41: In the Garden, Jesus knelt and prayed.
- Acts 20:36: Paul knelt when he prayed with the church elders.
- 1 Timothy 2:8: "Therefore I want the men in every place to pray, lifting up holy hands."

All of the above forms are common to the Muslim prayer ritual. In the Bible there is no reference to praying with one's eyes closed. Muslims pray with their eyes open. There is only one reference in the Bible to praying while being seated (2 Samuel 7:18, repeated in 1 Chronicles 17:16). Yet this is by far the most common posture of prayer for evangelicals, and one almost never used by Muslims.

Does it really matter that Christians have not followed biblical norms in prayer forms? Are we not free to choose according to personal preference? What we find in Scripture are historical records of how people prayed in ages past. In fact, apart from the obvious repeated exhortations to pray, there are few verses that could be classified as form commands. One of these is Matthew 6:5-7:

> *And when you pray, you are not to be as the hypocrites; for they love to stand and pray in the synagogues and on the street corners, in order to be seen by men. Truly I say to you, they have their reward in full. But you, when you pray, go into your inner room, and when you have shut your door, pray to your Father who is in secret, and your Father who sees in secret will repay you. And when you are praying, do not use meaningless repetition, as the Gentiles do, for they suppose that they will be heard for their many words.*

Even here the issue is not that all Christians must only pray in inner rooms. The point of the exhortation is that the Christian must avoid spiritual pride and hypocrisy. God's concern is the state of the heart, not the place or position of prayer.

A Muslim can hardly comprehend Christian prayer. I recall with great embarrassment one such clash of views which occurred in my home. My friend Dr. Ali was returning to Bangladesh upon completion of his stint as a visiting scholar at Harvard. He stopped in Manila and stayed in our home for several days. As per my custom, I was up early having my devotions in my office when suddenly the door opened and there stood Dr. Ali. I was praying in the most unorthodox position possible – leaning back in my chair with my feet on the desk. Noting my Bible, Dr. Ali assessed the situation and hastily withdrew. Because of his graciousness, he never mentioned the incident, but he must have wondered how one could ever be so deceived as to think he can pray in a sitting position with feet propped up on a desk. (My only consolation is that I was barefooted, as Muslims are required to be when they pray.)

While in an Asian country conducting a seminar on Islam, I was asked to lead a Sunday morning worship service in a contextualized Islamic-type liturgy. The Christian delegates happily entered in as we chanted the attributes of God, read biblical passages relating to prayer forms, and prayed prostrate on the floor. Following the service a Malay Muslim convert came up to me and excitedly exclaimed, "Oh, that was wonderful! I feel like this is the first time I have really prayed since becoming a Christian twenty years ago." Spirituality to him was at least partially related to worship in which prostration was an element.

Richard J. Foster links worship to physical expressions:

The root meaning for the Hebrew word we translate worship is "to prostrate." The word bless literally means "to kneel." Thanksgiving refers to an "extension of the hand." Throughout Scripture we find a variety of physical postures in connection with worship: lying prostrate, standing, kneeling, lifting the hands, clapping the hands, lifting the head, bowing the head, dancing and wearing sackcloth and ashes. The point is that we are to offer God our

bodies as well as all the rest of our being. Worship is
appropriately physical. (Foster 1978, 147)

The ritual of praying the rosary is very important to
many Roman Catholics. As a celebration of the 2000th
birthday of Mary, the mother of Jesus, Catholic leaders in
1985 placed an advertisement in a Manila newspaper which
said in part, "Pray the Rosary daily, whenever possible with
your family, especially from September 8 to December 8
this year" (Bahay Maria 1985, 11). Calvin Miller as an
evangelical would not be excited about using the rosary as
a prayer help, but he does speak of a lively imagination
being essential to worship: "My own imagination ever sees
new visualizations of God, high and lifted up, stooping to
my needs, giving me the Christ for whom I hunger" (Miller
1984, 68-69).

Other worship variations would include that of the
Pentecostals. The worshipers stand, raise their hands, and
corporately pray in unison. "Singing in the spirit" is, to me, one
of the most beautiful expressions of Pentecostalism. Black
churches also emphasize a more emotional style of worship.
The free leading of the Spirit is very important to this segment of
the body of Christ.

In my opinion, diversity in ritual is a distinct advantage
within Christendom. While teaching in Jos, Nigeria, I was
awestruck watching a rather heavyset African lady dance
before the Lord. During the congregational singing, she
moved out of her pew and began slowly dancing up and
down the aisles of the church. Her face was turned upward.
As her body swayed rhythmically she clapped her hands in
concert with the other believers. There was nothing sensual in

her actions. She was simply expressing her deep love for Jesus in a cultural context that approved of her particular worship form.

In all of creation, we see God's affirmation of variety. It seems to me, that the offering of our praise and love to Jesus in that same grid of variety is, assuredly, a sweet-smelling savor before the throne of God. Perhaps our Muslim friends should give deeper consideration to the Christian position on worship ritual and the reasons why we refuse to embrace and enforce a universal liturgy.

Spiritual Reality

Spiritual reality is an abstract not easily grasped. It requires a great amount of effort and faith to leap from the temporal to the eternal. Across the globe people exhibit the universal need to pray, but even the most devout people have trouble praying.

Some years ago the United Presbyterian Church, now known as the Presbyterian Church (U. S. A.), sent its missionaries a questionnaire requesting information on what they considered to be their greatest personal difficulty. Almost every missionary indicated his main struggle was having a successful devotional life. *Leadership* magazine did a similar survey among its readership. Over 50 percent of the readers admitted to some degree of frustration in the practice of prayer and Bible study.

In my survey of missionaries, by far the most serious spiritual struggle in life was identified as trying to have an adequate personal time with the Lord. Over 80 percent of the 390 respondents stated that at times they do not enjoy prayer. Close to 70 percent declared that there are occasions when they simply pray out of a sense of duty. In the same survey it was revealed that 101 missionaries pray, on an average, less than 10 minutes daily. Another 229 pray between 11 and 30 minutes. In the Elmbrook Church survey, 26 percent of the congregation indicated they had a specific prayer time less than twice a week.

An attendant problem is that of mind wandering. Not long ago I was sitting in my office when I took a mental excursion to an event of a few years ago. In my mind I replayed the Falkland Islands conflict between Argentina and Britain. Warships were being sunk. Helicopters were flying over battleships as decoys to incoming missiles. My heart went out to the suffering inhabitants of the island that was once so sleepy and peaceful. After a number of minutes, I was able to bring about a glorious victory for the British. Only then did I realize that I was in the middle of my early morning prayer time. What did the Falkland Islands have to do with my royal audience with the Lord? Once again Satan had been successful in his diversionary tactics in my devotional time.

Bishop H. B. Dehqani-Tafti has testified to the problem of concentration in prayer. He once visited a famous monk, known as Matthew the Poor, who lives in one of the ancient monasteries in the Egyptian desert. When the bishop asked about how one can better focus the mind on prayer, the monk replied, "Concentration relates to the whole of life. A man who is normally a scatter-brain cannot suddenly switch off all the noises within him and achieve full concentration. He has to learn the art of perpetual inner silence" (Dehqani-Tafti 1981, 101).

I am convinced Muslims strive with the same problems.

The devout Muslim will often find it difficult to maintain the five-times-daily regimen of prayer. This leads to a sense of guilt and failure. It would be interesting to do a survey that would indicate the percent of the faithful who strictly pray according to the dictates of Islam. My observation is that such a group would constitute a minority of less than five percent worldwide.

Even a very devout Muslim like Dr. Ali, who is amazingly faithful in prayer, finds it extremely difficult to arise before sunrise to commence his day by performing the *salat*. He has told me that he hopes Allah will have mercy and forgive him for being tardy by an hour or two. I have asked him whether he, too, struggles with mental concentration in prayer. He assured me he does.

Ghazali, in his writing, has referred to one of the Muslim "saints" who overcame these difficulties.

Amir ibn Abdullah was one of those who are humble in their prayers. He would sometimes pray while his daughter was playing the tambourine and the women of the house were chattering freely, but he was quite insensitive to the noise and did not even hear it. They once asked him: "Does anything come into your mind during the prayer?" "Yes," said he, "the thought that I am standing in the presence of God, Great and Glorious is He, and that I am bound for Paradise or for Hell." He was then asked: "Do you get any worldly thoughts, as we do?" To this he replied: "I would rather be made a butt for lances than get that sort of thing in my prayer." He was also in the habit of saying: "Even if the veil was lifted from the unseen, my faith could not be more

THE CROSS AND THE CRESCENT

certain than it is now." (Ghazali 1983, 50)

Spiritual Hunger

A missionary friend of mine in a Muslim setting frequently arises at three-thirty in the morning for a time of seeking God through prayer, Bible reading, and perusal of the classic writings on Christian spirituality. My friend's heart is hungry for the Lord. I detect, at times, a holy impatience in his words and actions. "Why isn't God giving that which will bring glory to Himself? Will those who hunger and thirst after righteousness not be filled?" Yet with all sincerity he continues his quest.

It appears this same conflict is at the root of the decision of Thomas Howard, the evangelical writer, to convert to Roman Catholicism. He comments, "I don't know whether I've ever met an evangelical who does not lament the desperate, barren, parched nature of evangelical worship. They're frantic over the evangelical poverty when it comes to the deeper reaches of Christian spirituality and what the mystery of worship is all about" (Woodbridge 1985, 50). The obvious follow-up question is whether Howard will find spiritual fulfillment in the liturgical Roman Catholic church. Quite apart from doctrinal distinctives between Catholics and evangelicals, does a worship form which is so repetitive and routine (at least from my point of view) present a creative and dynamic alternative to that which many conservative churches have to offer? Few question Howard's sincerity. There are other noted evangelicals poised for the leap as well. But are these believers grasping for reality within an institution instead of setting their focus on a Person? If so, they may find that Catholic worship will deteriorate into an insipid set of rituals even more lifeless than that which they have left behind. It seems that part of being fallen human beings is our capacity to make *any* form of worship into a lifeless act. This can happen among Roman Catholics, Pentecostals, and everyone else.

John Hyde, known as "Praying Hyde," was an American missionary in a predominately Muslim area of prepartition India. He was known as a man in vital contact with God. A friend described a time of prayer with Hyde:

> *I said to Mr. Hyde, "I want you to pray for me." He came to my room, turned the key in the door, and dropped on his knees, and waited five minutes without a single syllable coming from his lips. I could hear my own heart thumping and his beating. I felt the hot tears running down my face. I knew I was with God. Then, with upturned face, down which the tears were streaming, he said, "O God!" Then for five minutes at least, he was still again; and then, when he knew that he was talking with God . . . there came up from the depth of his heart such petitions for men as I had never heard before. I rose from my knees to know what real prayer was. (Kneeling Christian 1971, 64)*

Praying Hyde's influence among Christians in what is now the country of Pakistan is probably unparalleled. The older believers love to recount stories they have heard of the amazing exploits of this man of God. Hyde entered into a depth of spiritual hunger few have experienced.

Another one of these few is also from Pakistan. Bilquis Sheikh was a wealthy Muslim lady who knew almost nothing about Jesus Christ. After a dramatic conversion, she commenced her quest for reality in worship.

> *"Father, O my Father God," I cried, with growing confidence. My voice seemed unusually loud in the large bedroom as I knelt on the rug beside my bed. But suddenly that room wasn't empty any more. He was there! I could sense His Presence. I could feel His hand laid gently on my head. It was as if I could see His eyes, filled with love and compassion. He was so close that I found myself laying my head on His knees like a little girl sitting at her father's feet. For a long time I knelt there sobbing quietly, floating in His love. I found myself talking with Him, apologizing for not having known Him before. And again came His loving compassion, like a warm blanket settling around me. (Sheikh 1978, 42)*

Sufi Muslims understand this type of personal experience. But orthodox Islam would declare Sheikh's encounter to be but an outworking of a vivid imagination that has careened out of control. Spiritual reality, to many Muslims, is that which is regulated and regularized. God-awareness must be channeled through established ritual.

Alan Villiers tells of observing Muslim sailors who were performing religious rites on a ship as it sailed around Saudi Arabia. Water was hauled up from the sea for performing ablutions. The men then stood in lines, silently meditating before rhythmically commencing their set prayer ritual. Villiers was especially drawn to the faces of the sailors. As the prayer progressed, the lines softened and a tranquility settled over the usually severe faces of the men. "There was no hypocrisy in those strong faces which looked toward Mecca. It was obvious that their religion was a real and living thing. Their prayers were not simply a formula to be mouthed, but a form of very real communication with a very real god" (Villiers 1940, 30). Is it fair, then, for Samuel Zwemer to say, "Prayer is reduced to a gymnastic exercise and a mechanical act; any one who has lived with Moslems needs no proof for this statement" (Zwemer 1905, 100)? He goes on to say the Muslim sees prayer always as a duty, not a privilege. But my personal observation is that many Muslims happily regard prayer as both duty and privilege.

A missionary was flying on a commercial airline in the Middle East. The stewardess announced that a movie would be shown. From the write-up in the flight magazine, it was obvious that the movie was to be less than "religious" in content. As the missionary adjusted his headset and flicked the dial to the movie channel, he noticed his Pakistani Muslim seatmate get up to open the overhead rack. He pulled out his prayer rug and walked down the aisle to the bathroom, where he performed ablutions and, in a most confined space of solitude, went through his *salat*. The missionary was forced to compare his desire to relax and watch a movie with his companion's priority of prayer.

Kharraz, a Muslim writer, has written penetratingly of the reality of worship within *salat*.

When entering on prayer you should come into the Presence of God as you would on the Day of Resurrection, when you will stand before Him with no mediator between, for He welcomes you and you are in confidential talk with Him and you know in whose Presence you are standing, for He is the King of kings. When you have lifted your hands and said,

"God is most great" then let nothing remain in your heart save glorification, and let nothing be in your mind in the time of glorification, than the glory of God Most High, so that you forget this world and the next, while glorifying Him. (Smith 1950, 26)

The eschatological importance of prayer is seen in this Hadith: "Of all a man's actions, the first to be examined on the Day of Resurrection will be the Prayer. If it is found to be complete, it will be accepted of him along with the rest of his works, but if it is found wanting, it will be rejected along with the rest of his deeds" (Ghazali 1983, 23). There is then a salvific dimension to prayer that promotes observance.

It would seem that *salat* is a straightforward obligation, but the motives operating within the worshiper can be multiple and complex. These can include any mix of the following: a desire to be regarded by others as a pious person; fear that neglecting prayer will condemn one to hell; an obligation minus joy and reality; a habit performed without thinking; an overwhelming sense of gratitude and worship directed toward Allah.

The common denominator among Christians and Muslims is an awareness that worship is to be an experience of real encounter with God. Reality is a definite goal, but, sadly, an oftentimes unfulfilled goal.

Fasting

Muslims regard fasting as an integral component of worship. Each month of Ramadan finds millions of Muslims abstaining from food and liquids during daylight hours. I have never ceased to be amazed at how widespread is this discipline throughout the Islamic world. In more fanatical Muslim countries (Saudi Arabia, for example), the Ramadan fast is obligatory. Failure to follow the religious prohibitions and rituals will result in being fined and imprisoned. But for the most part Muslims willingly partake in this religio-social act that has no exact counterpart anywhere in the world.

My concern relates to Christian neglect in regard to fasting. The Bible clearly teaches abstinence from food and, on certain occasions, from water as well. In Exodus we read of Moses fasting for forty days without eating or drinking. David fasted for seven days prior to the death of his son. Esther asked her people to abstain from food and water for three days before she went in to see the king. The people of Ninevah refrained from eating and drinking in order to avert the judgment of God. Jesus fasted forty days and nights. In Acts, we read of the early Christians engaged in prayer and fasting. Abstinence from food moved believers toward repentance, humility, and a deeper desire for God.

I see three particularly helpful reasons for Christians who live among Muslims to practice fasting:

1. Spiritual benefits: Weakness in body seems to lead to an enhanced dependence upon God. One's spiritual perception becomes more sensitized. Also, there is usually extra time to spend in devotional exercises.

2. Empathy with the hungry: It is good to know what it is like to experience the gnawing pangs of intense hunger and thirst. Much of the world goes to bed each night without adequate nourishment. Our prayers (and deeds) for the unfortunate become more intense after "sitting where they sit."

3. Identification with Muslims: Often Muslims have told me they consider Christians to be spiritually lazy. Followers of Isa (the Muslim name for Jesus) do not pray five times a day nor fast one month a year. My Muslim friends are amazed and gratified when I tell them I have kept the total Ramadan fast two different years.

A number of missionaries favor following the Muslim ritual of arising one and a half hours before sunrise and eating breakfast and having prayer. This is followed by abstinence from food, liquids, medicine, and sexual relations until sunset. All prohibitions are then removed until the next morning. This is the only form of fasting which is regarded as legitimate by Muslims. This style of fasting is extremely difficult, particularly abstaining from drinking any form of liquid.

A few options on timing for Christian fasting are: 1. each Friday; 2. three Fridays a month, making a total of 36 days per year; 3. the month of Ramadan (30 days); 4. one Friday a month, which would be totally set aside for prayer and fasting; and 5. occasional fasting. The Assemblies of God have initiated a JUMAA Prayer Fellowship wherein 30,000 Christians have agreed to set aside Friday noon as a time to pray and fast for Muslims.[3] This is particularly appropriate for concerned laymen in the church.

For those desiring to follow the Muslim ritual of fasting, there are a few practical points to consider. The first few days of the fast are the most difficult. Our bodies must make adjustment to mild dehydration. Headaches and slight dizziness

[3]For further informaiton write: Center for Ministry to Muslims, Division of Foreign Missions, Assemblies of God, 1445 Boonville Avenue, Springfield, MO 65802.

are common. It is important to make the effort to rise early in the morning and drink several glasses of water. Yogurt is also good to eat, along with a reasonable amount of solids.

Brushing your teeth and washing out your mouth (without swallowing) several times a day is allowed. In the tropics a noon shower, where possible, is always appreciated. A midday siesta is highly recommended. If the pace of life can be slackened, this will facilitate feeling better. Plan to have a reasonable supper at sunset, but do not be excessive in eating. Drink plenty of liquids throughout the evening. (It is true, unfortunately, that a few individuals simply cannot fast.)

Above all, make the time of fasting a special occasion to seek the Lord. A good time for extra prayer is between the early morning meal and before the rest of the family arises. As you humbly share your experiences of fasting and prayer with your Muslim friends, you will find them genuinely appreciative of your hunger for God which is being expressed in terms they can best understand.

Results

Is prayer effective? In response to this question we find the scoffers scoffing and believers believing. There is a standoff between the antagonists and the protagonists. The skeptic points to a formula for farming to authenticate his agnosticism:

Seed + Rain + Hard Work + Prayer = A Good Crop and
Seed + Rain + Hard Work = A Good Crop
therefore
Prayer = Nothing

The godless person for whom no one is praying appears to recover as quickly as the devout Christian with his resources of countless praying friends. And what about the hundreds of other prayers which seemingly are divinely ignored? A pall of perplexity hangs low over the lives of countless Christians as they struggle with the contradiction between biblical assurances and real life. A shroud of unwelcome mystery seems to separate our finite understanding from God's sovereign will. It is at this crucial point of perplexity that more than one Christian has simply decided God is not holding up his part of the bargain. They have then slowly and sadly walked away into a dark night filled with alienation, loneliness, and conflict. But questions of universal consequence remain. Agnosticism answers nothing. It only changes the game plan from faith to an unresolved quagmire of the unknown.

Alexander Solzhenitsyn is my literary and moral hero. His *One Day in the Life of Ivan Denisovich* is one of the most gripping books ever written. In this novel based on events in Solzhenitsyn's life, we read of a dialogue on unanswered prayer between two prisoners in a Siberian prison, the Baptist Alyosha and Ivan Denisovich Shukhov. I record it in detail because of its relevance to the topic under discussion as well as for its literary pungency:

> *Alyosha heard Shukhov's whispered prayer, and, turning to him:*
> *"There you are, Shukhov, your soul is begging to pray. Why don't you give it its freedom?"*
> *Shukhov stole a look at him. Alyosha's eyes glowed like two candles.*

"Well, Alyosha," he said with a sigh, "it's this way. Prayers are like those appeals of ours. Either they don't get through or they're returned with 'rejected' scrawled across 'em."

Outside the staff quarters were four sealed boxes – they were cleared by a security officer once a month. Many were the appeals that were dropped into them. The writers waited, counting the weeks: there'll be a reply in two months, in one month.... But the reply doesn't come. Or if it does it's only "rejected."

"But, Shukhov, it's because you pray too rarely, and badly at that. Without really trying. That's why your prayers stay unanswered. One must never stop praying. If you have real faith you tell a mountain to move and it will move. . . ."

Shukhov grinned and rolled another cigarette. He took a light from the Estonian.

"Don't talk nonsense, Alyosha. I've never seen a mountain move. Well, to tell the truth, I've never seen a mountain at all. But you, now, you prayed in the Caucasus with all that Baptist society of yours - did you make a single mountain move?". . . .

"Oh, we didn't pray for that, Shukhov," Alyosha said earnestly. Bible in hand, he drew nearer to Shukhov till they lay face to face. "Of all earthly and moral things, our Lord commanded us to pray only for our daily bread. 'Give us this day our daily bread.'"

"Our ration, you mean?" asked Shukhov.

But Alyosha didn't give up. Arguing more with his eyes than his tongue, he plucked at Shukhov's

113

sleeve, stroked his arm, and said: "Shukhov, you shouldn't pray to get parcels or for extra stew, not for that. Things that man puts a high price on are vile in the eyes of Our Lord. We must pray about things of the spirit – that the Lord Jesus should remove the scum of anger from our hearts." (Solzhenitsyn 1963,153-154)

Without denying the validity of prayer for parcels, stew, and bread, I must agree with Alyosha in his sense of priorities. The real focus in prayer should be internal transformation. Attainment of a godly character is the greatest challenge of prayerful petition. It seems to me that the majority of time spent in prayer is materialistically oriented. We bombard the throne of God with selfish requests.

Anyone who knows me well is aware of my ongoing battle with pride. Even the cognizance of how little I have attained in life does not seem to deter an inflated sense of self-worth. Yet there was a time in my life when things were much worse. In fact, it is not an overstatement to say I was spiritually crippled by an overwhelming desire to be recognized and acclaimed. Much of this problem is rooted in an unhappy childhood that had more than its share of poverty and peer rejection. The psychological effects of those influences resulted in a deep insecurity that drove me to aggressively pursue attention.

I recall the trauma of sitting through elections during college days. More than once, I came away depressed because of being ignored during nominations for class officers. Each day after chapel I stood around the mailboxes, hoping that people would stop and talk with me. My silent cry was *Please love me*.

One early morning I became overwhelmed with the futility of my efforts to be recognized. Kneeling in an empty classroom, I petitioned my Lord for inner release from a sin so powerful that it was slowly but surely pulling me down into a pit of destruction. For an extended period, I confessed my wretchedness and cried out to God for transformation. Just after dawn the sun began to rise in the inner recesses of my soul. The rays of light diffused into the crevices of a weary mind. Suddenly I began to experience a release that can only be described as exhilarating. No longer did I feel the oppressive weight of pride casting me about in a storm of emotional turmoil.

I rose from my knees perplexed and joyful. By that evening I had confirmed, not sinless perfection, but a wonderful new salvation from a sin of the spirit that had so ensnared me. I continue the elusive quest for true humility, but I can gratefully testify to the power of prayer in effecting a release from the more overt manifestations of the spiritual disease of pride.

I like the way Harold S. Kushner sums up the value of prayer:

One of the things that constantly reassures me that God is real, and not just an idea that religious leaders made up, is the fact that people who pray for strength, hope, and courage so often find resources of strength, hope, and courage that they did not have before they prayed. (Kushner 1981, 128)

Having affirmed all the above, do we limit the fruit of prayer to the more subjective areas of the life of the one who is praying? It is gratifying that 81 percent of the parishoners at Elmbrook Church said they agreed or strongly agreed with the statement "I can tell of a specific answer to prayer within the past two weeks." Over 80 percent of the respondents to my missionary survey indicated that God "frequently" gives specific answers to their prayers.

Brian Lawrence, a missionary serving among Muslims in the Philippines, was kidnapped by Islamic extremists in the summer of 1986. In a note to me, Brian wrote about the part prayer played in his ordeal.

> *As I was forced to walk barefoot through the woods I reminded myself that what had happened was not a mistake of God, but part of his perfect plan for his children. A letter received from a prayer supporter in California told us how God had awakened her during the early morning hours of July 12 and directed her to pray specifically for me, Carol Ann [Brian's wife], and our unborn child. Until that time she had not even heard that Carol Ann was pregnant! Allowing for the time difference between here and there, she must have been praying for us just before I was abducted. God chose this willing servant to specifically bathe us in prayer during that difficult time. . . . How encouraging it was to hear my name on local and short wave broadcasts over the radio that my abductors stole from our house. It assured me that many were praying for us. Since my release, we have received letters from friends, and even strangers, in every continent. These dear ones assured us that they had heard of my kidnapping over the news media and were praying*

*for us and encouraging others to pray also. It is to
this prayer that I attribute my good treatment and
quick release, without ransom, after only six days.*

It would be quite possible to offer volumes of testimony
to substantiate the claims of Christians that God does indeed
hear and answer prayer. This belief has been a cornerstone
of Christian spirituality throughout church history. To
complete this chapter it is only fair to allow our Muslim
friends to give their testimony concerning Allah hearing
and acting upon their prayers.

The Fruit of Muslim Prayers

Sura 40:60 is a clear command and assurance: "Pray
unto me and I will hear your prayer." The *salat* contains
mostly a repetition of verses from the Quran. Following
this ritualized prayer, the worshiper is expected to spend
an additional amount of time in informal intercession. He
can pray for relatives, friends, and personal needs. It is his
belief that Allah is aware of his petition and desirous to
grant good gifts to his children. The basic prerequisite for
receiving answers to one's prayer is submission to Allah in
every area of life. I have prayed informally with Dr. Ali on
many occasions. He has been as intense and sincere in his prayers
as any Christian I know. He would always conclude by praying
for his fifteen-year-old son who is mentally retarded. It was a
touching experience to see an intellectual Muslim bow before
Allah and with choked voice pray for his beloved son's mental
healing. It was equally challenging to me to see how tenderly
and patiently he dealt with the boy even when his behavior was
somewhat frustrating. This seemed to parallel Paul's experience

of seeing prayer answered, not in the removal of the thorn, but in receiving the grace to endure it.

A Filipino Muslim once testified to me of the value of prayer in his life. Akbar was a person who had drifted far from his religious and moral roots. He was a successful businessman who had access to an abundance of money which funded a lavish and sensual life-style. Gambling was a compulsive habit. Prostitutes were used and discarded on a cyclical basis. Akbar divorced his wife and was happy to be free of legal restraints. He was sinking deeper and deeper into a self-dug pit of personal destruction. All that was beautiful and noble lost its luster. Soon the appetites of the flesh became impossible to satisfy. There was no satisfaction, no peace, no rest.

Akbar felt he had two choices before him. One was spiritual suicide and the other was spiritual salvation. He testifies that he chose the latter. He cried out to Allah for renewal, commenced the five-times-a-day prayer ritual, and cut loose from the sexual degradation which was so pervasive in his life. He stood before me a very different man than he had been just a few years previously. His friends all testified to me of the change they had observed in Akbar's life.

It is changed lives like these that are frustrating for us as Christians to ponder. Has the Quran and the prayer ritual radically altered Akbar's behavior? Or was it a psychological encounter based on a morally conditioned conscience? Where does common grace fit in regard to such an alteration in individual behavior? I must say, I find it difficult to conclude such a positive change is the product of Satanic influence. Once again we find life is full of perplexities which defy our most persistent probings. My prayer for Akbar continues to be that he may yet find Jesus as Lord. Though he may have experienced a moral transformation, I as a Christian am committed to praying and witnessing to the end that Akbar will become a Christian.

A Muslim scholar has written concerning the power of prayer in assisting man in overcoming evil.

> *Prayer helps man to fight against evil with patience and perseverance. It is a prescription which improves and purifies one's self and helps one to attain high moral qualities and to build a strong defense against evil. The Holy Quran refers to this miraculous effect of prayer in these words: "Establish regular prayer, surely prayer keeps (one) away from indecency and evil. And certainly the remembrance of God is the greatest (force against evil)" (29:45). (Rahman 1979b, 170)*

Another assurance of answered prayer comes from Ali Zain al-Abidin. It is set forth in poetic expression.

> *Praise be to Him who when I call on Him answers*
> *me, slow though I am when He calls me.*
> *Praise be to Him who gives to me when I ask Him,*
> *miserly though I am when He asks a loan of me.*
> *Praise be to Him to whom I confide my needs*
> *whensoever I will and He satisfies them.*
> *My Lord I praise, for He is of my praise most worthy.*
> *(Padwick 1961, 81)*

Ritual, reality, and results – the Christian and the Muslim affirm all three. It is now up to the discerning reader to reflect on the contradictory and complementary claims of Christianity and Islam in regard to worship and prayer.

THE CROSS AND THE CRESCENT

4

The Suffering World

If I were God . . . should I go further? Perhaps not. But I am compelled. Yes, with a trembling hand I assert the following: If I were God, I would create and not destroy. I would make love for Christ and man a norm and not an exception. I would see to it that every baby was born whole. I would banish earthquakes, hurricanes, and tornadoes. I would, in one stroke, annihilate pain and its horrendous fallout on mankind. I would manipulate technology so it would be only a dependable tool for the benefit of the human race. I would make people laugh and dance and be forever joyful. And then I would sit back on my throne, relax with eternal contentment, and say, "It is good."

Are these words presumptuous blasphemy or simply a Christian baring his soul in honesty? I trust they are the latter. Others stronger than me can close their ears and avert their glance. They can press for optimism, recommend a full-orbed, triumphant faith, or strongly emphasize God's mysterious sovereignty. Without denying any of the above, I cannot tune out the cries of the abused child, the brokenness of the faithful wife who has just been told she is married to an adulterer, or the sorrow of a newly widowed nineteen-year-old devout Christian girl.

Walk with me through these next pages. May the walk lead to an enhanced realism, a tenderness toward the hurting, and a stronger faith in our Lord. May it lead us to a deeper understanding of how Christians and Muslims respond to suffering in the world.

The Riddle of Evil and Pain

The headline of the Manila morning paper was crisp and to the point: "Four Missing-Six Injured-One Thousand Homes Razed-One Million Dollar Loss in Shantytown Fire."

Such a revelation of tragedy usually calls for a thirty-second pronouncement of sympathy. This fire was different. It occurred less than half a mile from our home. Billowing orange flames lit up the night sky for hours on end.

I had often driven by the squatter area called "Nazareth" and wondered what it would be like to live as a family of ten in an eight-by-ten-foot room bounded by quarter-inch plywood walls and a leaky tin roof. How could one adjust to the constant clamor of children, the incessant barking of dogs, the sorrowful weeping of an abused wife, the fear of thievery of one's hard-earned pesos, and the heartache of explaining to hungry children that Dad had just gambled away his wages in the cockfights.

Julie and I stood for two hours and watched the flames leap from one shack to another. Filipinos rushed out into the clogged adjacent highway and deposited any possessions they could salvage from the onrushing torrent of flames. A mother pensively sat in the middle of chaos and nursed her trusting infant. Nearby a young man rested his head on a huge generator he had helped pull from one of the nearby shops. Every few minutes he opened his red, swollen eyes to check his proximity to the flames. A cute girl, neatly dressed in her school uniform, was left to guard her parents' few belongings, which had been dumped in the road. She stared at me with a bewildered look of deep pain. It was as if she wondered what it would be like to be me – comparatively rich, well-dressed, comfortably housed, blessed with loving relationships. I stared back at her with an equally bewildered look of deep pain.

Scores of statues of Jesus and pictures of Mary were carried out of "Nazareth" with the same loving care as the families' most prized possessions. Yes, God must be protected from the fire. But what about God protecting the innocent poor from the fire? I looked up into the clear sky and could only think of one word – *rain*. "God of the heavens and of nature, please send a cloudburst of unimaginable intensity. Rebuke and dispel the fires of hell." Through the smoke the beautiful, ever so distant stars winked in a mockery of cosmic silence. The rain did not come.

The next morning, I shaved in painful reflection while downstairs the Christian radio station played the refrain over and over and over again. . . .

He's got it all under control,
He's got it all under control,
He's got it all under control.

The scene now shifts to a reflection I wrote up after returning from an evening of outreach and ministry to Muslims.

"The street was dark and isolated. I had just moved the Christian literature from the tables into the cupboards. It was seven-thirty and time to close down the Reading Center which is located in the midst of the Muslim community in inner-city Manila. As I put boards over the display window and closed the double door, I glanced down at the repaired bolt, which brought memories of the phone call telling me of the attempted break in. Were the thieves willing to risk a jail sentence to steal only a fan . . . or were they trying to send a message to the Christian missionary who had blatantly invaded their turf?

"As I walked down the lonely sidewalk I came to a small bridge over an unbelievably filthy canal. I looked to the right and surveyed 'Little Vietnam' in the distance. Over ten thousand Muslims are packed into an area measuring about half a square mile. Its acquired name derives from the violence that is headquartered within its walls. Delinquent Muslims move out in broad daylight robbing, raping, and killing. They then quickly return, secure in the belief that the police and military will not follow them into their 'city of refuge.'

"Closer to where I was standing on the bridge I observed scores of thin plywood shanties precariously hanging out over the murky waters of the canal. In each of these six-foot-square hovels are living as many as eight Muslim family members.

"Towering over this maze of restless humanity is the

minaret of the famous Golden Mosque. It was from the top of this same tower that a deranged Muslim in a midnight foray of madness began wildly shooting everyone in sight. After he had thrown a few grenades he was successfully subdued and arrested.

"As I walked over the bridge into the crowded Quiapo square, I was accosted by the 'Christian' contributions to the religiously mixed area. First I saw the short-term hotel which caters to the erotic drives of youth. For two dollars, a couple can enjoy the facilities of a bed and a bathroom for three hours. No questions asked.

"Then there were the ever-present peddlers of pornography. In the midst of the stench and deprivation of poverty, one can take a flight into the fantasy of sexual experience. Moral standards become anesthetized, and then it's only a short step away to thievery and drug abuse.

"Just outside the Quiapo Church of the Black Nazarene I boarded the bus and sat pensively viewing the crowd. Three young teenage girls were animatedly discussing the day's events. Dangling from their arms were garlands of flowers which they were selling to Catholics, who would then take them home and place them lovingly over the head of their patron saint. One of the girls became excited and angry as she told of one of the happenings of the day. As her voice rose, she roughly caressed her breasts several times. Now, there is anger and shame. Tomorrow she may be unable to resist the lure of the pesos for selling her precious body again . . . and again . . . and again.

"The bus lurched forward.

"Good night, Quiapo.

"Good night, Christians.

"Good night, Muslims.

"I'll see you tomorrow . . . in the night."

"In the night." Is the world consumed and terrorized by a night of stygian darkness?

A further experience reflects on a brief foray I made into what must be the nearest thing akin to hell on earth.

It is just twenty minutes away from the opulence of ex-President Marcos's palatial home. But hell is light years distant from that fairyland of three thousand pairs of shoes, five hundred brassieres, and full-length mink coats.

Hell is entered by walking thirty feet along a muddy path which opens into a labyrinth of narrow corridors tightly bordered by wooden shanties. One suddenly realizes he is walking on a sea of compressed garbage discarded by Manila's eight million residents. Karma to some, bad luck to others, and God's sovereign plan of predestination to the more religiously inclined - these are the rationale advanced to explain why some are favored to be born in Malacanang Palace while others are destined to draw their first breath of noxious air in hell, more commonly known as the Tondo Garbage Dump, colloquially referred to as "Smoky Mountain."

As soon as I rounded the corner I could see, off in the distance, twenty-five-foot-high mounds of refuse with dark blue smoke billowing forth from fissures that cut across the three-quarter-mile square plot. I was told that internal combustion sparks the flames that produce the smoke that in turn blackens the lungs of the eight hundred families who live in the dump. My "tour" took place on one of the warmer (ninety-six degrees) Manila mornings. Sweat poured down my face as I pushed through the smoke, being ungrateful for the wind which was blowing the blasting hot air off the mountains of burning garbage straight into a community of five thousand dirty, coughing, poorly-clothed, malnourished, God-created Filipinos.

Here I found people with no reason to laugh or play or dance. Yet there they were: gleefully calling out, "Hi, Joe"; children and adults deeply engrossed in a most competitive game of Bingo; a pretty girl managing a small store overlooking a decorated ten-by-twenty-foot area, which becomes the community's dirt dance floor once a week; a teenager laid out in his tiny room, engrossed in watching one of the two or three TV sets in the dump area; a man just released from prison who now attends a weekly Bible study; a little girl, partly obscured from sight by smoke, crying, ever so alone in the middle of one of the garbage heaps; the small baby in a hammock who had almost been killed by her father, who held her responsible for the death of his wife due to childbirth complications; and so many little hands reaching out to be held, affirmed, loved. One little girl just hugged and hugged my legs as though I were her most precious doll.

Slowly and reflectively, I returned to my five-year-old Toyota, which to any of my newfound friends represents a wealth equal to that of a Marcos palace. Arriving home, I took a bath, changed my clothes, shined my muddy shoes, and sat down to a more than adequate lunch. And then I tried to pull it all together.

But for the grace of God, I could have been born in that representation of hell on earth. Yet what about God's grace and those who were born there?

A little touch, a squeeze, and a smiling "Hi" – how hungry they were for the warmth of human love. But who wants to walk the corridors of hell to share love?

The Holocaust

In late 1987, Julie and I visited Auschwitz, Poland, fulfilling a desire to empathize with a segment of humanity that had been subjected to the most ingenious plan man had ever invented to erase a race of people from the earth. I have often contemplated how an intelligent, cultured, and professedly Christian nation could ever descend to such depths of depravity.

My heart swarmed with overwhelming emotion as I sat on the hotel bed and tried to give vent to my feelings.

"It is now just a few hours since Julie and I boarded a 'tour bus' in Krakow and journeyed for ninety minutes through the lovely Polish countryside. Soon the infamous rail line came into view. The ever-efficient Nazis had strategically located the Auschwitz camp at a rail junction at the dead center of their killing empire. Within a few minutes we were standing in front of the awesome gate that welcomed four million newcomers. With a minimum of effort one could conjecture visions of the moment of eternal decision being made by a Gestapo doctor as he gave temporary reprieve to the healthy. The rest were sent to a large courtyard where they were told to quickly undress and run in the nude to the 'showers.' Packed into the large room, men, women, and children received not the refreshing cool water to revive their tired aching bodies, but rather the 'coup de grace' of cyanide pellets that sent them hurtling into eternity.

"As we walked through the camp, as we surveyed the double fence of electrified barbed wire, as we relived one of man's cruelest and most barbaric moments, we felt emotionally drained and physically nauseated.

"One of the most devastating areas was the death block where prisoners were either tortured or shot to death. One cell was dedicated to starvation and another to darkness. Yet another was a two-by-two-foot enclosed area that was entered by crawling in through a small enclosure in the bottom. Four prisoners then stood jammed against each other for the duration of their sentence. The death block barracks contained pathetic messages scribbled on the ceiling by the condemned from the top of their three-tier bunk beds. The final indignity for twenty thousand prisoners was to strip and line up against an outside wall and be shot."

And what about God? *The Deputy* is a drama in which a Nazi physician speaks to a confined priest in Auschwitz:

Since July of 42, for fifteen months, weekdays and Sabbaths, I've been sending people to God. Do you think He's made the slightest acknowledgement? He has not even directed a bolt of lightning against me. Can you understand that? You ought to know. Nine thousand in one day a while back.

Later the doctor reports that though he challenged "the old Gent" to answer, "not a peep came from heaven" (Schilling 1977, 203-204).

On a Sunday afternoon in the Buchenwald camp during World War II, a group of intellectual Jews came together for the purpose of putting God on trial. The charge? "Neglect by God of His chosen people, the Jews." Witnesses came forth to argue persuasively both for the prosecution and the defense. The judges were incarcerated rabbis. With a unanimous verdict, God was found guilty and was condemned.

The Nuclear Age

Our Japan Airlines plane skirted Mount Fuji as we headed south toward Hiroshima. Our flight took us almost directly over the point where, at nineteen hundred feet at eight-fifteen on the morning of August 6, 1945, a foretaste of Armageddon visited planet earth. From the plane we looked down at the famous "Peace Dome" with its grotesquely exposed steel girders.

Later in the day Julie and I stood mesmerized as we gazed at the Peace Dome from a distance of a few feet. We walked through the Peace Park. The names of all persons killed by the bomb, from 1945 to the present, are written on a scroll preserved in a special concrete memorial. A massive bell is rung in the park each morning at exactly eight-fifteen. A perpetual flame spews forth from a torch, reminding.

In the Peace Memorial Museum we walked through the corridors of pain and agony. We silently observed:

- An actual picture of the desolation, taken four hours after the "visitation."
- Rosaries forever fused together into a melted blob.
- The indelible imprint of a person's shadow burned into steps of stone.
- Ragged uniforms taken from the dead.
- A film which pungently described the plight of a seriously retarded forty-year-old woman. Her misfortune? She was a six-month-old fetus in her mother's womb on August 6, 1945.

Today we totter on the precipice of a gigantic chasm that accommodates a nuclear arsenal with the force of more than two million Hiroshima bombs. God help us - and God help the men who have the authority to order the simultaneous pushing of buttons that will raise mushroom clouds, not over just a city, but over a planet.

A Potpourri of Pain

A few glimpses of tragedy from my personal diary. . . .

- I was driving the young MK (missionary kid) to the hospital to visit his baby sister. He looked at me and whispered, "She'll be OK, won't she, Uncle?" Two hours earlier Wade had inadvertently shot an arrow into the air that landed in the eye of his baby sister. She lost the eye.
- The telephone call was subdued. My brother quietly informed me his youngest daughter had just given birth to a Down's syndrome girl. After hanging up, I angrily accused God of not really caring.
- If we had had a son, we would have named him Danny, for Danny Raass was a special friend born of very special parents. Danny once visited us in Miami. He laughed and ran around the living room with our daughter, Lindy. Danny was blind with a golf-ball-size tumor protruding out of his head. He died at age seventeen. I preached his funeral. Danny was a special friend.
- Tom Payne was one of my Sunday school boys. He married a beautiful girl and fathered a lovely daughter. His business prospered. He had everything to live for. And then the "big C," cancer, came for a terminal visit. Payne's name was prophetic. Few have agonized with such excruciating pain. In his early thirties he was finally delivered and translated into the presence of the Lord. Today his dad has crippling multiple sclerosis.

- Merrette Wigand's body slowly began to deteriorate, another case of multiple sclerosis. On furlough, we saw her, bedridden and unable to speak. Soon she could only write with her finger on the blanket, "When?" What terrible suffering she and her husband, Warren, endured. At the triumphant funeral I was able to pay tribute to God's adequate grace as experienced by two very precious saints.
- Eight men from my home church went out for a pleasant afternoon of fishing on the lake. Who sent the sudden squall? Why? Only one survived by clinging to an overturned boat in turbulent waters. Hundreds attended the funerals. No clichés. Just tears.
- Phil Armstrong, newly retired founder-director of SEND International, and I had lunch together at a Holiday Inn in Detroit. He looked piercingly into my eyes and with a laryngitis-laced voice asked, "Phil, where to from here?" Within a short time, Phil was bouncing around in a small plane in a storm over Alaskan waters in the middle of the night. "Goodbye and thanks. We are going in." Those were the last words of the pilot on his radio. Not a trace of the plane or Phil or the others on that flight has ever been found. Phil's question was answered by an authority much higher than that to whom he originally addressed it.
- Beautiful, indescribable Kashmir. Julie and I had just enjoyed a most relaxing vacation in the lovely mountains. We had met an elderly British missionary doctor. She was poised for retirement after a lifetime of selfless ministry in India. The day before we were to leave a friend came to our hotel room and requested we join the search party for the doctor. She had gone out to climb a mountain and had not returned. We soon found her mangled body

just below a sheer cliff. The planned joyful party to celebrate the doctor's retirement was cancelled. A memorial service took its place.

• The Fillmans are friends of ours. Don and Dolly, one late evening, were kneeling in prayer by their bed. Their adopted son took careful aim through the window, squeezed the trigger, and sent a bullet crashing into Don's head. Somehow he survived . . . and somehow he forgave.

• Ray Schaeffer and I used to have long talks together. He was the director in Bangladesh of the Australian Baptist Missionary Society, and we had many common concerns and interests. His devoted wife died of cancer. With his second wife, he went for a missionary visit to Irian Jaya. A few months later I flew over the fateful spot. Another storm. Another crash. The pilot, Ray, and his wife translated from Irian Jaya to eternity.

Do you have the explanation for these perplexities? Lawrence Sanders thinks he does:

Do you know the answer to all the heavy questions that have baffled the world since Adam? I have the answer: Think of God as a clown, the Divine Clown that solves everything. Undeserved suffering. Injustice. Pain. It all suddenly makes sense if you think of God as a clown. An earthquake kills a thousand people? Slapstick. A bridge collapses in Bolivia and thirty innocents are drowned? A great act. Are you following me? An infant born with leukemia? Hard to top. The Divine Clown. Think about it. When the idea sinks in, you can sit back and applaud the performance. (Mr. & Ms. 1984, 8)

Can you identify with the writer of Ecclesiastes?

Then I looked again at all the acts of oppression which were being done under the sun. And behold I saw the tears of the oppressed and that they had no one to comfort them; and on the side of their oppressors was power, but they [the oppressed] had no one to comfort them. So I congratulated the dead who are already dead more than the living who are still living. But better off than both of them is the one who has never existed, who had never seen the evil activity that is done under the sun. (Eccles. 4:1-3)

Have I dug the pit too deep? Are the illustrations too overwhelming? After reading these preceding pages, are you overcome with despair? Read on. Let us consider first the Muslim response and then ponder the Christian and his interaction with the problem of pain and purpose. Spirituality simply cannot be sealed off from the harsh realities of everyday life.

Muslims and Fatalism

It is all very simple: *Everything that occurs in the life of a Muslim is the will of Allah.* All is foreknown and foreordained. Devoted followers of God only submit and never question. The potter unilaterally molds the clay. The puppeteer manipulates the puppets according to his own desire.

As my Muslim friends have told me, "Allah is the Alpha and Omega. What can human beings do to influence the acts of a sovereign God?"

Samuel M. Zwemer takes this attitude a step further as he searingly critiques Islam as an institution.

God wills both good and evil; there is no escaping from the caprice of His decree. Religion is Islam, i.e., resignation. Fatalism has paralyzed progress. Hope perishes under the weight of this iron bondage; injustice and social decay are stoically accepted; no man bears the burden of another. (Zwemer 1907, 95)

It pains me to read such a sweeping generalization. Zwemer is one of my favorite Islam scholars. I possess eighteen of his books. He spent most of his life in witness among Muslims. Yet he often writes from a colonialist mentality that cuts deep into the very fiber of Islam. How well would the West hold up against a similar analysis of the social sins of a culture long exposed to Christian influence? E. Stanley Jones does little better.

Islam, great and noble in many ways, has nevertheless sterilized the life of vast portions of the East, because its acceptance of inequalities and sufferings as the will of God lays a paralyzing hand on any civilization that adopts it. It is an opiate. (Jones 1933, 61)

Thus we are drawn back to Karl Marx's position that

religion is an opiate. Has Jones forgotten that the original charge was leveled primarily against Christians? Have not we, as Christians, historically and theologically encouraged submission and acceptance as a legitimate response to the higher acts of God? More on this subject will be explored in the next section of this chapter.

There is enough truth in what Zwemer and Jones are saying to cause us to investigate further. Kim Gustafson has sought to set forth determinism or fatalism in graph form.

Islamic Determinism

May produce attitudes of:	Resulting in:
Contentment, peace, patience, and tolerance	Acceptance of divine order; happiness; and status quo
Pessimism	Lack of confidence to alter his life; negative on change and/or progress
Passivity	A sense that God, the uncontrollable factor about which he can do nothing, is forcing life to go on as it is
Corruption	Relegation to fate of his personal responsibility for any mistake, failure, or sin
Complacency	Lack of originality and creativity; a craving for the past or tradition
Devaluation of the	Acceptance of hard and

present life   frustrating environment, holds
                                little belief in progress; finds
                                salvation only in the hereafter
                                (Gustafson 1985, 8)

Theological Perspectives

Several verses in the Quran refer to the sovereign outworking of God's purposes.

And whomsoever it is Allah's will to guide, He expandeth His bosom unto the Surrender, and whomsoever it is His will to send astray, He maketh His bosom close and narrow as if He were engaged in sheer ascent. (Sura 6:126)

Thou sendest whom Thou wilt astray and guidest whom Thou wilt. (Sura 7:155)

He maketh whom He will to enter His mercy. (Sura 76:31)

Islamic theology is primarily based on the Quran. It is clear from these and other verses that God is the first and last cause. The will of Allah superintends every activity of man. He even causes, in some instances, His creatures to go astray. These particular verses have caused Muslim theologians to be stretched into hermeneutical gymnastics.

The Hadith (Tradition) is the fleshing out and personalizing of Scripture. From actual recorded happenings, the Muslim can see the Quran applied to life. What did the Prophet say and do in specific experiences of life? How did he interpret quranic injunctions within an actual historical-cultural setting? These following Hadith interact with the subject of God's sovereignty:

> *There came to him a messenger from one of his daughters, telling him that her child was on the verge of death. The Prophet told the messenger to tell her, "It is for Allah what He takes, and it is for Allah what He gives, and everything has its fixed time (limit)." (Bukhari [Vol. 8], 391)*

A further incident reflects on the same theme:

> *The Prophet came up to us and sat and we sat around him. He had a small stick in his hand. Then he bent his head and started scraping the ground with it. He then said, "There is none among you and no created soul, but has place either in Paradise or in hell assigned for him and it is also determined for him whether he will be among the blessed or wretched." (Bukhari [Vol. 2], 250-251)*

It is noted that all responsibility for one's future destiny seems to be placed on Allah. Does this indicate God has a capricious nature?

Another Hadith speaks of knowledge that is unique to Allah:

> *The Prophet said, "The keys of the unseen are five and none knows them but Allah: (1) None knows (the sex of) what is in the womb, but Allah; (2) None knows what will happen tomorrow, but Allah; (3)*

None knows when it will rain, but Allah; (4) None
knows where he will die, but Allah (knows that); (5)
and none knows when the Hour (Judgment) will be
established, but Allah. " (Bukhari [Vol. 9], 353-354)

Is there another side to Muslim belief ? Most assuredly
so. It is highlighted in this Hadith:

Narrated Ali: We were in the company of the
Prophet in a funeral procession at Baqi al-Gharqad.
He said, "There is none of you but his place in
Paradise or in the hell Fire is assigned for him."
They said, "O Allah's Apostle! Shall we depend (on
this fact and give up work)?" He said, "Carry on
doing (good deeds)." (Bukhari [Vol. 6], 442)

Here one sees the theological tension emerging in the
form of an antinomy. An antinomy can be described as a
contradiction between what appears to be two true
statements. The followers of Muhammad were seeking to
be logical. If their destiny was sealed by Allah, then why
not relax and go the way of the flesh? Why fight the battle
for morality and higher ethics? One's eternal destiny in
paradise or hell is predestined by the higher counsels of
God. Who can alter the will of God?

Did the Prophet engage in double-talk? Why are the
disciples encouraged to continue in good deeds as if their
eternal state depended on it? Anyone familiar with one of
Christendom's most divisive theological controversies will
immediately understand the Muslim problem. The free will
of man versus the predestination of God has been hotly
debated among Bible-believing Christians for centuries.

This one doctrinal issue has split more than one denomination and brought many new ones into being. But perhaps the majority of Christians affirm both free will and predestination. This paradox allows for an encounter with the God of mystery. Is this where Muslims have ended up?

A helpful statement on this subject has been written by William C. Chittick:

> *An unbiased look at many periods of Islamic history shows no signs whatsoever of a "fatalistic" streak in the Moslem peoples. And in fact, by sifting through the Koran and the prophetic sayings, one can find at least as many references to man's free will, power of choice, and responsibility as to his predestination. The Moslems were fully aware that to tell someone he is predestined in every sense, and then to ask him to practice religion, involves blatant absurdity. Man's true situation, especially from the point of view of his own existence and awareness, lies somewhere between the two extremes. He is predestined, but he chooses the path he is going to follow by his own free will. If he were not free, God would be an unbelievable tyrant, rewarding and punishing people for acts for which they were not responsible. But God is just, putting everything in its proper place. (Chittick 1983:113)*

Two respected Christian scholars of Islam have summed up Muslim thought with these succinct words. "In the end, then, the Quran simply holds fast to the complementary truths of God's omnipotence and man's responsibility without reconciling them intellectually. This is basically also the position of the Bible" (Bell and Watt 1970, 152).

It is necessary to give the last word on this doctrine to one of the most outstanding scholars in the Muslim world. Seyyed Hossein Nasr interacts with the charge that Muslims are fatalistic:

> *Were Islam to be fatalistic it would not be able to conquer half the known world in seventy years. It is actually absurd to call one of the most virile, patriarchal, and energetic civilizations which the world has known fatalistic. . . . What is, however, emphasized in Islam is that freedom in an absolute sense belongs to God alone. Nevertheless, we share in this freedom and therefore bear the responsibility of having to choose. Were this responsibility not to be incumbent upon us there would be no real meaning to religious faith. (Nasr 1966,19-20)*

Practical Considerations

In light of the above, how do we find grassroots Muslims handling the heavy subjects of evil, pain, and suffering? In the sense of first cause, the Muslim always attributes the problems of life to God. "It is the will of Allah" is a kind of panacea statement of resignation. It has been uttered millions of times from lips of Muslims. But the analysis does not stop at this point. The next attribution of responsibility is directed toward man. Wherever possible, curses are then made toward the individuals or institutions that are regarded as a more direct source of the problem.

Herein lies the difference between Christians and Muslims.

Christians first seek a human cause and then proceed to godly resignation. Muslims reverse the process; they begin with interaction with God and then go on to assign human blame.

The Muslim propensity toward resignation to Allah's will appears to produce a resilient race of people. My wife and I lived for twenty years in Bangladesh, formerly East Pakistan. This battered Muslim country of more than a hundred million people was forever expecting the next tragedy. A constant source of amazement to me was to observe the Bangladeshis in dynamic interaction with calamity.

In November 1970 a massive hurricane churned in the Bay of Bengal and then slammed into the southern coastal area of East Pakistan. Winds of 135 miles per hour created a fifteen-foot-high tidal wave that encompassed a breadth of over twenty miles. This wall of water moved ten miles inland totally obliterating everything in its path. Thousands of day laborers had been brought into the area to harvest crops. They were all sleeping in grass and bamboo huts that fateful night. Warnings had been grossly inadequate. There was nowhere to flee.

Within eight hours, Bangladesh had been divinely awarded the distinction of having endured the world's worst natural disaster of this century. Five hundred thousand precious, God-created men, women, and children, on that moonlit night, were transported to eternity via the surging, angry waters of the Bay of Bengal.

Dawn came. Desolation reigned. The land had been brutally raped. No houses, no animals, no crops in the field, no trees, and few people were left to testify as Noah and his family did in days of old. Soon word began to filter through to us in the capital city of Dhaka. Resources were mobilized. A compassionate world responded with an unbelievable outpouring of assistance.

It was my privilege to work with Baptist missionaries in the sinking of tubewells in the affected area. Fresh drinking water was the greatest need of the people. As I walked among the dazed Muslim survivors, I particularly noted their reaction to the catastrophe they had just endured. Shock and pained expressions were in constant evidence. But a calamity that is nature-related is far removed from the control of man. Only Allah can empower the winds, rain, and tides. So I found little perplexity or questioning. The emphasis was on the will of God, a will not to be interrogated, but to be accepted.

A subtle shift in perception occurred in 1971. That was the year of the insurrection. After twenty-four years of subservience under the political yoke of West Pakistan, the East Pakistanis mobilized their meager resources and commenced a successful war of independence. It was a joy indescribable to be in Dhaka at the moment East Pakistan became Bangladesh. I sent out a "birth announcement" to our many praying friends who had supported our sojourn during those terribly tragic days.

"March 25, 1971, to December 16, 1971 - a nine-month full-term waiting period which included fourteen days of agonizing labor, followed by the bloody Caesarean birth of the world's eighth-largest nation.
Name: Bangladesh
Size: 75 million people
Disposition: Extremely jubilant
Prognosis: Democratic, socialistic, and secularistic"

Achieved, but not without great cost. No one will ever be able to calculate the losses involved in the war for independence. I saw hundreds of dead bodies thrown into huge piles at the University of Dhaka. On one trip in the countryside I surveyed whole villages burned to the ground.

While driving around Dhaka, I frequently had to divert my six-year-old daughter's attention while we drove past a dead person who had been indiscriminately shot by a nobody made somebody through the power of an ancient, yet deadly, rifle. I visited the bunkers where soldiers had kept the beautiful Bengali girls as sexual playthings.

During those gruesome nine months we walked among the living dead. No hope, no joy, no laughter. The nights were filled with the sound of rifle fire and grenades. Days were spent sharing the latest rumors as well as listening to twelve shortwave radio news broadcasts trying to ascertain the true situation in the country.

Talk – empty, vain, repetitive talk – was a catharsis of sorts. So often I would verbally probe into the depths of a Muslim friend's soul. "How can Muslims engage in such a genocide against their fellow believers?" I would ask. As we listened to the call to prayer wafting above the sound of the machine guns, my friends would wage battle between memorized theology and practical realities. They wanted to rest comfortably in the sovereignty of Allah. But somehow the words would not come. The immediate was too pressing. Angrily the answer came: "Those sons of a pig are not Muslims. They are heathen who will burn forever in hell." Perhaps it was ultimately Allah who was allowing the people to suffer, but it was hard for the Bengalis to see beyond the one who was pulling the trigger or throwing the firebomb.

Yet another perspective needs to be mentioned. Not long ago Abdul from Kabul stopped by our Reading Center in Manila. He spoke movingly of the carnage taking place in his beloved Afghanistan. His family lives in constant danger. No one moves outside their home after dark. I once again requested an interpretation of the purpose for the tragedy. Without hesitation Abdul ascribed his people's suffering as a direct result of their rebellion against Allah. His words came forth in a torrent, "The Afghans are not good Muslims. They are dishonest, wine drinkers, and adulterers. God is angry and is punishing us. If our people repent and turn to Allah, then the turmoil will cease and there will be peace." This is not the first time I have heard such a Muslim rationale for pain and suffering.

So in Islamic thought, God is never far from being recognized as first cause, even though He uses a variety of instruments to accomplish His will. The Christian, I feel, struggles on more fronts and in a deeper, more profound manner.

Christians and the Cosmic Struggle

Catherine Marshall, the renowned Christian author, articulated her pain as she endured the death of her husband and two grandchildren.

> *"How can God permit such things to happen?" is the cry that rises from our hearts. If He exists at all and is a loving God, He would not want such evils to befall us. Yet how could He be God and not have the power to prevent these disasters? These are the most difficult of all questions for those embarked on the Christian walk. Certainly for me this problem of evil has been a real stumbling block. (Marshall 1974, 3)*

Many have struggled with these heart-wrenching issues only to conclude that God has set boundaries to His power. He allows circumstances, nature, and the natural powers of degeneration to take their toll. He is neither directly involved nor responsible. This explanation seems to satisfy Rabbi Harold S. Kushner, who has written a touching story of his son Aaron, who died at age fourteen of progeria, otherwise known as the disease of "rapid aging." Aaron never grew beyond three feet tall; he lost his hair and looked like a shriveled old man at the time of his death at puberty. *When Bad Things Happen to Good People* put Kushner on the *New York Times* best-seller list for eight months. Kushner describes his conclusion in these pungent words:

> *I believe in God. But I do not believe the same things about Him that I did years ago, when I was growing up or when I was a theological student. I recognize His limitations. He is limited in what He can do by laws of nature and by the evolution of human nature and human moral freedom. I no longer hold God responsible for illnesses, accidents, and natural disasters, because I realize that I gain little and I lose so much when I blame God for those things. I can worship a God who hates suffering but cannot eliminate it, more easily than I can worship a God who chooses to make children suffer and die, for whatever exalted reason. Some years ago, when the "death of God" theology was a fad, I remember seeing a bumper sticker that read "My God is not dead, sorry about yours." I guess my bumper sticker reads "My God is not cruel; sorry about yours." (Kushner 1981, 134)*

However much we may protest Kushner's conclusions, we must interact with his sincere quest to deal with life's overwhelming mysteries. His search for a credible, intellectually satisfying answer was nurtured in the crucible of watching a beloved son slowly evolve into a dying old man. Can anyone contemplate what agony those parents endured for thirteen years?

So where does all of this bring us? Do we agree with the great seventeenth-century mystic, Madame Jeanne Guyon, when she stated, "If knowing answers to life's questions is absolutely necessary to you, then forget the journey. You will never make it, for this is a journey of unknowables – of unanswered questions, enigmas, incomprehensibles, and most of all, things unfair" (Guyon 1984, 37). This view seems to lead us into a maze of "Christian agnosticism." It is a self-contradictory phrase, but has particular relevance to a sincere person seeking, without a great deal of success, to apply faith to suffering. Mystery and agnosticism. Are they closely allied adversaries who seek to torment the struggling believer?

In my missionary questionnaire, I sought to probe this question among those who are so often confronted with suffering in some of its most crude and wrenching forms. "Do you ever question God regarding evil and suffering?" Over 69 percent of the respondents indicated some level of concern. "Does the danger of nuclear war bother you?" This query was personalized but should have brought to mind the devastating effect such a war would have on mankind in general. Therefore, it was a surprise to me that 54 percent stated they never were bothered by such a danger. The reason for this may be reflected in another question. Over 90 percent of the missionaries said they have absolute assurance of eternal life. This confidence may lessen concern over nuclear issues.

Scripture

John Stott, the great Anglican preacher, was the guest speaker at a convention in Dhaka, Bangladesh. I took him out for lunch one day and "unloaded" on him my concern about God's role in human suffering. His response was centered on two events of history: the Fall and the Cross. Stott sees the Fall and its effect throughout Scripture as all-encompassing. Man's character has been utterly, although not irredeemably, affected. Even animals and nature have been altered from that which was good and changed into potential forces of evil.

Stott then dwelt on the importance of God suffering with and for His creation. A good summary of his position is set forth in his article "God on the Gallows."

I could never myself believe in God, if it were not for the Cross. In the real world of pain, how could one worship a God who was immune to it? I have entered many Buddhist temples in different Asian countries and stood respectfully before the statue of the Buddha, his legs crossed, arms folded, eyes closed, the ghost of a smile playing round his mouth, a remote look on his face, detached from the agonies of the world. But each time, after a while I have had to turn away. And in imagination I have turned instead to that lonely, twisted, tortured figure on the cross, nails through hands and feet, back

lacerated, limbs wretched, brow bleeding from thorn
pricks, mouth dry and intolerably thirsty, plunged
in God-forsaken darkness. That is the God for me!
He laid aside his immunity to pain. He entered our
world of flesh and blood, tears and death. He
suffered for us. Our sufferings become more
manageable in the light of his. There is still a
question mark against human suffering, but over it
we boldly stamp another mark, the Cross, which
symbolizes divine suffering. As P. T. Forsyth wrote:
"The cross of Christ . . . is God's only self-
justification in such a world" as ours. (Stott 1987,
30)

Is it legitimate to probe Stott a bit further on the
thousands of years of pre-Cross history? If he had lived
before God died on the gallows, would he still be able to
say, "That is the God for me!"? His writings make me
wonder.

Scripture does not avoid these problems in all their
mystifying dimensions. Psalm 73 highlights some of these.
But as for me, my feet came close to stumbling;

My steps had almost slipped.
For I was envious of the arrogant,
As I saw the prosperity of the wicked. For there are no
*   pains in their death;*
And their body is fat.
They are not in trouble as other men;
Nor are they plagued like mankind.... Behold, these are
*   the wicked;*
And always at ease, they have increased in wealth.

149

Surely in vain I have kept my heart pure,
And washed my hands in innocence;
For I have been stricken all day long,
And chastened every morning. (Ps. 73:2-5, 12-14)

The psalmist begins his slippery descent into a melancholic morass of introspection. The wicked are doing just great! New chariots, palatial dwellings, power over the poor, gourmet delicacies, and warehouses overflowing with grain. "But, God, they are evil men! They deny you and your righteousness. Where, O where is your justice?"

The psalm continues,

When I pondered to understand this,
It was troublesome in my sight
Until I came into the sanctuary of God;
Then I perceived their end.
Surely Thou dost set them in slippery places;
Thou dost cast them down to destruction.
How they are destroyed in a moment!
They are utterly swept away by sudden terrors!
(Ps. 73:16-19)

Does the believer unlock the mysteries of God by philosophy, reason, or logic? Or does he humbly present himself in the sanctuary of God? Spiritual complexities can best be understood in the context of a spiritual environment. Faith perception becomes focused and sharpened. Yes, the poor groan under the repressive yoke of the oppressors. But the end is not yet! In God's own time the evil ones will be cast down to destruction and destroyed in a moment. And then comes the delightfully refreshing affirmation of a soul set free and liberated through the process of applied faith:

> *Whom have I in heaven but Thee?*
> *And besides Thee, I desire nothing on earth.*
> *My flesh and my heart may fail,*
> *But God is the strength of my heart and my portion*
> *   forever*
> *For behold, those who are far from Thee will perish;*
> *Thou hast destroyed all those who are unfaithful to Thee.*
> *But as for me, the nearness of God is my good;*
> *I have made the Lord God my refuge,*
> *That I may tell of all Thy works. (Ps. 73:25-28)*

Not a voice incapacitated and paralyzed, but rather a spirit soaring and proclaiming all of the good works of the Lord. What a transition! A seeker of God works through his reactions of disgust and anger. He flees to the sanctuary of God. There, in quietness and humility, he begins to perceive the great designs of divinity. New dimensions to an earthbound world view begin to emerge. The result? Another believer bows, rises, and then goes forth pressing ever onward in the battle of faith.

The Word of God, it seems to me, is always pushing us forward into the spiritual coliseum. We are hesitant and frightened. The amphitheater is jammed with hostile unbelievers. They spit forth their profane jeers and insults. Emotionally they whip us down. But standing before us is a more immediate danger. The lions roar and pace around us, casting their razor sharp claws dangerously close to our shivering bodies. Will we be consumed?

Physically and emotionally we are promised tribulation. One

could wish for better news! I well recall giving a devotional to an informed and spiritually minded group of businessmen. About midway I observed that the psalmist may never have seen the righteous forsaken or his seed begging bread (Ps. 37:25), but that this had been my repetitive experience in Bangladesh, where Christians have not been spared the terrible deprivations that come from crops ruined by drought or flood. Immediately, one of the men interrupted me and said with great emotion, "Phil, that is the Word of God. How can you deny its truth? God says He will not allow His children to go hungry and beg! How can you bring His Word into question?"

Here we had a cultural clash. America is an overwhelmingly wealthy nation. My friend had never seen a hungry Christian and simply could not imagine one existed. But I had to gently remind him of Paul being without food and clothes (2 Cor. 6). Then on to a chronicle of terrible suffering endured by God's choicest servants as recorded in Hebrews 11. Lastly, I spoke of dedicated Christians hiding in caves and forests in Viet Nam and Cambodia. These would only be representative of hundreds of thousands throughout the world who are suffering, even though they are children of the King! A later illustration I could now cite refers to a financially well-off Christian in his thirties who lives in a predominantly Muslim country. This believer, in an attempt to better equip himself to witness to Muslims, attended my seminar on evangelizing Muslims. He has recently been arrested on a charge of "proselytization of Muslims." Part of the proof produced against him was his attendance at the seminar. Today he is serving out a two-year prison sentence with no recourse to appeal. His wife and children anxiously await his release.

Physical prosperity of the righteous may indeed be hinted at in a few places in the Old Testament. But as we come into the dispensation of the New Covenant, we see men like Stephen, John the Baptist, and James paying for spiritual reality with their lives. The Book of Acts is replete with illustration after illustration of one great promise of God: not deliverance from trials, but *peace within tribulations*. For authentication, we can refer to no higher source than that of Jesus Christ.

"These things I have spoken to you, that in Me you may have peace. In the world you have tribulation, but take courage; I have overcome the world." (John 16:33)

As I continue scripturally to contemplate suffering, I, like Stott, am driven repeatedly back to the Cross. What a symbol! What a reality! It is all so mysterious, and yet so compelling. I recently made a trip to Bataan, a peninsula of the island of Luzon in the Philippines. It was here the Americans and Filipinos made a last desperate stand against the Japanese. Thousands lost their lives in March 1942 on that blood-drenched piece of tropical real estate. On Good Friday, in the blazing heat, the earth shook convulsively. Religious soldiers with emaciated bodies looked heavenward and wondered if that was a message of groaning coming from the Cross. In a few days it was all over except for the infamous death march.

I made my pilgrimage to the top of Mount Samat, Bataan's 2,000 - foot-high mountain. There the view is fabulous. One can look across the bay and see Manila. In another direction is Corregidor where MacArthur and others held out briefly and vainly in their rock fortress. Towering over the scene is a gigantic three-hundred-foot-high cross. World War II veterans can climb to the top of the cross and look over the lush countryside where so many of their companions died. I could not help but think of the hymn which speaks of the Cross "towering o'er the wrecks of time." It stands in its glory as Japanese come by the scores to lay wreaths of repentance all over the Bataan peninsula. Can it not be said that, somehow, the Cross prevailed?

When Elie Wiesel was awarded the 1986 Nobel Peace Prize, the committee cited him as "one of the most important spiritual leaders in the world." Here is a man who suffered deeply in a concentration camp during World War II. And he has done all of this without the appropriation of the work of the Cross. Thinking through this, I wrote him a letter, an excerpt of which follows:

> *As I read Night again this weekend, I couldn't help but think of one of the names attributed to Jesus Christ. "Man of Sorrows" truly depicts one aspect of the character and temperament of Jesus. Without doubt, you as an informed Jew have considered the life and claims of the Jewish Man of Sorrows. But I couldn't help but write a note to you to once more commend Him whom I regard as Savior and Messiah. It seems to me, by virtue of Christ's acceptance of our weight of sin and grief, He can uniquely allow us to apply to ourselves the appropriate words with which you concluded Night, "Free at last." At least, for myself, in a world poised at the precipice of violent self-destruction, I have found a real measure of liberation from depression and darkness in the words of hope which Jesus gives, "In the world you shall have tribulation, but in Me you shall have peace." Thus, my faith in the atoning*

work of Christ on the Cross offers light at the end of the tunnel of life which otherwise could be full of despair and defeat.

Wiesel graciously wrote back a handwritten note on his Boston University stationery. "Thank you, thank you for your good words; they mean much to me. Best wishes to you. Elie Wiesel." I continue to pray that it will be the Cross that will mean much to this great prophet of warning that God has given to the world in the latter part of the twentieth century.

Before I proceed to share testimonies of Christians who have been victorious in suffering, I would like to quote a well-known Christian leader. J. Richard Chase, president of Wheaton College, is an honest man of God who is willing to make himself vulnerable before his constituency. In an editorial in a Wheaton College *Bulletin*, he opens his heart in regard to the problems of questions and faith.

Should we wrestle in private and praise in public? In our public relations-oriented world, that is the temptation; but I do not think God needs the help of slick contemporary Christian rhetoric. If I am troubled, God will continue to be God. He can handle our honesty; can we?. . . .

I will continue to praise Him in want or in plenty, for He is God. Though mystified by the reality of cold comparisons of hard human data, and irritated by spokesmen for God who purport to explain away the mysteries of God so that life is neatly packaged and God is contained in our image, yet will I serve

Him. I can live with tough circumstances and the inadequacy of our best rational response to tough questions. With the Apostle Paul in Romans 8, the comfort that comes from the knowledge that the Spirit of God is praying in my behalf and the ultimate hope of eternity are sometimes my only help. But it is divine help . . .

In the final analysis, though, it is my heart that aches and my mind that grows weary in wrestling God in order to pin Him beneath human thought. I long for physical help and greater insight, but I most need comfort, forgiveness, and love; that He readily provides. (Chase 1987,2)

Victory

It was my privilege to have Joseph Stowell, gifted president of Moody Bible Institute, as my pastor for six years. Joe has written an excellent book on suffering, *Through the Fire*. One of his observations relates to the last chapter of life.

It's like a book with a good ending. The beginning is a story of choices. In the middle the plot thickens and much seems confusing, unfair and hard. Don't put the book down! Read the last chapter. Our best chapter may be just ahead or in eternity. But it is always a chapter of victory and joy. (Stowell 1985, 66)

It is now time in this chapter to talk about those who have persevered. There is much to learn from those who have trod the hard paths. E. Stanley Jones was a very special man of God. He died in 1973 in India at the age of eighty-nine after suffering a debilitating stroke. Just before his death he wrote:

When I came into this Way of the Kingdom, my first feeling was to hug myself that I had sense enough to do it. I still feel that way at the age of eighty-eight and sitting in a rehabilitation hospital recovering from a stroke. My eyesight is cut in half, my speech is barely intelligible. My locomotive powers are almost nil. I am having to learn to walk again like a baby. But am I unhappy? If so, I haven't discovered it. I belong to an unshakable Kingdom and an unchanging Person. My feet are on the Way. Jesus is the Divine Yes when there isn't much yes in my surroundings to rejoice in, except in him. In him is the embodiment of the Kingdom. If it isn't, it just isn't. But I am happy because my happiness isn't based on happenings, but is based on him, the Eternal. (Jones 1975, 53)

Leighton Ford, the well-known evangelist, had a son who had everything to live for. At twenty-one years of age, Sandy appeared to have the world before him. Intelligent, popular, mature, and spiritually on fire for the Lord, Sandy was a lover of life. His mom and dad were ever so proud of their son. And then one terribly dark day their child walked out of their home and into eternity. Leighton has recorded his pilgrimage of grief.

During the months following Sandy's death, to cope with my grief and sense of loss, I kept a journal.

Through a series of "conversations" with Sandy, I continued to express my grief and bring our relationship to a close. In one of those chats, I said, "Sandy, you've been dead two months earth-time."

"I feel as if I have been alive forever, Dad. It's a lot like one big long today."

"It's not a matter of time, Sandy, except that time heals. It's more a matter of nearness. I guess I'm concerned that as our time goes on, we will lose any sense of nearness."

"But why, Dad? You're moving closer to eternity every day. You're no longer moving from, but to me! And besides, the 'Wall' between us is so thin - you would laugh if you could see it."

"I think more of you than when you were at Chapel Hill."

"Sure! I know you do. I hear those thoughts."

"Night, son! Enjoy the stars!"

"It's morning here, Dad. Enjoy the light!" (Ford 1985, 171)

Leighton Ford has penetrated the darkness. For such a testimony we are indeed grateful.

Barbara had long been on the shut-in list of our church. One stormy afternoon I drove out to the rest home to pay her a visit. I wasn't prepared for what I found. Barbara was the nearest thing to a human vegetable I have ever seen. She was coiled up in a fetal position, making continual unintelligible grunts. There was no possibility of her senile mind initiating or responding. She was incontinent. At each meal someone had to laboriously spoon-feed her. Often the food would be regurgitated.

Standing beside Barbara was her husband, Jim. The picture of that man is indelibly etched on my mind. Jim lovingly stroked his wife and whispered sweet cooing words of love to her. He fed her, changed her diapers, and just kept loving her. He softly told me how much he appreciated all that Barbara had done for him throughout his life. Now it was his privilege to repay her. Each day Jim walked in the harshness of Detroit weather from his apartment to the rest home to deliver his bouquet of Christian love to his beloved. Meeting Jim and Barbara made more of an impression on me as a newly married young man than all the sermons on conjugal love that I have ever heard.

In England I spoke in a church pastored by John Grindell. In the front of the sanctuary were several spastic young ladies in wheelchairs. Their bodily motions were uncontrollable. Heads were flung from side to side. Hands were thrown about wildly. Saliva dripped down the faces. But there was an indescribable radiance about the girls, for these precious ones had been redeemed by the blood of the Lamb. Their minds were sharp. Comprehension was 100 percent. It was only their bodies that refused to respond to mental commands. What a challenge to see them pressing on in life! The church provided a warm, loving atmosphere for their spiritual nurture. The parishioners cared not at all about the offbeat grunts that accompanied each congregational song. Love in action.

Jim McKinley is one of the most dedicated missionaries I have ever met. He has served faithfully for years in Bangladesh with the Southern Baptist Mission. It was his youngest daughter I referred to earlier in this chapter who lost an eye in the bow and arrow accident. Jim and his family of five children endured the 1971 Pakistan-Bangladesh civil war. He was always in the middle of the action seeking to help his suffering friends.

At the commencement of the war Jim and his family were in a small town, seemingly far removed from direct warfare. It was not so to be. One day the planes came and bombed their nearby marketplace. Jim's daughter Cherie wrote a poem about that tragic day.

Roaring out of the Bengal sunset they came,
Two black dots on a warm summer evening.
Some children stop their playing to set clear eyes
*   upon them,*
In awe watching the pair, soaring over rice fields
*   and straw huts*
Like finches looking for someplace to rest their
*   wings.*
But suddenly, as they spot the tiny town,
Their nature changes, and now, like vultures,
They screech and dip down upon it.
A piercing wail rings out and then,

BOOM!. . . BOOM!. . . BOOM!

The children scatter like frightened ants into their
*   houses,*
Amid the constant shattering and blasts.
Flinging themselves upon the floor,
They lay frozen in fear,
Their faces ghastly, their blood cold, their heads
*   buzzing with the question, "Why?"*
While outside the vultures peck at their prize.

A mother tries to comfort a child with shaking hands.
The only steady comforting sound is the thunk,
*   thunk, thunk of the father's feet*
Pacing the floor. Again and again the planes dip,

BOOM!. . . BOOM!. . . BOOM!

Then in the same mysterious way they appeared,
They are gone.
All is quiet, the world seems dead.
But ... off in the distance comes the clattering
*   of wheels on the old road,*
And the jingling of bells.
Like water from a broken dam,
The living gush into the countryside,
Trying to escape from the smell of death and blood.
Some crying, some with faces of white stone,
They all plod along together.
Not saying a word,
Not having to, because their grief is written
*   on their faces.*
Slowly, they filter away.
The night comes, the stars twinkle,
A cool breeze blows from the south.
The only irritating sound is the crickets
*   which seem to say ...*
LOVE YOUR ENEMIES ...
*   LOVE YOUR ENEMIES...*
*   LOVE YOUR ENEMIES.*
*   (McKinley 1978, 104-105)*

It wasn't so easy for Jim to get a hold on forgiveness. But his daughter's poem opened his heart. He shares the experience:

Cherie had relived the day the jet planes of the Pakistan Air Force first struck Feni. It took me about thirty minutes to read the poem. Feeling was deep. But I thought she, with God's help, had come through beautifully in her struggle against hate, hate toward the Pakistani soldiers. My thirteen-year-old daughter understood love and forgiveness better than I, her missionary father. Hatred hounded me continually – hatred against military forces that were treating Bengali people as if they were lower than the lowest form of animals.

But Cheri's poem helped me to pray more earnestly for the strength to love and forgive men who were brutal in their behavior to others.

I think Cherie both shamed me and embarrassed me through her beautiful experience. But the help I received was worth that shame and embarrassment. (McKinley 1978, 105)

Such is an encounter of spirituality in the crucible at the deepest level. I close these reflections with two very personal experiences, the first of which I have never before recorded in writing. These are only shared in the hope they will be helpful to fellow pilgrims who are as weak as I am.

In 1959, as a senior in college, I was overcome with nervous tension. It appeared I was having a nervous breakdown. That hardly seemed possible at twenty-one years of age. I was overwhelmed with incomprehension. What was

God doing? Why? My life was on the altar. I was headed toward Bangladesh to serve the Lord. It appeared Julie was to be my helpmate in Christ's service. All was neatly in place. And now this!

For months I waged a lonely struggle. After all, it was a "shame" for a Christian to have emotional problems. All one needed to overcome these tensions was a greater trust in the Lord. Such was contemporary thinking.

Two critical decisions loomed on the horizon: our marriage, and our plan to go to one of the world's most difficult mission fields. Was the Lord flashing a green, a caution, or a red light? A long talk with Julie in a car parked on a little island looking toward beautiful Miami Beach settled for us the rightness of our commitment to each other.

Eight months after marriage, with visa in hand and support fully pledged, we were faced with the second decision. If I was hardly able to run with the footmen, how would I ever make it with the horsemen? The emotional stress still plagued me. One late night we called a surgeon friend and asked him to visit us. After patiently hearing my full story, he flashed the green light. I was reassured that God's grace would be adequate.

The next thirteen years were tough. At times I would think it was impossible to press on. There were instances when I was preaching and thought I would have to give up and sit down. The option of throwing in the towel was considered. All during those dark years Julie was my solace and constant comforter. She never gave up on me. It is totally impossible to repay her gift of love to me.

Slowly, healing came. By 1974 I was basically restored, with only stress-related headaches and back pain that have lingered on through the years. All during that time, apart from Julie and a doctor friend, no one had any idea of my continuing heartache and perplexity. Only recently have I felt the liberty to share the experience, in the hope that it might assist someone else in the family of God. Through it all the presence of the Lord never left me. I praise Him for His grace to endure the "thorn" and accept it without ultimate understanding.

The other experience also reflects the mercy of God. In October 1982, Julie had a hysterectomy at a mission hospital in Bangladesh. As per routine, samples of her tissue were sent to a pathologist, the best in the country. Julie and I returned to our up-country town of Kushtia. Two weeks after the operation we received the startling news that the pathology reports showed that Julie had cancer and indications were that it had spread throughout her body. We were told to immediately return to the U.S. for treatment.

The next week was a whirlwind of excitement and confusion as we tried to pull things together for an emergency furlough. The biggest issue to us was the spiritual dimension. Could we have grace to be a godly example to our intimate Muslim friends and missionary colleagues? After all, we had spent twenty years preaching God's enablement. Now it was our turn to prove it.

The Lord gave an indescribable peace. We were amazed. On the way to the U.S. we stopped by Manila to pick up our daughter, who was in the twelfth grade at Faith Academy. In Detroit we had every need met by our loving friends at Highland Park Baptist Church. Extensive tests were made both on Julie and on the tissue specimen we brought home with us from Bangladesh. In a week the doctor called with conclusive word that Julie did not have cancer. There had been a mix-up by the Bangladeshi lab technician.

The cancer belonged to some unknown person in Bangladesh, not to Julie.

The three of us sat on the floor of our bedroom with such a mixture of emotions. We were tremendously relieved about the absence of cancer. But what was the Lord doing and why? The three of us had just undergone the most serious trauma of our lives. We were suddenly pulled out of our ministry. Lindy was deprived of high school graduation with her friends at Faith Academy. Our supporters had been put to a significant amount of trouble. And where to from here? It was a real down experience for the three of us.

Today, do we understand it any better? Can we look back and see any rationale in it all? No, not really, except to see it as an opportunity for growth. We will never forget the peace and grace given to us in our hour of desperation.

And so we continue on. That is the real message of faith in adversity. And that is the real essence of spirituality within the crucible of suffering. Enfolded in the love of the God of the Cross, the pilgrim of the Way presses on with tenacity and joy. A veil of divine mystery may, at times, separate us from the Divine Yes. But faith refuses to be conquered. We wait with great expectancy for the day when, once again, the veil will be split and faith will gloriously be absorbed into radiant light.[4]

---

[4]Philip Yancey's *Disappointment with God* is a gripping and at times agonizingly frank book that deals with these questions: Is God unfair? Is God silent? Is God hidden? I highly recommend this treatise on God and suffering.

5

Sin and Holiness

R. C. Sproul speaks of sin as "cosmic treason." What could be more serious than a premeditated insurrection of the created against the Creator? Standing in opposition to man's natural bent toward soul rebellion is God's standard of holiness. "Pursue sanctification without which no one will see the Lord" (Heb. 12:14). The word *holy* in its various forms occurs more than six hundred times in the Bible. Aaron, as he ministered before the Lord, wore a turban on which was attached a plate made of pure gold. Engraved on the plate were these pungent words: "Holiness unto the Lord." All Israel was made aware of God's will for national and personal behavior. How far they strayed is a matter of historical record for all to ponder.

Holiness cannot be explored without examining its antithesis. In this chapter both sin and godliness will be opened to our scrutiny. Spiritual warfare and also spiritual victory will be probed from Christian and Muslim perspectives.

Spiritual Warfare

Muslims and Christians hate sin. Using that as a premise, I assume the Christian reader will understand the general biblical definition of sin. But many will not be aware of how Muslims regard the subject of violating the expressed will of Allah.

Sin, to the Muslim, is not an inherited trait. Adam and Eve had a choice set before them. They could have walked in the path of Allah and righteousness or, listening to the voice of Satan, they could have chosen to do evil. It is interesting, in light of last chapter's discussion of predestination, that Muslims attribute sin to personal choice, not to the will of God. The choice of good or evil lies before every Muslim. He does not have to choose corruption. (Muslims do not believe, as most Christians do, that Adam and Eve's choice affects us now. For Muslims, sin is not *inherited* from Adam. It is strictly the individual's own choice to sin.)

Satan's activity and influence, however, is very real and pervasive. One Hadith states, "The Prophet said (to them), 'Satan reaches everywhere in the human body as blood reaches everywhere in one's body'" (Bukhari [Vol. 3], 140). Sin is categorized according to degrees, much as in Roman Catholic theology. A minor sin can be said to become major in dimension under any of the following conditions:

1. Persistence in committing sin.
2. Treating it lightly.
3. Taking pleasure in it.
4. Being boastful of doing evil.

Muslim leaders decry the lack of godliness found within the Islamic community. One scholar comments,

An important cause of the decline of Muslim... is their evil habits. The noble qualities inculcated by Islam are on the wane among them. Gone is the strength of character and all other virtues from their midst which the early Muslims had acquired for themselves. (Arsalan 1944, 52)

There is a natural propensity to look for a scapegoat. Decadent Western cultural influence provides Muslims with an easy answer, particularly in "Christian" countries where Muslims are a numerical minority. But Islam finds it more difficult to explain overt sin within the context of a predominantly Muslim nation. In a conversation with a Muslim from Saudi Arabia, I gently probed into the area of sin and hypocrisy. With an enthusiastic flair, my friend began to denounce the waywardness of his fellow countrymen. He summed it up by stating that half of the Saudis are genuinely Muslim while the other half are blatant hypocrites.

While in Nigeria I acquired a newspaper article castigating the sins of Muslims who go to Mecca on the *Hajj*.

The Alhaji goes to the holy city to throw stones at Satan. He comes back a smuggler after a good spiritual refreshment before Allah. The corruption that mounts on religious exercises in Nigeria is

becoming unbearable for God. Think of the Alhajis who deal in cocaine. Can you imagine pilgrims who obtained their papers for the journey by offering bribes? They come to the prayer ground with dirty hands. The biggest magnates and dealers in beer in Nigeria are religionists. Think of Alhajis going to buy a few bottles of beer in a kettle which appears like the usual kettle with water for prayers. Think of the immoralities of adulteries in the name of Allah's license for a maximum of four wives. ("Nigerian Religionists Rethink" 1985, 3)

Julie and I enjoy an occasional weekend at an inexpensive resort a few hours drive from Manila. Sitting around the pool on a sunny Saturday afternoon, we noticed two Muslim families. The ladies were covered from head to foot in traditional veils while the husbands were enjoying the pool dressed in skimpy bathing suits. They were also imbibing beer. Later, in the parking lot, we observed that their car bore Saudi Arabian diplomatic license tags. If they had had beer in their possession in their own country, they would have been imprisoned. But in the Philippines they felt they could be quite blatant about drinking alcoholic beverages.

In our reading center in Manila I meet a variety of Muslims. Many are indifferent to religion, while others will argue vociferously concerning the absolute superiority of Islam. It would appear that many of the latter group seek to faithfully obey the tenets of the Muslim faith. Yet others fail. I particularly recall a drunken Muslim lawyer stopping by to have a chat with me. He was thirty years old, a father of two children, and separated from his wife. I had seen this personable, intelligent young man in a sober state. Now he stood before me a broken man asking for Allah to have mercy on him. His excuse for being drunk was that he could not sleep without the assistance of alcohol. He repeatedly mumbled, "God give me sleep, God give me sleep, I can't sleep, I can't sleep."

Just down the street from our center is a Muslim community infamous for drug dealing. A Christian acquaintance went into the area to meet a Muslim friend. In the span of a few minutes he was offered drugs five times. All of this takes place in the shadow of a large mosque and quranic school that dominates the whole neighborhood.

At times it seems to me Muslims get bound up in trite legalisms while failing to deal with the roots and fruits of serious sin. I could not help but smile at the response given by a beautiful young Muslim girl to my query as to why she was not praying during the evening prayer time. She held out one foot and her eyes moved shyly between my face and her toes. That did not seem much of an answer to my question. Finally I said, "I give. What do your toes have to do with your not praying?" With a touch of embarrassment in her voice, she whispered, "I am wearing toenail polish and I am prohibited from doing my absolutions and praying until I take it off."

While on a visit to Senegal I particularly desired to visit Touba, a small town that contains one of the largest mosques in all of Africa. A Muslim sect centered around the memory of Sheikh Ahmadu Bamba dominates the area. At the outskirts of town our car was stopped by Senegalese policemen. They made us all get out of the car and be subjected to a body search. They then went through all of our bags. The sign along the road said that all cigarettes and liquor would be confiscated. Possession of cigarettes in the town of Touba would be punishable by a beating and three month's incarceration. Nowhere else have I observed such a prohibition against smoking in the Muslim world.

The following poem entitled "I Wonder" was printed in a Muslim newspaper. The plagiarism is obvious to those who recognize the writing as originally centered around Jesus Christ. Yet it is interesting to see how sin is described and how Muhammad is the author's functional equivalent of Christ.

If the Prophet Muhammad visited you,
Just for a day or two.
If he came unexpectedly,
I wonder what you'd do.
Oh, I know you'd give your nicest room,
To such an honored guest,
And all the food you'd serve to him,
Would be the very best,
And you would keep assuring him,
You're glad to have him there,
That serving him in your home,
Is joy beyond compare.

But . . . when you saw him coming,
Would you meet him at the door
With arms outstretched in welcome,
To your visitor?
Or . . . would you have to change your clothes
Before you let him in?
Or hide some magazines and put
The Quran where they had been?

Would you still watch X-rated movies,
On your TV set?
Or would you rush to switch it off,
Before he gets upset?
Would you turn off the radio,
And hope he hadn't heard?
And wish you hadn't uttered
That last loud, hasty word?

Would you hide your worldly music,
And instead take Hadith books out?
Could you let him walk right in,
Or would you rush about?
And I wonder ... if the Prophet spent
A day or two with you,
Would you go right on doing the things you always do?
Would you go right on saying the things you always
     say?
Would life for you continue
As it does from day to day?
Would your family conversation
Keep up its usual pace?

And would you find it hard each meal
To say a table grace?
Would you keep up each and every prayer?
Without putting on a frown?
And would you always jump up early
For prayers at dawn?
Would you sing the songs you always sing?
And read the books you read?

And let him know the things on which
Your mind and spirit feed?
Would you take the Prophet with You
Everywhere you plan to go?
Or would you, maybe, change your plans
Just for a day or so?

Would you be glad to have him meet
Your very closest friends?
Or would you hope they'd stay away
Until his visit ends?
Would you be glad to have him stay,
Forever on and on?
Or, would you sigh with great relief,
When he at last was gone?
It might be interesting to know
The things that you would do
If the Prophet Muhammad, in person, came
To spend some time with you. (Badr 1985, 1)

Many Muslim Filipinos have encountered the severity of Saudi Arabian law in regard to the punishment of sin. One such Filipino overseas worker would take a Coke with him to jewelry shops in Jeddah. He would ask to look at a large selection of expensive gems. When the salesperson's attention was diverted, he would slip a few jewels into his Coke bottle. He was successful until the third time. He was apprehended with the result that his right hand was cut off and he was deported to the Philippines. Back home, the chastened Filipino constructed an elaborate story of an automobile accident in which he lost his hand.

Much could be said about pride. I have sought to

objectively evaluate this sin of the spirit that seems particularly prevalent among Muslims. One conclusion is a nationalistic orientation that says what I am and possess is superior. This tendency, of course, is common to the human race. Another rationale for pride is the underdog mentality. Islam, for centuries, has been subjected to colonial exploitations. It resisted any conquering of the spirit. Muslims kept believing that one day their faith in themselves and Allah would be vindicated.

More to the point of this chapter is the theological consideration. Does not exclusivistic doctrine tend to make adherents rigid and prone to pride? Even nominal Muslims are generally dogmatic about the truth of Islam. They may not pray five times a day or keep the Ramadan fast, but they will fervently affirm Islamic theology. The Quran presents a "one way" salvation. Evangelical Christians possess a similar view of the Bible, but it is usually tempered by a clear exhortation toward love for those outside the faith.

Do Muslims regard pride as sin? Is humility viewed as a weakness or a virtue? I will never forget the occasion when I was sitting around a table drinking tea with educated Muslims. One of them looked at me and sneeringly remarked, "You Christians are taught that it is a virtue to turn your cheek when someone strikes you." He got no further before the group erupted in mocking laughter. They all began to denounce such a response to an unprovoked attack. "We Muslims fight back. No one is allowed to get away with striking us," they affirmed.

Islam teaches aggression is to be met with force. Does this worldview engender a harsh, proud spirit? In this regard, is there much difference between Muslims and Jews? In both theology and practice there are marked similarities in what an unbiased observer would see as the pride factor. The underlying causes are very close as well.

How do we evaluate the priests of Islam? They certainly can be extremely dogmatic, and this at times seems to indicate pride. Al-Ghazali, writing over eight hundred years ago, commented on the dynamics of a haughty attitude.

A proud man will not tolerate any other to be on equal terms with himself. In private and in public he expects that all should assume a respectful attitude towards him and acknowledging his superiority treat him as a higher being. They should greet him first, make way for him wherever he walks; when he speaks everyone should listen to him and never try to oppose him. He is a genius and people are like asses. They should be grateful to him seeing that he is so condescending. Such proud men are found especially among the Ulama. (Ali 1920, 70)

Possessing wealth does not appear to be a sin. What is evil is the misuse of money by disregarding the obligation of giving 2.5 percent of one's wealth (zakat) back to Allah. A Hadith speaks to the subject in lucid terms.

Allah's Apostle said, "Whoever is made wealthy by Allah and does not pay the zakat of his wealth, then on the Day of Resurrection his wealth will be made like a bald-headed poisonous male snake with two black spots over the eyes. The snake will encircle his neck and bite his cheeks and say, I am your wealth, I am your treasure. (Bukhari [Vol. 2], 276-277)

Few imams are men of wealth. Rather, they are expected to maintain a low financial profile. Dedication to the work of Allah is to involve sacrifice and self-denial. As expected, urban mosques give higher salaries to their imams than their rural counterparts, but overall there is little observable struggle in the area of financial greed among Muslim clergy.

Christians and Sin

Believers in Christ make lofty professions. The indwelling Holy Spirit is said to cause us to walk triumphantly in the midst of a hostile and evil world. Jesus on the cross is proclaimed as the path to an ongoing state of forgiveness. Peace is trumpeted as a trademark of the Christian. Joy, even in the midst of cataclysmic adversity, is held forth as an achievable experience.

Having acknowledged the above as an ideal, what indeed is the reality? Joseph M. Stowell of Moody Bible Institute comments,

I left seminary several years ago with an unflinching commitment to the doctrine of the perseverance of the saints. I soon discovered that on a practical level, the saints don't persevere all that well. As a young pastor, I noted that God's flock was often more committed to comfort than to character, to convenience more than to commitment, to cash more than to Christ. It was a unique brand of disposable discipleship. (Stowell 1985, 142)

What a large chasm often exists between belief and practice. The sensitive believer struggles to be authentic. He is so often trapped in ambivalence. "We are a mixed breed, shadow and light, weak and strong, foul and clean, hate and love, all at the same time. Our middle name is ambiguity" (Smedes 1984, 118). The Muslim looks on and ponders, *Why do Christians assert that which they do not possess? How can followers of Jesus claim to be superior in behavior to Muslims?* Conclusion: Christianity is a charade!

Tough words. Naz is a Pakistani Christian studying at the Asian Theological Seminary in Manila. One day he came to me in an agitated mood and blurted out, "Phil, I have met a highly educated Muslim Pakistani who is spending some time here in Manila. I really desire to witness to him of Christ's love and redemption. But what can I say? All around are Christian churches and those who profess to be believers. Yet, the bars, massage parlors, and prostitutes undercut anything I can say about the Christian message. The Philippines is perhaps the most blatantly sinful country in all of Asia, and at the same time, it is the only nation which is 'Christian.' The Pakistani will only mock my witness and point to the relative absence of overt social sins in his Muslim homeland." Such is the dilemma of seeking to bring some degree of parity between Christian profession and Christian deeds.

A number of Jordanians were living together and attending a local college. All were practicing and witnessing Muslims, with the exception of John, who was a Baptist. John became spiritually cold and ceased attending church. He began smoking and drinking. One of his orthodox Muslim friends had been scrutinizing John's life. He went to him and severely rebuked him, telling him such a life-style is displeasing to God.

Pride and a desire for institutional power have been the downfall of many men of God. I was given a tour of the headquarters of a large, well-known Christian development organization. It was an overwhelming experience to walk into the president's office. The room was massive. The decorations were lavish. Over to one side was a wall completely covered from top to bottom with awards and recognitions that had been given to the president. He was pictured with well-known personages from around the world. My heart sank with a sense of outrage and embarrassment. What a contrast between what I was seeing and the pictures of starving orphans that this organization uses in their magazine advertisements, and television specials. Within a short time, the president became entangled in his own ego and today is out of the mainstream of evangelical ministry.

Calvin Miller describes the process by which a man of God is seduced by satanic deceit:

We may be sure of this: Satan's offer of personal power will always be couched in the interest of God and others. We all like to think of ourselves as generous and self-giving. We all like to hear others tell us how humble or spiritual we are. Such comments separate us from God. Compliments are the parents of egotism and egotism seldom stops celebrating its own power long enough to marvel at God's. (Miller 1984, 34)

Distressing news began to filter through the circuit that an organization in the Midwest concerned with Muslim evangelism was undergoing internal disintegration. Soon an announcement was made that a group had split off, and now two missions were vying for the financial support of the same constituency. A friend wrote me that one of the leaders caused these problems by his "vile temper and underhanded ways." He went on to lament, "This incident is one of the messy, unfortunate and painful realities of life in a yet imperfect world and partially redeemed church."

Without a doubt, much of the true story has been carefully concealed from trusting supporters. This lack of integrity continues to astound me. The Christian public would be amazed if they became privy to much of what goes on behind the scenes in certain organizations. My friend, quoted above, has come to accept all this as "painful realities in a yet imperfect world." But can the Muslim onlooker be expected to be so understanding? He is always pushing us against the wall to prove our assertions of superiority. Our eloquent words all too often fail the test of applied reality.

In many countries where Protestants have not penetrated, Muslims have only the Roman Catholic church as an example of Christianity. They are perplexed as to the use of images in worship, since such aids are prohibited in Islam. How, they wonder, can the priests remain moral while enduring a lifetime of celibacy? This is regarded as abnormal. And why is Mary called "the Mother of God"? God can have neither mother, father, nor son. Many Muslims would agree with the following assessment:

Bishops are real signs of contradiction. They practice the opposite of what the gospel proclaims. The gospel teaches humility: "No one among you should be called preacher or father." Yet they insist that priests should be called Reverend Fathers and they are to be called at least very Reverend Monsignores or Excellencies, not to mention their Eminences or His Holiness, just one step short of God Almighty. All of them are to be dressed up as pompous clowns, while the priests are not to neglect their ceremonial robes in order to add splendor to their shows. The Son of Man died naked on the cross, but they display golden crosses in order to inspire the masses to suffer with greater devotion. (Doyo 1985, 18)

A friend and I drove up to the bishop's house in a city inhabited by many Muslims. It was a beautiful, rambling building surrounded by a lush garden. The entrance of the robed bishop was as that of a potentate. Everyone stood and offered obsequious gestures. Young girls came from all over the building and bowed before the bishop and then kissed his huge ring. It was a demonstration of honor and respect that seemed all out of proportion for a mere mortal to whom had been entrusted the task of servant leadership.

A 1987 issue of *Life* magazine devoted seven pages to spectacular full-color photos of six television evangelists. Jimmy Swaggart, the fallen evangelist, was quoted as saying, "We really don't have that much" while pictured jogging in front of his $1.5 million house. Robert Schuller is reported to be living on his $15,000-per-speech fees, plus royalties from best-selling books. Oral Roberts was born in a two-room cabin but now drives a Mercedes-Benz and owns three houses, the largest of which is a 6,328-square-foot Tulsa mansion. Pat Robertson is shown in front of his $300,000 Georgian home. Jerry Falwell is purchasing a home with a pool and indoor waterfall. The Bakkers hardly deserve comment!

To a faithful Muslim this is all obscene. They would evaluate such men in terms of CEOs of large corporations, but not as men of God called to deliver a heavenly message to a needy world. They would, in all of this, only see incongruity, not continuity with the teaching of God's Word.

While on a speaking tour of Nigeria I was handed a letter and envelope. If I had not personally seen those two pieces of paper, I could never have been convinced of their contents. A small evangelical church of thirty members located in a Muslim area was requesting financial assistance in building a parsonage. At that time they did not have a pastor, but they evidently felt the need for a home that would be a definite drawing card for a gifted person. The letter was asking for $275,000 to be donated for the project! Evidently these Nigerian brethren had obtained their information on pastoral housing costs from *Life* magazine.

Missionaries are not exempt. I had an acquaintance in a poor country tell me he was considering the purchase of a $25,000 car for his private use. The nationals among whom he works commute in crowded, dilapidated buses.

One spiritual leader in an underdeveloped Muslim country remarked, "Why do missionaries from the mission always preach about heaven? They have nothing to anticipate. Everything they could possibly desire in heaven, they already have here."

I had a small part in leading a Muslim Pakistani doctor

to Christ. It was my desire to see him find his first employment in a mission hospital where he could be discipled in a Christian atmosphere. It was a shattering experience to receive from him this assessment of the hospital: "I had joined the hospital with a zealous mission. Soon after joining someone told me that it is a 'United Corruption Hospital.' I thought he was biased, but after eight months of stay there I realized that remark was quite true. Probably 90 percent of the workers are corrupt, from the security guards and janitors up to the administrator and the board of directors. Most consultants are busy in making money – by hook or crook. The personnel of the hospital does not even realize the mission of the hospital."

My friend left that "Christian" environment and has gone to work for a totally Muslim hospital.

An assessment of Christian and Muslim sins could go on indefinitely. But there is one further focus of human weakness that should be touched on. It is set apart as a special consideration.

Sex

Couldn't our hormones or chromosomes have been arranged so that mates would more easily find sexual satisfaction with just one partner? Why weren't we made more like animals, who, except for specified periods, go through their daily routine with hardly a thought of sex? I could handle lust better if I knew it would only strike me in October or May. It's the not knowing, the ceaseless vulnerability, that drives me crazy. ("The War Within" 1985, 33)

Sex, at least to the male, is a relentless presence. It is a lurking force that, in its perverted form, is ever ready to wage combat over all that is pure and moral. How easy to empathize with the anonymous author who has written of his "ceaseless vulnerability." A glib rehearsal of the exciting, proper usage of God's gift of sex can be as sounding brass to a God-seeker caught in a terrible web of lust. He would gladly trade the thirty-minute periods of sexual ecstasy for a life freed of the constant battle for mental and physical morality. Origen, one of the early church Fathers, responded to this debilitating conflict by having himself castrated. He felt there was no other way for him to break loose of fleshly allurements that were slowly causing a disintegration of his spiritual life. While certainly not advocating such an extreme measure, I, along with millions of other men, can understand the intensity of Satan's special tool, which has successfully been utilized in bringing the moral downfall of innumerable men of God.

Sex is interpreted differently within the variety of ethnic groupings found around the world. Morality will mean one thing to a Zulu animist and another to a Brazilian Roman Catholic. To some, religious codes and strictures play a key role in sexual understanding. To others, common sense and humanistic concerns are the key to a good sexual identity. But to almost all, there is the recognition of the necessity for sexual control. Islam and Christianity are both very concerned about sex. Islam has mandated strict moral regulations with severe punishment prescribed for offenders. The Bible denounces perverted sex more often than any other sin, with the exception of idolatry.

Christians and Temptation

In 1970 I was invited to a Christian conference in Singapore. On a Sunday afternoon I bade my wife and small daughter farewell at the Dhaka, Bangladesh, airport. Two hours later I landed in Bangkok, Thailand. Thai Airlines provided overnight accommodation at a reasonable hotel in a nice section of the city. After checking in, a young man took my bags up to my room. As soon as we were alone he offered to send a beautiful girl to the room for five dollars. I refused the offer and decided to take a short walk before supper. As I went out the front door of the hotel the bell captain gave me a card showing me how to get to one of the "best massage parlors" in town, I continued my walk out along the busy street.

Soon a young Thai lady appeared, took my arm and began to tell me, in glowing terms, what she had to offer. Convinced of my lack of interest, she left. In rapid succession, three taxiloads of Thai girls pulled up at the curb and sought to entice me to pile in and experience ultimate sensual sensations. All of this occurred within thirty minutes, far removed from the infamous red light districts of Bangkok.

My pace quickened as I retreated to my hotel room. I was wet with sweat as I knelt by my bed, read from Psalms, and thanked God for deliverance. Not one person in Bangkok knew me. So easily I could have capitulated to the base instincts that all men carry within them. Only a keen love for God and family put up the roadblocks.

Satan is a master at understanding man's vulnerability. He is constantly awaiting the proper context of weakness during which he can bombard the believer with an allurement which can barely be resisted. Such was the situation with Paul, a sincere Christian I've known for many years. One late evening in Manila the phone rang and I suddenly found myself talking with Paul some eight thousand miles distant. He was in a state of extreme agitation. A beautiful young woman had invited him to spend the next night with her. She had graphically verbalized the sexual delights they would experience in her waterbed. Paul, speaking to me at three in the morning, was overwhelmed with a desire to have sex with this woman. She was enticingly eager. He was ready to throw over his own virginity for what he acknowledged would probably be a one night stand.

I sought to probe every possible way to bring Paul to his senses. We talked of his commitment to Christ and to his godly family. His church and employment relationships were discussed. I spent some time downgrading the girl, a professing believer, who was prepared to use sex as a recreational tool rather than a vital part of a lifetime commitment of marital fidelity. And what of guilt that would plague Paul the rest of his life? There was everything to lose and ever so little to gain.

Finally, after forty minutes of intense conversation, Paul began to move toward an understanding of what a loss he was about to accept into the very fiber of his psyche. He went to the brink, and by God's grace, he turned back.

In Manila "short-time motels" do a booming business. Five dollars pays for a room for three hours. An extra few dollars pays for the rental of a video machine and a pornographic film. These motels are ringed by high walls in order to guarantee clients' confidentiality. The proprietor of one of Manila's largest motels must have a religious sensitivity. Each Christmas season he constructs an elaborate manger scene at the head of the driveway. At least 95 percent of his customers are adulterers and fornicators. He has made it convenient for the immoral to pay their regards to the baby Jesus on the way into the den of Satan.

The Secret Life of Hannah Whitall Smith by Marie Henry is a sad book. Smith's *The Christian's Secret of a Happy Life* is a classic book on spirituality; it has sold millions of copies. This book had been a great help to me in the early days of my spiritual pilgrimage. One evening I was reading an autobiography of Bertrand Russell and noted his aversion to his difficult mother-in-law, a wealthy Quaker mystic from Philadelphia. That rang a bell, and I found after some quick research that Hannah Whitall Smith's daughter had married Bertrand Russell, and soon thereafter she became an atheist like her renowned husband. I then had to try to understand all the negative things Russell had to say about Hannah. Marie Henry's book provided the answers.

Hannah was married to Robert Pearsall Smith, who became a famous evangelist. During his career he suffered a nervous breakdown. While recovering, he was led into a "spiritual discovery." This special insight centered around the receiving of sexual thrills at the time of intense hungering for God. After he recovered he went to England on a speaking tour during which time he was widely acclaimed as a powerful evangelist.

One late evening at a Bible conference a young lady in need of spiritual counsel came to Smith. He shared with her his new insight about sex and spirituality. The next morning the girl went to the leaders of the conference and related Smith's views on sex. Immediately the scandal spread, and Robert Smith began a journey into repeated adultery and total denial of the faith.

All of this had a deep effect on Hannah. Although she

remained loyal to Robert, she became embittered and difficult to live with. None of their children walked with God. And it all began with a sexual aberration in the name of spiritual reality.

A minister fell deeply into the trap of anonymously attending sex shows in Boston. His schizophrenia began to eat into his soul. He describes his disintegration as a person:

What shocked me was my trip up the coast the next two days. I followed my usual practice of staying in homey inns with big fireplaces, and of eating by the water-front and watching the sailboats bob in the shimmering sea, of taking long solitary walks on the rocky promontories where huge waves crashed with thunder, of closing my eyes and letting salt spray splash across my face, of stopping at roadside stands for fresh lobster and crab. There was a difference this time: I felt no pleasure. None. My emotional reaction was the same as if I had been at home, yawning, reading the newspaper. All romance had drained out, desiccated.

The realization disturbed me profoundly, By all counts, those wonderful, sensuous experiences rated far higher than the cheap thrill of watching a fat, nude, pock-marked body rotate on plywood. And yet, to my utter disbelief my mind kept roaming back to that grimy booth in Boston. Was I going crazy? Would I lose every worthwhile sensation in life? Was my soul leaking away? Was I becoming possessed? ("The War Within" 1985, 41)

There is a good ending to this man's torment. He went to his wife and confessed his attendance at the burlesque shows. She was able to forgive him with the result that their marriage was saved. He was finally able to break loose from sexual bondage.

A number of queries concerning sex were asked on the missionary questionnaire:

Question	Frequently	Infrequently	Never
Do you have sexual fantasies of lust?	57	215	112
Do you read sexually stimulating literature?	4	127	258
Do you attend R-rated movies?	1	61	322
Do you attend X-rated movies?	0	12	375

Have you remained sexually moral since becoming a missionary? Yes: 372; No: 10

Another survey was conducted by Christianity Today. They asked their readers, "Since you have been over 21, have you ever done anything with someone (not your spouse) that you feel was sexually inappropriate?" Responses were:

Laypersons	Yes: 45 percent	No: 55 percent
Pastors	Yes: 23 percent	No: 77 percent
		(Stafford 1987, 36)

These statistics indicate sexual temptation is a serious

struggle for Christians in all walks of life. This is reflected as well in the divorce rate among evangelicals. Many churches now cater to people with broken homes through special Sunday school classes and care groups.

There is no one totally competent to offer advice on sexual matters. One Christian leader has written some of evangelicalism's best books on marriage and family. The disclosure of his adulterous affair sent shock waves through the worldwide Christian community. Recognizing my own vulnerability, I would still like to set forth several urgent considerations in regard to maintenance of sexual purity.

- Biblical morality must become an integrated part of our total being.
- Our relationship with Jesus is to be continually revitalized through an application of spiritual disciplines.
- For those who are married, there must be a mutual commitment to keep the sparkle and freshness of "first love" within the relationship. Children are not to absorb so much parental love that it detracts from marital intimacy.
- Loneliness, discouragement, arguments with one's mate, extended absences, and proximity to sexual temptation all set up one for a moral fall. This recognition leads to mental and spiritual alertness when faced with unavoidable circumstance.
- Flee! Lingering in the presence of the tiger of lust will lead one to be devoured. The enticement of sex has always been to lead the tempted person just one step further than he has already gone.

These steps never end until there is complete moral

disintegration.

Millions of Christians have testified, through the centuries, to the reality of a victorious sex life. In days of blatant moral testing, the renewed challenge to purity is urgently pressing itself upon the Christian community.

Muslims and Sex

While in Istanbul, Turkey, I had the privilege of taking a walk through the heartland of Islamic history. Topkapi Palace was the official residence for powerful sultans who ruled the Ottoman Empire for over four hundred years. To one side of the ostentatious buildings is the "harem," which contains four hundred rooms. It was difficult for me to reconcile theological Islam with the stories of some of the Muslim sultans who had forty wives at one time. It was evident that sex was a high priority item for the leadership of the Muslim world.

Orthodox Islam is opposed to fornication and adultery. Muslims are allowed to have four wives at any one time depending on their ability to treat each with equality. Divorce is permitted. An embarrassment to many Muslims is the controversy surrounding *muta* (temporary marriage). An authoritative Hadith states,

We used to participate in the holy wars carried on by the Prophet and we had no women (wives) with us. So we said (to the Prophet), "Shall we castrate ourselves?" But the Prophet forbade us to do that and thenceforth he allowed us to marry a woman (temporarily) by giving her even a garment, and then he recited: "O you who believe! Do not make

*unlawful the good things which Allah has made
lawful for you." (Bukhari [Vol. 6], 110)*

Ayatollah Khomeini comments of muta, "A woman may
legally belong to a man in one of two ways: by continuing
marriage or temporary marriage. In the former, the duration
of the marriage need not be specified; in the låtter, it must
be stipulated, for example, that it is for a period of an hour,
a day, a month, a year, or more" (Khomeini 1979, 94). Jim
Dretke tells of Saudis who go to Iraq for weekends of sexual
pleasure. Taking advantage of *muta*, a Saudi marries a young
Iraqi girl for a specified amount of money on Friday evening.
On Sunday afternoon he divorces her. He has had his "legal"
sex, and she has been paid a generous amount for the use of
her body.

In fairness, it must be said that to most Muslims *muta*
is a totally unacceptable practice. They deny that the one
rather obscure quranic verse on the subject gives license
for temporary marriage. Also, the Hadith citations
condoning *muta* are said to be of questionable repute. *Muta*
is not widely practiced in the Islamic world.

Sexual sin, however, is not at all uncommon. One oil
company in Saudi Arabia regularly checks out its Saudi
employees for venereal disease. Among the men who leave
the country for vacations it was found that half of them had
syphilis or gonorrhea. Dudley Woodberry, professor of Islamics
at Fuller Theological Seminary, and his wife Roberta told me of
the time in Riyadh when their twelve-year-old son was
propositioned by a sheikh in a limousine for the princely sum of
$250.

A highly educated Egyptian lady wrote of one of the

Muslim leaders of a Persian Gulf state who selects a beautiful young virgin to sleep with one night each month. This girl then becomes highly desirable as a wife due to her relationship with the sheikh. She receives a generous allowance for the rest of her life.

The video revolution has taken its toll on Muslim morality. It is not uncommon for X-rated movies to be shown in small rooms where customers can crowd in and enter a world of fantasy that they could never have imagined existed. These improvised "theaters" are proliferating at an amazing rate throughout the Muslim world. A missionary friend lives across the street from one such establishment. He daily observes Muslim young men entering the bamboo "theater" for their early afternoon titillation. This trend will definitely have an effect on traditional family values within Islam.

The conflict between the traditional and the liberated was related to me by a person who was amazed at what he saw at a Cyprus beach resort. A family had come from a Muslim country to Cyprus for a vacation. On the beach the mother was dressed in a long black veil. Lying next to her was the teenage daughter with her breasts uncovered. This would certainly not be regarded as typical, but perhaps as a trend for the Western-influenced, nominally religious Muslims of the future.

In Manila I have seen an Arab walking through the five-star Philippine Plaza Hotel with one arm around a prostitute and the other hand going through his prayer beads. Many discos and massage parlors in Manila's red light district have their signs written in Arabic as well as English. An acquaintance told me of an Arab resident in the Philippines who religiously keeps the Ramadan fast in the daytime and then breaks it with a bottle of beer in the evening. His nights are spent with prostitutes.

In front of our reading center in the Islamic area of Manila I have seen a Muslim young man caress a girl's buttocks as they walked down the street in broad daylight. The girl was arrayed in conservative Muslim dress.

A heavy-set Filipino Muslim judge was bragging to me of his pilgrimage to Mecca. He used to be a heavy drinker, but on the day he boarded the *Hajj* ship nineteen years ago he prayed for deliverance from a desire for alcohol. Allah granted that prayer, and he never drank beer or wine again. I pressed him in the area of morals. He confessed very openly to committing adultery with prostitutes. This was justified because his travel necessitates absences from his wife. He said he had sex by contract, not out of love for the prostitute. Therefore, it was purely a sexual-economic issue, one that was of benefit to both parties. In response to my question about how God views such acts, he just smiled and said Allah is merciful and will graciously forgive sinners.

Another Filipino Muslim I spoke with was upset when I mentioned polygamy. He was opposed to the practice and had forbidden his sons to take multiple wives. It was his view that no one can treat more than one wife equally. Love must be exclusive. When I mentioned Muhammad's many wives, he replied, "We aren't prophets." It is my observation that polygamy is uncommon throughout the Muslim world. Divorce is fairly widespread but still significantly less frequent than in Western "Christian" countries.

Muslim mystics throughout the centuries have exhorted faithful believers to sexual purity. One such mystic was Kashf al-Mahjub, who wrote in the twelfth century.

It behooves the seeker of God to spend his whole life, day and night, in ridding himself of incitements to passion which show themselves through the senses, and to pray God to make him such that this desire will be removed from his inward nature, since whoever is afflicted with lust is veiled from all spiritual things. If anyone should repel it by his own exertions, his task would be long and painful. The right way is resignation. (al-Hujwiri 1982, 209)

Jim Dretke relates the moving story of an Arab Muslim who attended the Sunday morning worship service where Jim pastored. He noted Abdul had partaken of the elements during the Communion celebration. Following the service Jim went to Abdul and in the conversation mentioned the Communion. Abdul quickly related what had happened to him the previous night. A group of student friends at his university had taken him to a nude bar in Hollywood. There, completely undressed girls had danced just a few feet from him. He had broken out in a nervous sweat and was unable to sleep that night. The next morning he decided to go to a religious place and see if he could find forgiveness and peace. Jim had represented Communion as a symbol of God's mercy and cleansing, so out of a deep sense of need Abdul had partaken. Jim told him that he felt the Lord would be pleased with his action.

My Muslim friend Dr. Ali has traveled rather extensively. He told me of a very attractive lady he met at an educator's conference in India. She offered to go to bed with him. While at Harvard as a visiting scholar, a student at the university made an overture to him that most likely included sex. In these and other instances Ali refused, telling the women that he is a devout Muslim and happily married.

In contrast to Dr. Ali, I know of a renowned Christian missionary who has had a number of emotional, if not physical, affairs with women other than his wife. Yet Ali, without the Bible, Christ, or the Holy Spirit, has been enabled to remain a faithful husband and father. He gives credit to Allah and the guidance given to him by the Quran.

All of this should be a challenge for a new effort to be made by Christians to matching a high commitment to biblical purity with that which is demonstratably true.

Spiritual Victory

The sign on the gate of a retreat center an hour's drive from Manila enticingly reads, "House of Spirituality." Every time I drive past that house I find myself mystified and challenged. Can I just drive in the gate, knock on the door, enter, go out to the back porch, and begin to absorb spirituality as I look out over the gorgeous vista of a lake, a dormant volcano, and petite villages lying peacefully two thousand feet below? With my lunch, can I order a pound of spirituality? Or will it come as I imbibe the fresh, cool air where nothing seems to impede my prayers between earth and heaven? In the tranquil garden, among the blooming roses and sweet scent of the gardenias, will it be there that I encounter genuine lasting spirituality? Or may it not be finally realized in the warm fellowship between myself and the saintly inhabitants of the House of Spirituality?

Could it be, could it just be, that the spiritual reality for which I long is to be wrapped in a very different package, a package containing Manila's humidity, sweat, noises, smells, cries, and groans? Could it be a spirituality hammered out on the anvil of perplexity, empathy, discouragement, and even failure? The quest continues.

Christians and Victory

Yes, the quest continues. Spiritual victory seems to come in small increments, not in gargantuan leaps. But how grateful I am that it does come! We are not left to grope about in a morass of continual defeat. The few illustrations that follow are but a sampling of those who have walked with God and experienced His enablement.

Dave is an extremely gifted intellectual seeking to live out his Christian testimony within a sensitive Muslim setting. He had been invited to speak at a Christian conference in a very remote rural area. One dark night Dave was driving down a dirt road when his way was blocked by an ox cart. Suddenly he was surrounded by screaming Muslims who mistakenly assumed he was the thief who had just taken part in a robbery in a nearby village. It was so dark that no one could see his face and ascertain that he was a foreigner. Dave relates his story:

The first fellow screamed that I had murdered someone, another said robbery. Others smashed the windshield in on top of me. I was dragged from the car. "Kill him - kill him - kill him" seemed to be the chant from every side. Then they began to beat me, mostly from behind. I was slammed to my knees. I guess I was hit enough so that I didn't notice when

*a fellow plunged an arrow like a spear into my arm.
I took the most difficult blow smack on the left eye,
which completely closed the eye. Within a short time
help arrived and the one hundred shouting villagers
realized they had made a tragic mistake.*

Dave then had to determine his response.

*I told one of the Muslims that according to the
teaching of Jesus Christ, I also love those who beat
me. I asked him to communicate my love to the
villagers and to say that I had forgiven them
completely. This is a society without grace. When
grace is shown, it is something of a total amazement.
That grace was important in practical ways as well.
The police arrived. I found out later that the local
chief had something of a vendetta against those
villages. This would have been a perfect opportunity
to trash a few villages and to gain certain other
"benefits." But he needed me to register a case. I
refused.*

Dave went on to speak of the mental comparison he made
of his undeserved suffering and that of Christ on the cross. In a
new dimension, he was able to enter into the reality of the love
of Jesus as He bore the insults and blows of an angry crowd.
They too did not know whom they persecuted. The words of
forgiveness from the cross provided the perfect model for Dave
in his moment of extreme trial.

During my China tour our group had a unique opportunity.
One late evening, in the interior of a city, we unobtrusively made

our way to an old, dingy apartment building. Making our way up the unlit back stairs, we passed a number of open doors where people were pressed into very small rooms. We filed into the appropriate two-room apartment and quickly closed the door. Standing before us was one of the sweetest elderly ladies I have ever met. This grandmother was full of vibrant faith and zeal.

Taking our seats on the floor or on rickety chairs, we were riveted in our attention as she shared her story with us. She is a doctor. Prior to 1949 she was head of obstetrics in a mission hospital. Following the Communist takeover, her life became extremely difficult. During the Cultural Revolution she was made to do the work of an orderly, mopping floors and emptying bedpans. Later, at a very advanced age, she was ordered to go from village to village as an itinerant medic. Now she sat before us as one who had so victoriously endured the fires of testing and had come forth as pure gold.

There was no rancor in her spirit, only a humble forgiveness toward those who had mistreated her. Every day she goes to the nearby park and seeks to fulfill her goal of winning one soul to Christ each day. On a weekly basis twenty-five ladies crowd into her apartment for Bible study. There will be a grand reception in heaven for this precious saint.

In our home church we enjoy the friendship of a number of godly families who have upper-bracket incomes. I am always amazed at how down-to-earth and humble these Christians are. One evening we were invited to a dinner at the home of Henry and Betty Frank, a very special couple who came to Christ later in life. The Franks had also invited Don and Ginny Otero, a relatively new couple in the church.

After dinner I was sitting in the living room, engaged in casual conversation with Don. In response to my question about his profession he told me he was "with" a certain corporation. I pushed him a bit and he casually mentioned the company has 3,400 employees, does 270 million dollars in annual sales, and is the third-largest corporation of its kind in the world. His identification of his relationship with the company had been totally vague, so I asked him what particular responsibility he held. Don looked down at the carpet and quietly replied, "I'm the president." I was awestruck, not with his position, but with his humility. Later, I had the opportunity to visit Don in his corporate headquarters and to tour two of his plants with him. He gave me one of several small crosses he had specially made to wear in his lapel as a witness to his Christian faith.

In speaking of Ken Taylor, author and founder of Tyndale House Publishers, a Christian magazine publisher has written this tribute:

> *Here was a successful publisher who could be living luxuriously but has given away more than 24 million dollars for the gospel and drives around town in a little Chevette. His wife, Margaret, throughout their marriage, has made the sacrifices with him. Ask anyone who knows them and you will get the same answer: both are humbly and patiently committed to the ministry of the Word and each other. Now that's heartening to know about the translator of the Living Bible and chairman of Tyndale House Publishers. (Myra 1985, 12)*

Ken and Margaret visited Bangladesh where Julie and I had fellowship with them on a few occasions. Years later, we were living in Wheaton for a few months. One day the phone rang and it was Ken inviting us to his home for dinner. We were not even aware that he knew we were in town. Following that delightful occasion they accepted our invitation for a meal in our home. We had done nothing of significance for the Taylors in Bangladesh, yet they graciously extended their love and time toward us.

Humility and servanthood are not easy disciplines to incorporate into one's life. Cliff Richard, the famous British singer, is a gracious Christian who exudes humility. During a series of concerts in Bangladesh we hosted a reception for him in our home. In a most natural way, he picked up the teapot and went around the room serving everyone.

Romans 6 gives a vision of victory as it mentions Christ or God nineteen times. It is exhortative but not complete. Chapter 7 focuses on the word *sin* for another nineteen count. A massive struggle is going on between the old and new nature. Sin and righteousness seem locked in mortal combat. Then chapter 8 marches triumphantly on the scene. The Holy Spirit, mentioned nineteen times, at last prevails. The good news of liberation comes in verse 2. "For the law of the spirit of life in Christ Jesus has set you free from the law of sin and of death." This is a good biblical basis for Christian victory.

By now the reader may well have grasped that a central motif of my writings on spirituality is *endurance*. In our bedroom hangs a stunning reproduction on papyrus of the Great Judgment Day as perceived by Egyptians five thousand years ago. On the wall of a king's tomb had been painted this very dramatic picture of a woman's works being weighed on a scale while the judge looks on. Details of the woman's deeds are being written in the background. Though the picture's theological doctrine is inadequate, it still contains elements of biblical truth. What will be the state of our deeds at the time of final judgment? Will they be consumed as wood, hay, and stubble or come forth as perfected gold and silver? The process of endurance to the end is of paramount importance to our appearance at the Judgment Seat of Christ.

Robertson McQuilkin, former president of International University, is an impressive and mature Christian leader who has been tested deeply over the years. His desire to persevere is beautifully articulated in a poem he has written entitled, "Lord, Let Me Get Home before Dark."

It's sundown, Lord.
The shadows of my life stretch back
    into the dimness of the years long spent.
I fear not death, for that grim foe betrays himself at
    last, thrusting me forever into life:
Life with you, unsoiled and free.

But I do fear.
I fear the Dark Spectre may come too soon -
    or do I mean, too late?
That I should end before I finish or
    finish, but not well.
That I should stain your honor, shame your name,
    grieve your loving heart.
Few, they tell me, finish well . . .
Lord, let me get home before dark.

The darkness of a spirit
    grown mean and small, fruit shriveled on the vine,
    bitter to the taste of my companions,
    burden to be borne by those brave few who love me
    still.
No, Lord. Let the fruit grow lush and sweet,
    A joy to all who taste;
Spirit-sign of God at work,
    stronger, fuller, brighter at the end.
Lord let me get home before dark.

The darkness of tattered gifts,
    rust-locked, half-spent or ill-spent,
A life that once was used of God
    now set aside.
Grief for glories gone or
Fretting for a task God never gave.
Mourning in the hollow chambers of memory,
Gazing on the faded banners of victories long gone.
Cannot I run well unto the end?
Lord, let me get home before dark.

The outer me decays -
    I do not fret or ask reprieve.
The ebbing strength but weans me from mother earth
    and grows me up for heaven.
I do not cling to shadows cast by immortality
I do not patch the scaffold lent to build the real, eternal
    me.
I do not clutch about me my cocoon,
    vainly struggling to hold hostage
    a free spirit pressing to be born.

But will I reach the gate
in lingering pain, body distorted, grotesque?
Or will it be a mind
wandering untethered among light fantasies or
grim terrors?
Of your grace, Father, I humbly ask . . .
Let me get home before dark.

May this be our prayer as well.

Muslims and Obedience

To a Muslim, a life of victory over the base desires of the flesh is a simple matter of submission to Allah and obedience to his dictates. In fact, a well-known gospel hymn title, "Trust and Obey," could be the overall theme for Islamic sanctification. Muslims are excited about the fact that the requirements for obedience are so clearly enunciated in Islam. The Quran gives the overview, the Hadith supplies the model, and the Five Pillars provide the specifics.[5] What more could an earnest seeker of God desire?

Bishop Stephen Neill has accurately assessed the Muslim view of obedience.

In modern Muslim propaganda in the West, nothing

---

[5]The Five Pillars of Islam are the five obligatory duties imposed on all Muslims. These are: 1. The *Shahadah*, the confession of faith in Allah and His Prophet; 2. *Salat*, the five-times-daily prayer ritual; 3. The *Zakat*, giving a prescribed percentage of harvest and income to charitable Muslim causes; 4. observing the fast during the month of Ramadan; and 5. the *Hajj*, pilgimage to Mecca in Saudi Arabia.

is more strongly emphasized than the feasibility, the viability, of Islam. Men can turn and obey, if they will. Islam makes only reasonable demands upon men. This is part of the mercy of God - he knows what men can do, and does not lay upon them burdens too heavy to be borne. A constant contrast is drawn between the unpractical idealism of Jesus, suitable perhaps, for ascetics and those who can flee entirely from the world, and the practical down-to-earth regulations of Islam. And the Muslim objects strongly to Christian stress upon the sinfulness of man. This seems to him to be mere evasion. By pleading his weakness man tries to excuse his failure to obey, and so to withdraw himself from the just judgment of God on disobedience. Instead, he should gird himself to the riot overwhelmingly difficult effort of obedience. (Neill 1970, 68)

Obedience is the goal, but what is the reality? According to Muslims, it is about equal to or a bit better than that which is found in the worldwide Christian community. The devoted minority find the path to spiritual victory. A significant majority pay only lip service to Islamic faith and practice. Allah will one day judge the nominal and the hypocritical Muslim.

There are many claims made by Islam that proclaim the results of the path of godly obedience. About one group it is stated, "Due to their prayers they mastered their lusts and lascivious passions and due to the high pleasure they derived from reading the Koran they did not care for sensuous pleasure" (Valiuddin 1980, xix). The Bektashis, a prominent Turkish Muslim order, don a girdle and recite a seven-point liturgy.

I tie up greediness and unbind generosity.
I tie up anger and unbind meekness.
I tie up avarice and unbind piety.
I tie up ignorance and unbind the fear of God.
I tie up passion and unbind the love of God.
I tie up hunger and unbind contentment.
I tie up the power of Satan and unbind divineness.
(Cragg 1976, 17)

Christians look on Muslims and are prone to criticize what appears to be a strong legalistic system of religious bondage. They question if inward purity and good deeds are as important in Islam as legislated ritual. Islam does address this issue. A rather severe Hadith states,

The Prophet was once informed of a woman who used to offer prayers regularly and kept fasts very often. She gave alms frequently but her neighbors were sick of her abusive tongue. The Prophet said, "Such a woman deserves only the fire of Hell!" (Ismail 1980, 17)

Ali Bin Uthman al-Hujwiri's statement is exceptionally clear.

Outward and inward purification must go together; e.g., when a man washes his hands he must wash his heart clean of worldliness, and when he puts water in his mouth he must purify his mouth from

*the mention of other than God, and when he washes
his face he must turn away from all familiar objects
and turn towards God, and when he wipes his head
he must resign his affairs to God, and when he
washes his feet he must not form the intention of
taking his stand on anything doubly purified. In all
religious ordinances the external is combined with
the internal; e.g. in faith, the tongue's profession
with the heart's belief. (al-Hujwiri 1982, 292)*

Al-Ghazali is my favorite devotional writer within
Islam. This Sufi mystic was always seeking to place Muslim
spirituality in the context of the inner man.

*Do not neglect your inner being, which lies at the
heart of all purification. Endeavor to purify it with
repentance and remorse for your excesses, and a
determined resolution not to commit them in the
future. Cleanse your inner being in this way, for
that is the place to be examined by the One you
worship. (Ghazali 1983, 44)*

There are many examples of selfless acts performed by
Muslims. An American oil worker in Saudi Arabia was
driving through the remote desert and suddenly realized he
would not reach the next town before his car ran out of gas. As
it was getting dark, he started to experience a real sense of
panic. At that moment he saw a new GMC truck parked
alongside the road. He pulled up and explained his problem
to the Saudi driver. Both men looked in vain for a hose by
which to siphon gas from the truck. Suddenly the Saudi
placed a bucket near the gas tank, took out his knife and

plunged it into the steel thereby releasing a stream of gasoline. That American will never forget that sacrificial gesture of kindness.

I recently received a letter from Dr. Ali. One particular paragraph means a great deal to me. "You are my brother. No matter whether you are an American or profess the Christian faith. The bond of friendship between you and me is everlasting." Islam at its best!

Frank Laubach spent a number of years among the Maranao Muslims of the southern Philippines. This famous literacy expert loved Muslims.

When anybody tells me that it is hard to make friends among Moslems I know better. They do get angry when we throw stones at their religion, but who can blame them when we ourselves are so horribly unlike our Christ? I have found among Moslems as loyal and true friends as among any Christians in the world." (Laubach 1960, 65)

The writings of Jonathan and Rosalind Goforth are among my favorites. During the Boxer Rebellion in China the Goforths were desperately seeking to make their way to the safety of the coast. Along the way they had been beaten and stabbed. As they stumbled through one village a large, friendly crowd surrounded them.

One poor old man insisted on my taking a pair of his old shoes, so worn as to scarcely hold together, saying they might keep my feet from the rough ground. Women came with old soiled children's garments, urging that the nights were cool and the children might need them. "Why were they so kind?" one man was asked. He replied, "We are Mohammedans. Our God is your God and we could not face Him if we had joined in destroying you." (Goforth 1937, 138-139)

Sir John Glubb was a keen observer of Muslims. His comment about their behavior is instructive:

I am a Christian. But I have lived more than half my life among Muslims, sometimes entirely among them with no Christian anywhere near. I know that Islam can produce fine men, and even saints, and that the "image" of Muslims entertained by most people in the West is completely untrue. (Glubb 1971, 8-9)

While my allegiance to Christ and Christianity remain unshakable, I still consider it a great privilege to have spent half of my life among Muslims, twenty of those years living in their towns, eating their food, and speaking their language. I have wept and laughed with my Muslim friends. I have been sometimes exhilarated, sometimes frustrated by their behavior. Their religion at varying times and in varying circumstances has challenged me, annoyed me, and dumbfounded me. Muslims have provided many new and instructive experiences for me. To them I am eternally grateful. My life is richer and much fuller because of my walk among them.

6

Mysticism and Spiritual Power

Webster's technical definition of the word *mysticism* is, "The belief that direct knowledge of God or ultimate reality is attainable through immediate intuition or insight." Note that the mystical experience is not limited to institutional religion. I read about one physicist's dynamic awakening through coming into mystical harmony with the elements of nature. This was a spectacular encounter with the ultimate reality. The scientist felt his quest was complete.

Mysticism, however, is usually God-directed. The "person" or "concept" of God is extremely varied. Each organized religion has its own definition. And within each religion, varied interpretations abound. Add to this the subjective mystic who comes on the scene as a law unto himself. He is dynamically in tune with the unseen. He is able to hear communications from God, which are inaccessible to the average devotee. His claims are as dogmatic as they are unverifiable. The mystic is a person of strident independence. No mere mortal is qualified to scrutinize or criticize his revelations.

Joseph Fletcher's remark that mysticism is something that begins in mist and ends in schism is not far off the mark. The mystic will usually attract followers. But this is often done in the context of divisiveness. Many nonmystical people will stand aloof and mock. Another group will join the crowd for a time and then be drawn to another mystic who is more dramatic. And then there is a large body of people who are simply confused. In the babel of confusion they ask, "Who really speaks the Word of the Lord?"

In light of all this controversy, what makes mysticism so attractive? E. G. Browne has capsuled its allurement in a few brief words:

There is hardly any soil, be it ever so barren, where mysticism will not strike root; hardly any creed, however formal, round which it will not entwine itself. It is, indeed, the eternal cry of the human soul for rest; the insatiable longing of a being wherein infinite ideals are fettered and cramped by a miserable actuality; and so long as man is less than an angel and more than a beast, this cry will not for a moment fail to make itself heard. Wonderfully uniform, too, is its tenor: in all ages, in all countries, in all creeds, whether it come from the Brahmin sage, the Persian poet, or the Christian quietist, it is in essence an enunciation more or less clear, more or less eloquent, of the aspiration of the soul to cease altogether from self and to be at one with God. (Smith 1931, 2)

Is it possible to be a Christian or a Muslim without being a mystic? While not seeking to be overly technical, it must be stated that any encounter with the unseen is a mystical experience. We are really dealing with degrees, not only degrees of mystical belief but also of mystical practice. The level of practice is where the controversy is centered. Let the mystical monk, alone in his desert cell, have all the supernatural encounters he likes. He bothers no one, misguides no one. But when a television evangelist promotes a certain type of mystical experience in 146 countries, it is quite another matter.

A few citations from the Bible highlight the legitimacy of mystical claims. Moses saw God in the burning bush and on Mount Sinai. Our Lord commanded His followers to eat His flesh and drink His blood. The controversy concerning these mystical words continues unabated - Paul was dramatically apprehended by the Lord on the road to Damascus. His experience of ascending to the third heaven is all a mystic could ever hope for! Paul's very mystical phrase "in Christ" is recorded 164 times. Writings of a mystical bent include David's Psalms, the Song of Solomon (which has been given many mystical interpretations), and the Gospel of John's opening discourse on the Logos.

And what can be said of Muslims?

It would appear, then, that Muhammad, from what he saw and heard around him of Christian asceticism, and from the judgments of Christian mystical teaching which came to his knowledge, laid the foundation, perhaps all unwittingly, of a doctrine of mysticism, based on asceticism, which was further developed by the early traditionalists, and later became that fully-developed system of Islamic

Mysticism which we know as Sufism. (Smith 1976, 152)

Islam, like Christianity, has its tension between the orthodox and those of mystical bent. The orthodox, the theological purists, are uncomfortable with the mystics, the "libertarians" who claim to encounter Allah outside the mainstream of Islamic ritual. Muslim fundamentalism, without doubt, is on the rise, yet a majority of Muslims are influenced by some form of Muslim mysticism.

How do we as Christians regard these Muslims? Sir Norman Anderson, the British expert on Islamic law, comments, "My study of Islam. . . convinces me that one cannot deny that some of the great Muslim mystics have sought the face of God with a wholeheartedness that cannot be questioned; and I do not doubt that in some cases it was God himself whom they were seeking, not self-justification or a mystical experience per se" (Anderson 1984, 152). In this chapter I will seek to elucidate practices of both Christians and Muslims who are disposed toward mysticism. It is up to the reader to evaluate their validity.

Experience and Ecstasy

Experience authenticates doctrine. It is the application and internalizing of what is taught. The mystic is highly experience-oriented. He wants to feel. His pulse quickens, his face flushes, his hands tremble. What was once cold, logical teaching now begins to take hold in the deep recesses of the soul. God is at work. A reality is being shaped that can transform a life. Subjectivity is gradually replaced by an affirmation: "I know . . . and am persuaded."

Hollywood actors are told to portray their roles as "excess within control." I wonder if this exhortation has religious significance. Ecstasy in Christian worship can easily cross the border into unbridled excess. Emotion can accelerate and become self-perpetuating. It becomes an end in itself and not a means to an end. It dead-ends as an experience instead of leading toward a higher reality. Emotion is manipulated toward a goal as defined by the manipulator. But all ecstasy is not of this nature. Quiet inward joy also creates a feeling of ecstasy.

With these words of introduction, I go on to briefly illustrate these concepts within the Christian grid. Actual experiences are the flesh and blood of life. We will understand by reverently standing in the shadows and observing, evaluating, and reflecting.

Seppo Syrjanen relates a Muslim's encounter with the voice of God:

When I sent my reply [to the Bible correspondence school] to the question on St. Matthew chapter 11, I was going along the street and I seemed to hear someone calling me: "Come to me, I will give you rest." I thought that what I had read in the morning was just repeating itself in my mind, but still I continued to hear the voice. The next day I heard this voice again and again. I made great efforts to put it out of my mind but I could not do so: for this was not just something imaginary or a repetition of words. On the third day I heard the voice very close to me, I felt the presence of the speaker and I shut the shop doors and knelt in secret before the Lord

*Jesus and received him as my personal Savior.
(Syrjanen 1984, 133)*

A very powerful story of a young Muslim Pakistani
woman meeting Christ is related by Gulshan Esther in her
book *The Torn Veil*. Gulshan was born into a wealthy and
devout Muslim home. As an infant she had typhoid fever,
which left her paralyzed on her left side. Her loving father
sought the best medical assistance for her both in Pakistan
and in England. He took her on the *Hajj* in the hope that
Allah would touch her body and give healing in Mecca.
Nothing happened until she was back in Pakistan alone in
her own room. Suddenly a bright light filled the bedroom.
She was so frightened that she covered herself with her
shawl. She relates what happened next:

> *I came out from my shawl to look. But the doors
> and windows were fast shut, with curtains and
> shutters drawn. I then became aware of figures in
> long robes, standing in the midst of the light, some
> feet from my bed. There were twelve figures in a
> row and the figure in the middle, the thirteenth, was
> larger and brighter than the others.*
>
> *"Oh God," I cried and the perspiration broke
> out on my forehead. I bowed my head and I prayed.
> "Oh God, who are these people, and how have they
> come here when all the windows and doors are
> shut?"*
>
> *Suddenly a voice said, "Get up. This is the path
> you have been seeking, I am Jesus, Son of Mary, to
> whom you have been praying, and now I am standing*

in front of you. You get up and come to me.

I started to weep. "Jesus, I'm crippled. I can't get up."

He said, "Stand up and come to me. I am Jesus." When I hesitated he said it a second time. Then as I still doubted he said for the third time, "Stand up."

And I, Gulshan Fatima, who had been crippled on my bed for nineteen years, felt new strength flowing into my wasted limbs. I put my foot on the ground and stood up. Then I ran a few paces and fell at the feet of the vision. I was bathing in the purest light and it was burning as bright as the sun and moon together. The light shone into my heart and into my mind and many things became clear to me at that moment.

Jesus had put his hand on the top of my head and I saw a hole in his hand from which a ray of light struck down upon my garments, so that the green dress looked white.

He said: "I am Jesus. I am Immanuel. I am the Way, the Truth, and the Life. I am alive, and I am soon coming. See, from today you are my witness. What you have seen now with your eyes you must take to my people. My people are your people, and you must remain faithful to take that to my people."

He said, "Now you have to keep this robe and your body spotless. Wherever you go I will be with you." (Esther 1984, 60-61)

Gulshan has had remarkable opportunities to share her faith and healing with thousands of people in a number of countries.

But there are also aberrations. For an interesting agnostic view on healing, peruse James Randi's *The Faith Healers*. J. C. Ryle has written of the "Athenian love of novelty." He goes on, "There is an incessant craving after any teaching which is sensational, and exciting, and rousing to the feelings. There is an unhealthy appetite for a sort of spasmodic and hysterical Christianity" (Ryle [1883] 1979, xxviii). It is interesting to note that these words were written a century ago. Times have not really changed.

In the Los Angeles area Julie and I visited a church in order to hear a special speaker from Indonesia. As we walked in we were greeted by loud Christian music. Toward the back two attractive young girls were dancing in circles, clapping their hands, and kicking their legs up in the air. When a known person of the congregation came in, the girls would grab him or her and dance together for a short while. Everyone seemed to enjoy the experience. I wondered if anyone else was having as much trouble as I was concentrating on worshiping the Lord.

In the African context, a Christian women's meeting is described thusly:

> *The air is heavily charged with emotion. Women stand up and speak out their troubles, sometimes wailing or screaming, sometimes in frenzied whisperings. Their bodies tremble. Their eyes are tightly closed or fixed heavenwards. Talk is of miracles, of the sick and the dead . . . until one will start shaking violently in preparation for the moment when "she is taken by the Spirit" and begins to speak. The other women listen intently, in close*

participation, and while the speaker slowly works herself up to a high pitch of emotion, the feelings of the listeners find in her a channel through which they pour themselves out. (Parrinder 1976, 85)

Unilateral guidance "from the Lord" can also be a problem. Syed, a Syrian believer, told me of his unique encounter with Sam, a Canadian Christian. Sam went to Damascus in response to what he said was the direct command of God. He found Syed and requested him to take him to the street called Straight. Once there, Sam began walking down the middle of the street, alternatively speaking in unknown tongues and in prophetic utterances. In a loud voice he cried out that God was going to destroy Damascus within one year's time. He called upon all to repent.

Somehow Sam and Syed survived that experience. Sam then wrote letters to the president and other leaders of Syria warning them of imminent destruction. He also went around the churches and urged all Christians to leave the city prior to God's impending judgment. Within six days Sam left Damascus. Six years later the city is still intact.

Muslims and Ecstasy

On a recent visit to Bangladesh, I was walking with Dr. Ali in a rural area. We met a group of Sufis belonging to the Baul sect. After engaging them in pleasant conversation for a short time, Ali asked them to sing for us. They formed a circle and began to sing, accompanied by one of the men playing a banjo-like instrument. Slowly and quietly they sang. Then the tempo began to increase. The voices became louder, and their feet began to move with the music. Quickly a crowd gathered. Within minutes an ecstatic event had commenced. The people moved in closer and began to clap their hands. Devout faces looked heavenward. Hands were raised.

The words being sung could have been taken from a Christian hymnal. "Forgive me, O God, of all my sins and look at me, your servant for all time. I am a poor creature who has gone astray but now I seek forgiveness from you, the Savior and Lord of the whole world." One could have wondered if he were attending a charismatic worship service rather than an impromptu meeting of Muslim mystics.

The word *wajd* is the Sufi equivalent of ecstasy. It actually means "finding," i.e., the pursuit of and apprehension of God. Ecstasy results when the great encounter takes place between the created and the Creator. Actually, a better word than *ecstasy* would be *instasy* because the mystic is not taken out of himself, but rather into the depth of himself (Schimmel 1975, 178).

> *Ecstasy is attained through the repeated enunciation of short invocations, with control of the breath, co-ordinated with body exercises, balancing, and inclinations. This is done to the accompaniment of both vocal and instrumental music, for music helps to free the physical effort from conscious thought, since both mind and will must be suspended if ecstasy is to be attained. All this is so ordered that it induces a special experience whereby loss of consciousness is regarded as 'union,' an emotional identification of seeker and sought. To some this experience became a drug for which soul and body*

craved. For the ordinary lay member, participation in the ritual of the dhikr, which for him only occasionally leads to the trance-ecstasy, provides at lowest a release from the hardships of everyday existence, and, at a high level, some measure of freedom from the limitations of human life and a glimpse at transcendental experience. (Trimingham 1971, 200)

The dancing of the so-called whirling dervishes of the Middle East has always been a problem for orthodox Muslims, who have said dancing is an illegitimate attempt to induce an ecstatic state. The dervishes' approach to intimacy with Allah is denounced by orthodox Muslim scholars and by more moderate Sufis. As the dervishes see it, dancing is a direct result of the Sufi coming into dynamic confrontation with the Divine One. Rapture overwhelms the devotee and turbulence begins to invade the body. The outworking of this ecstatic moment is an unrehearsed, spontaneous movement that the onlooker defines as dance. To the dervish, however, it is more a response than a dance.

Many persons were thrown into ecstasy upon hearing a verse of the Koran or a heavenly voice (hatif) or poetry or music. Many are said to have died from the emotion thus aroused. I may add by way of explanation that, according to a well-known mystical belief, God has inspired every created thing to praise Him in its own language, so that all the sounds in the universe form, as it were, one vast choral hymn by which He glorifies Himself.

Consequently those whose hearts He has opened and endowed with spiritual perception hear His voice everywhere and ecstasy overcomes them as they listen to the rhythmic chant of the muezzin, or the street cry of the saqqa shouldering his waterskin, or, perchance, to the noise of wind or the bleating of a sheep or the piping of a bird. (Nicholson 1975, 63-64)

Does not this come terribly close to pantheism? This is why some Sufis have been charged with being pantheists, in that they see, feel, and experience God in everything. Both for Muslims and Christians it is hard to draw the line between pantheism and seeing God's presence in creation. God is the Creator and is most certainly discernible in His creation. Should not we experience awe as we stand in the midst of a violent storm and see God's power unleashed through nature? I have seen my Sufi friends soar into ecstasy as they watch the wind bend the mango trees and cause the palm branches to come crashing to the ground. The mystic is God-intoxicated. Allah is everywhere.

A very interesting eleventh-century writing of Abu Saiid Abul-Khair, a Sufi master, comments on the practical value of emotion in worship as an aid in helping young people overcome their worldly passions and desires:

It is in the nature of young people that they are not free of desires. These dominate them and control their bodies. If they clap their hands and stamp their feet, the intensity of their desires will be lessened and they will be better able to control their outward

actions. It is better to release some of the excessive
intensity of their emotions (in the name of God) in
dance than to have to let it out among people, with
possible injury to oneself and others. (Nurbakhsh
1978, 59)

I can recall a visit to one of the largest and most beautiful mosques in Cairo. The setting was formal and sedate. The guide directed me to an enclosed area over to one side of the mosque. There I discovered an ornate room with walls covered with tiny blue tiles in intricate patterns. Over to one side sat a mystic who was deeply engrossed in his pursuit of Allah. His face was contorted with a grotesque look of pain and ecstasy. He kept throwing his head in all directions. His mouth was mumbling Arabic phrases of praise. Hands moved upward and outward, seemingly out of control. Here was an Egyptian Muslim wildly in quest of his Beloved. His shabby dress indicated he was from the poorest strata of society. No matter. His soul was being fed and clothed by the highest potentate of the universe. Such is the power of Muslim mysticism.

Meditation and Dreams

Bumper stickers with the words "Think God" abound on cars in Manila. Are we being exhorted to participate in a meditation exercise that will negate our real life worries and problems? Frank Laubach would evidently respond strongly in the affirmative:

This concentration upon God is strenuous, but
everything else has ceased to be so. I think more

clearly, I forget less frequently. Things which I did with a strain before, I now do easily and with no effort whatever. I worry about nothing, and lose no sleep. I walk on air a good part of the time. Even the mirror reveals a new light in my eyes and face. I no longer feel in a hurry about anything. Everything goes right. Each minute I meet calmly as though it were not important. Nothing can go wrong excepting one thing. That is that God may slip from my mind if I do not keep on my guard. If he is there, the universe is with me. My task is simple and clear. (Harkness 1973, 145)

This level of spiritual encounter is most likely reserved for the favored few. The more common use of meditation will be in the form of a discipline. Calvin Miller writes of the necessity of kenotic meditation. The word kenotic comes from Greek meaning "to empty." Miller suggests we clear our minds of swimming images and obscene and irrelevant thinking.

We must deal with the froth and spin of unceasing mental images. This is not easy, but as I move closer to this imageless state of being, my mind slows down to a cleansed level of quietness. At this point, I am able to receive the welcome of the Host with undivided attention. (Miller 1984, 36-37)

Meditation has become a revived art in the West, but not through Christian influence. Hindu teaching has influenced many persons of repute in America. It is not uncommon to hear of corporate executives sitting in a yoga position and engaging in meditation during lunch breaks. Their aim is to cultivate inner tranquility and to get "in touch with themselves" at soul level.

Dreams have been used as a means of divine communication through the centuries. The Fathers of the early church believed that dreams were used by God to impart revelation. "Ambrose, Augustine, all of the Doctors of the Church, both East and West, considered the dream a source of revelation, as the Eastern tradition still does. These men all believed that dreams gave access to the same realm of reality which one could penetrate in meditation" (Kelsey 1976, 167-168).

Bilquis Sheikh tells of the first dream that set her on a quest for new life in Christ:

> *Normally I never dream, but this night I did. The dream was so lifelike, the events in it so real, that I found it difficult the next morning to believe they were only fantasy. Here is what I saw.*
>
> *I found myself having supper with a man I knew to be Jesus. He had come to visit me in my home and stayed for two days. He sat across the table from me and in peace and joy we ate dinner together. Suddenly, the dream changed. Now I was on a mountaintop with another man. He was clothed in a robe and shod with sandals. How was it that I mysteriously knew his name, too? John the Baptist. What a strange name. I found myself telling this John the Baptist about my recent visit with Jesus. "The Lord came and was my guest for two days," I said.*

*"But now He is gone. Where is He? I must find him!
Perhaps you, John the Baptist, will lead me to him?"*
*That was the dream. When I woke up I was
loudly calling the name, "John the Baptist! John
the Baptist!" (Sheikh 1978, 25)*

Ruth Veltkamp ministers among the Muslim Fulani tribespeople of Nigeria. In probing the areas of their felt needs, she discovered that all of the Muslims seemed to experience nightmares that greatly disrupted their sleep. They attributed those nightmares to demonic influence. Ruth would ask the Fulanis if they would like to be delivered for one night and to have a really good sleep. The answer would always be in the affirmative. She told them that she would need to pray in Jesus' name for their deliverance. They readily agreed.

The next morning the Fulanis would be asked how the night went. Without exception the Muslims would testify to restful sleep. Ruth would then relate the gospel to the Fulanis and assure them that Jesus would continue to give them deliverance from demonic influence if they would only ask Christ to come into their heart and become a permanent guarding influence over their minds. Many have accepted the offer.

A white-robed person often makes an appearance in Muslim dreams. An imam in Nigeria encountered such a man in his sleep. The person told the imam that he would give him salvation and through him save many others. The next day he began to study about Jesus in the Quran. The passages spoke deeply to his heart. Soon he had a recurrence of the former dream.

He went to a Christian and asked him about the meaning of the dream. The Christian told him that it was Christ in the dream. The imam then became a follower of Jesus. As a result of being open in his profession of faith he was severely persecuted. Once he was secretly given poison to drink. But in answer to prayer, he was healed. The former imam has led eleven Muslims to Christ and is in the process of discipling them.

Muslims and the Subconscious

The inward man is the focus of the Muslim mystic. In order to "tune in" to the inward man, the mystic needs some measure of peace and quiet. One saying of the Sufis is, "The hen does not lay eggs in the marketplace." So a retreat, either physical or mental, is often called for.

Contemplation is useful for severing all worldly connections, complete abstraction, spiritual intoxication and all absorbing thought, total effacement or annihilation. This is how it is done: the seeker thinks that he is dead, has turned into a heap of dust which is scattered by the wind. He imagines also that the sky is cleft asunder, the stars scattered, and the sun with its dazzling light is extinguished, the form and composition of all things destroyed and God alone remains. This contemplation is helpful in producing the state of fana or total effacement in God. (Valiuddin 1980, 103)

Samuel Zwemer related the story of his encounter with a "Muslim St. Francis." The mystic was dedicated to a life of poverty and meditation. As Zwemer talked with him, he sat in a sort of trance, with his hand moving quickly through a rosary of ninety-nine beads that depicted the names of God. At one point the mystic said, "After all, one does not need a rosary to count the ninety-nine names; they are graven on our hands." Zwemer was somewhat astonished by this bold statement. The Muslim went on to spread his palms and point to the Arabic numerals (81 and 18) which are the lines in every person's left and right hands. These two figures add up to 99. The mystic then concluded, "That is why we spread our hands open in supplication, reminding Allah of all His merciful attributes, as we plead His grace" (Zwemer n.d., 114-115). That application of God as found in one's body is typically Sufi.

Another Muslim mystic, Tawakkul Beg, tells of his encounter with God as he followed the instructions of his spiritual guide:

Thereupon, he made me sit before him, my senses being as though intoxicated, and ordered me to reproduce his own image within myself, and, after having bandaged my eyes, he asked me to concentrate all my mental faculties on my heart. I obeyed, and in an instant, by the divine favor and by the spiritual assistance of the shaykh, my heart opened. I saw, then, that there was something like an overturned cup within me. This having been set upright, a sensation of unbounded happiness filled my being. (MacDonald [1909] 1970, 198)

Beg was led into this experience of intoxicated happiness through unorthodox Muslim procedures. Islam would fervently condemn the command to reproduce the

Shaykh's image in Beg's mind. But a mystic is extremely pragmatic. If the desired effect is gained, that is what is important.

A missionary acquaintance in West Africa told me of his Muslim friend who always speaks glowingly of his deep love for Allah. When the Muslim was asked how he came to have such a seemingly vital relationship with God, he replied, "I was in the process of going through my prayer beads thousands of times. One late night I saw this most beautiful vision of Prophet Muhammad. My heart was immediately filled with love for him. The effect of that vision has never left me. It totally changed my life."

Muslims believe dreams frequently communicate God's message to them in a personalized manner. This belief comes near to being a universal act of superstition. Dreams, at times, become regulatory and can lead to aberrant behavior. On the other hand, dreams can be religiously reinforcing with resultant positive behavioral changes. Such subjective experiences and interpretation of experiences can best be analyzed in terms of observable long-term deeds.

Annemarie Schimmel, professor of Indo-Muslim culture at Harvard University, is an expert on mystical Islam. Her books deserve a wide reading among evangelicals. They are full of valuable insights into the world of Muslim mystics. She has written of the relationship of the Muslim to the Prophet which can be enhanced through dreams.

Blessings for the Prophet and the loving repetition of legends connected with him may also grant the faithful Muslim the greatest boon one can hope for in this life, the vision of the Prophet in a dream.

*Such dreams play an extraordinary role in Islamic
piety to this day. They are always true, for Satan
can never assume the Prophet's form. These dreams
console the faithful; they can bring healing in cases
of illness or melancholia. To dream of the Prophet
might be an initiatory experience for the Sufi, or it
might help someone to solve a theological problem.
(Schimmel 1985, 79)*

An example of such a dream occurred to Yunus Emre
in Anatolia. He reflects,

*In an inspired dream tonight
I saw Muhammad.
In the clean mirror of the heart
I saw Muhammad.
The angels stood in rows and rows,
They donned green garments beautiful
And they exclaimed: "Muhammad!" - Thus
I saw Muhammad.
Muhammad gave a bowl to me.
Intoxicated was I then -
The Lord bestowed such grace on me:
I saw Muhammad.
I, like a drop sunk in the seas,
Found healing for my suffering:
Today I was greatly blessed -
I saw Muhammad!
(Schimmel 1985, 213-214)*

Dreams of Christ have led Muslims to become Christians,

but the reverse has also happened. A small number of Christians have become Muslims through the intermediary role of dreams. Dr. Abdul Germanus, professor and head of the Department of Oriental and Islamic Studies at the Budapest University, tells of an encounter with Muhammad in a dream, which directly led to his becoming a Muslim.

> *One night Prophet Muhammad appeared before me. His long beard was reddened with henna, his robes were simple but very exquisite, and an agreeable scent emanated from them. His eyes glittered with a noble fire and he addressed me with a manly voice, 'Why do you worry? The straight path is before you, safely spread out like the face of the earth; walk on it with trusty treads, with the strength of Faith."* *(Germanus 1976, 41)*

These dreams and visions set the stage for the last section of this chapter, which is even more pungent and mystifying.

Supernaturalism

Alan Tippett, the renowned Australian missiologist, poignantly comments on spiritual power. "A missionary geared to a metaphysical level of evangelism in his generator cannot drive a motor of shamanistic voltage. It is a tragic experience to find oneself with the right kind of Power but the wrong kind of voltage" (Tippett 1960, 413). It is this type of thinking that has caused a great deal of controversy within mainline evangelicalism. The Pentecostal and charismatic movements have added their dimensions of influence. The end result is that the whole subject of supernaturalism in its more spectacular forms has opened a missiological grid that was once regarded by many as borderline heresy. It is interesting to me to carefully observe cultural dynamics at work in the area of biblical hermeneutics. The Bible has not changed in two thousand years. But interpretations of that changeless Scripture seem to be extremely prolific according to the historical, cultural, preferential, and pragmatic *zeitgeist* of each succeeding Christian generation. At least Christianity is not boring!

In the New Testament we find the term *signs and wonders* nine times. The word *signs* on its own is found an additional three times, while *wonders* is recorded in two further instances. In the Gospels Jesus performed twenty-three healings. He exercised nine commands over the forces of nature such as calming the storm or walking on water. He raised three people from the dead. There is never a recorded instance where Jesus refused anyone who came to him for healing.

Catherine Marshall gives her understanding of a biblical perspective on physical health:

> *He did not once say in regard to health, "If it is God's will." There is no beatitude for the sick as there is for others like the bereaved, those who suffer persecution, the peacemakers. Nor did there ever fall from Jesus' lips any statements that ill health would further our spiritual growth or benefit the Kingdom of God. Rather, He not only wants to heal our diseases, He also wants us to stay healthy. (Marshall 1974, 166)*

The understanding of the position of the early church Fathers on the supernatural has been controversial. Selective writings have usually been quoted to reinforce the opinions of scholars on both sides of the supernatural fence! Irenaeus (140-203), the bishop of Lyons, is often quoted.

For some do certainly and truly drive out devils, so that those who have thus been cleansed from evil spirits frequently join themselves to the Church. Others have foreknowledge of things to come, they see visions, and utter prophetic expressions. Others still, heal the sick by laying their hands upon them, and they are made whole. Yea, moreover, as I have said, the dead even have been raised up, and remained among us for many years. And what shall I more say? It is not possible to name the number of gifts which the Church, (scattered) throughout the whole world, has received from God, in the name of Jesus Christ. (Wimber 1986, 158)

In contemporary times evangelical seminaries have begun to have courses slanted toward the supernatural. Trinity Evangelical Divinity School has a course titled "Power Encounter in Missionary Ministry." Fuller Theological Seminary's course "Signs and Wonders" attracted several hundred students each time it was offered under the direction of John Wimber. It has now been considerably revised and is taught exclusively by Fuller faculty.

Illustrations of the results of a "signs and wonders" ministry abound. I have met Mel Tari, the Indonesian evangelist, and I would be hesitant to declare the following story to be a figment of his imagination, although I must admit the rational, scientific side of me leans toward incredulity:

We were in a village called Amfoang where a man had died. He had been dead not only for a few minutes but for two days. The family invited us to the funeral because there were many people planning to come - as a matter of fact, hundreds - and they said, "Maybe you would have a word of comfort to give to the family." So we went.

When we arrived there, there were more than a thousand people. That man had been dead for two days and was very stinky....

When we were there and sitting with the mourners, suddenly the Lord said, "Now please go and stand around that dead person, sing songs and I will raise him back from the dead...."

Then I said to the Lord, "Oh Lord, please give me a simple heart, and move in our midst." So we decided in unison that we would obey the Lord....

On the sixth song, that man began to move his toes - and the team began to get scared. We have a story in Indonesia, that sometimes when people die they wake up and hug a person by their coffin and then die again. However, we just went ahead and sang. When we sang the seventh and eighth songs, that brother woke up, looked around and smiled.

He didn't hug anybody. He just opened his mouth and said, "Jesus has brought me back to life! Brothers and sisters, I want to tell you something. First, life never ends when you die. I've been dead for two days and I've experienced it." The second thing he said was, "Hell and heaven are real. I have experienced it. The third thing I want to tell you is, if you don't find Jesus in this life you will never go to heaven. You will be condemned to hell for sure."

After he had said these things, we opened our Bibles and confirmed his testimony by the Word of God. He not only found Jesus Christ as his Savior, but in that area more than 21,000 people came to know Jesus Christ as their Savior, because of the ministry of this man. (Tari 1971, 76-78)

John Wimber of Vineyard Ministries has stated that he has personally seen twenty-five blind persons made to see. In *New Paths in Muslim Evangelism*, I have told of observing a young Bangladeshi Muslim girl, blind from birth, blink her eyes and for the first time in her life say, "Father, I can see, Father, I can see." This was the context of a "healing meeting" in which the power of God was quite evidently at work. This incident was the first time I was able to personally verify such a dramatic healing.

A recent letter I received tells of God's intervention in the life of a Filipino Muslim lady.

This young woman was very ill. She prayed, "God, you who created me, show me who you are and if I get well I will serve you."
She then saw a vision of Jesus Christ in the clouds. After this experience she met a Christian from a nearby university and subsequently accepted Christ.

With the genuine also come the anomalies. There are many evidences of this in regard to ministry in the healing realm. One television celebrity seen around the world sends a "blessed cloth" to all those who donate financially to his outreach. This cloth has been power-anointed by the evangelist. His avid followers are exhorted to place the cloth inside their pillow or sew it into their clothes. By doing this they can be assured the power of God will be transmitted to them through the cloth.

In Manila there was widespread publicity for the 1985 "Jesus Miracle Crusade" of evangelist Wilde E. Almeda. In one large newspaper advertisement the public was urged to attend with these words:

> *Sick of cancer? Leukemia? Rheumatism? Asthma? All ailments pronounced incurable? Blind, Crippled or Deaf? Are you a Drug Addict? Do you have marital and heart-breaking problems? Do you want to be happy and be assured of eternal life? Do you want baptism in the HOLY SPIRIT and BE BORN AGAIN?*
>
> *The GOSPEL will hinder famine, chaos, criminality, disorder and anarchy. The GOSPEL is a great deterrent against atomic attack and will make you ready for heaven with proofs; the LAME will walk, the BLIND can see, the DEAF will hear; homosexuals will become normal coupled with signs, wonders and miracles.*

Reportedly, a very famous miracle occurs frequently in Roman Catholic circles.

Time and again in the course of the centuries has the world been amazed by a most extraordinary phenomenon, which has been called Stigmatization. The open wounds of the Savior in hands and feet and side, even the piercing of the head to mark the crown of thorns, have been reproduced in the bodies of certain of God's servants. Blood has flowed forth of these wounds, sometimes on Fridays about those hours when the Saviour hung tortured and bleeding on His Cross, and at other times, more or less continuously. It has been seen and testified to, by witnesses so numerous and so reliable, as to exclude all possible doubt about the fact. (Williamson 1921, 154-155)

In another newspaper, mystical necklaces are advertised as the path to love, fortune, and protection. One "necklace of fortune" guarantees luck in business, lotteries, games, and loves. "Very effective lucky prayer and instructions are included." All for two dollars. Other necklaces are to protect one from danger, human ills, and enemies. All of this is available from Peter's Mystical Book Center.

The Philippines is famous for psychic healers. These men perform amazing feats. The most renowned of the healers was Tony Agpaoa, who established a luxury resort in the mountains north of Manila. Julie and I were able to visit Tony's kingdom and to observe some of the "psychic operations."

The day we were there was a special day for thirty Canadians who had traveled halfway around the world to be healed by Tony. We followed the lame and diseased into the resort chapel where prayers were offered and hymns were sung accompanied by a guitar. Then we went to the "hospital" where the operations were to be performed. Each person had his blood pressure checked. They were then assigned to either Tony or his sister for their psychic healing encounter. Julie and I watched Tony's sister perform her surgery.

The patient was stretched out on a bed with her midriff exposed. The doctor, wearing a short-sleeved blouse, put her empty hands on the patient's stomach region and began pressing and twisting. Suddenly "blood" began to flow out from beneath the doctor's hands. She then pulled out the "offending organ," which looked like chicken entrails to us. They were deposited in a plastic bucket while the blood was wiped up with pieces of cotton. There was no sign of any incision. The lady was pronounced healed and the next patient called in. The man with the guitar in the outer room continued to play and hum Christian songs.

As we left the resort we drove past a pen full of chickens.

Tony Agpaoa soon thereafter died of a heart attack.

Muslims and the Supernatural

The Hadith presents various stories relating to the miraculous. Most of these refer to the Prophet.

An Ansari woman said to Allah's Apostle, "O Allah's Apostle! Shall I make something for you to sit on, as I have a slave who is a carpenter?" He replied, "If you wish." So, she got a pulpit made for him. When it was Friday the Prophet sat on that pulpit. The date-palm stem near which the Prophet used to deliver his sermons cried so much so that it was about to burst. The Prophet came down from the pulpit to the stem and embraced it and it started groaning like a child being persuaded to stop crying, and then it stopped crying. The Prophet said, "It has cried because of [missing] what it used to hear of the religious knowledge." (Bukhari [Vol. 3], 174-175)

At another time rain was very scarce. Muhammad's disciples enjoined him to pray and ask Allah for relief from the drought. This being done, it began to rain so hard that the followers of the Prophet could hardly reach their homes. So much rain became problematic. Another disciple requested Muhammad to again intervene with the forces of nature. "On that, Allah's Apostle said, 'O Allah! Round about us and not on us.'" Anas added, "I saw the clouds dispersing right and left and it continued to rain but not over Medina" (Bukhari [Vol. 2], 69-70).

Muhammad was reported to have multiplied food on one occasion. "By Allah, whenever we took a handful of the meal, the meal grew from underneath more than that handful till everybody ate to his satisfaction; yet the remaining food was more than the original meal. Abu Bakr saw that food was as much as or more than the original amount" (Bukhari [Vol. 4], 504).

The most spectacular miracle that the Prophet was involved in was his observation of the split moon. The one Quranic verse on the subject states, "The hour drew nigh and the moon was rent in twain. And if they behold a portent they turn away and say: Prolonged illusion. They denied (the Truth) and followed their own lusts" (Sura 54:1-3). The Hadith clarifies Muhammad's role, "During the lifetime of the Prophet the moon was split into two parts and on that the Prophet said, 'Bear witness (to this).' Narrated Anas that the Meccan people requested Allah's Apostle to show them a miracle, and so he showed them the splitting of the moon" (Bukhari [Vol.4]:533).

These citations are an embarrassment to many Muslims. They prefer to deal with the passage as Marmaduke Pickthall does in the explanatory note found in his translation of the Quran. He refers to "a strange appearance of the moon in the sky, as if it had been torn asunder" (Pickthall 1953, 379). This figurative interpretation is totally inadequate for more literalist Muslims. They point to the Quran, which indicates that a holder of this view is one who denies the truth and follows his own lust.

Muhammad was reported to possess powers of healing. In the Hadith, Salama is said to have had a wounded leg. The people were concerned and brought him to the Prophet. Salama gives his firsthand testimony, "Then I went to the Prophet and he puffed his saliva in it [the wound] thrice, and since then I have not had any pain in it till this hour" (Bukhari [Vol. 5], 366).

This ability extended to the Prophet healing his wives. From this passage it is clear that Muhammad saw Allah as the source of healing power:

Narrated Aisha: The Prophet used to treat some of his wives by passing his right hand over the place of ailment and saying, "O Allah, the Lord of the people! Remove the trouble and heal the patient, for You are the healer. No healing is of any avail but yours; healing that will leave behind no ailment." (Bukhari [Vol. 7], 428)

It should be clarified that Muhammad's participation in acts of divine healing are rare in the Quran and Hadith. The norm is the Prophet's recommendation of various indigenous remedies for healing. Some of these strike us twentieth-century persons as extremely odd. Maurice Bucaille, a French physician and a convert to Islam, has sought to give a rationale to these seventh-century prescriptions for healing as found in the Hadith.

We should not be surprised however to find that at a time when there were limited possibilities for the scientific use of drugs, people were advised to rely on simple practices; natural treatments such as blood-letting, cupping, and cauterization, head-shaving against lice, the use of camel's milk and certain seeds such as black cumin, and plants such as Indian Qust. It was also recommended to burn a mat made of palm-tree leaves and put the ash from it into a wound to stop bleeding. In emergencies, all available means that might genuinely be of use had to be employed. It does not seem - a priori - to be a very good idea, however, to suggest that people drink camel's urine. (Bucaille 1979, 245-246)

The Hadith clearly states that the Prophet advised the sick to be healed by drinking the urine of a camel. Never have I heard a Muslim give a good explanation of that problematic command.

Exorcism

Dr. Ali has written me of his firsthand observation of an exorcism ceremony. This would be typical of that which is found throughout the rural areas of much of the Muslim world.

The possessed person was a beautiful young lady 30 years old, married with two children. Her behavior had always been exemplary. She was very religious and modest. She suddenly became abusive and would run around in an almost naked condition. Her "fits" included stomping on the floor and jumping from one place to another. In desperation, the family called in a faqir (Muslim holy man). Dr. Ali's account follows:

> *The faqir was a middle-aged bearded man with a thick moustache and long loose hair. His eyes were sharp and penetrating. His teeth were broken and uneven. He was continually chewing betel leaf and occasionally puffing marijuana.*
>
> *The first thing he did was to look straight into the eyes of the patient. The moment the young lady saw the faqir she shrieked and went to a corner. The faqir had a small looking glass and a stone ring. He asked the patient to look through the magic glass, but she violently refused. The faqir then read a mantra and blew it over her. He again asked her to look through the glass. The woman made a sign that she could find an object in the looking glass. The faqir shouted at the top of his voice hurling abusive words toward the evil spirit who was believed to have possessed the village woman. His whole body began to shake and tremble. He recited some incantations taken from the religious books of the*

Muslim and Hindu community. He was using the names of Allah, Hari, Mahadev, Muhammad, Krishna, Fatima, Ali, and Ma Kali. He drew a circle around himself and the patient. He then burned turmeric and asked her to inhale. He also brought an old shoe and asked the patient to inhale the smell. The woman refused and got violent. The faqir then hit her with a broom and followed this by putting hot mustard oil into her ears. The faqir was repeatedly asking the identity of the spirit. The patient refused to comply with the words of the faqir. Then the faqir burned mustard seed and read a mantra over it. This brought the desired result. There was a burning sensation all over the body of the woman. She agreed to talk. Below is the exchange of words between the faqir and the patient or the spirit who possessed her:

Faqir: Who are you? Where do you live?

The patient, with a strong nasal accent, said: I am Kalu, I live in the bamboo groves behind the house.

Faqir: Why have you come into the body of this woman?

Patient: She is beautiful. I like her.

Faqir: Leave her immediately,

Patient: No, I shall kill her husband.

Faqir: I order you to leave her body.

Patient: I shall not go.

Faqir: See how I will force you to leave.

The faqir began to mutter a mantra. Then he brought out a root of an herb which he kept in his bag. Meanwhile his associates started beating a tin can which made a roaring sound. The faqir also flogged her cruelly. She acquired much strength. Her hair was dishevelled and her clothes were falling off her body. At last, she was forced to eat the root of the herb which she chewed and swallowed.

The faqir said: Would you leave now? Have you seen I am more powerful than you?
Patient: Yes, I shall leave her. Don't torture me any more.
Faqir: What sign will you make of your departure?
Patient: I shall leave her. Don't worry.
Faqir: Carry, with your teeth, an earthen pitcher full of water from the house and break it when you leave her.
Patient: Yes, I will do as you order me.

Then the woman, with her teeth, carried an earthen pitcher full of water and broke it after going five or six yards. Following this she fainted. The faqir quickly sprinkled water in her face. She was taken to a room where she slept for hours, after which she became normal.

The faqir then asked the husband to make a sacrifice and to offer a small amount of money to a shrine of a Sufi saint which was known to the family.

In Islam there is a high level of appreciation for such power practitioners. It does not matter that they are theologically syncretistic. The Muslim village people are pragmatists. They only want release from evil spirits. In my book *Bridges to Islam* I sought to document many illustrations of Muslims as they engage in power encounter. The Muslim world is full of so-called folk Muslims who step out of orthodox paths in order to find more immediate and dramatic forms of release from binding influences.

Conclusion

Mystical belief and practice are common to all mankind. Mysticism is as old as religion, and it is as contemporary as the Christian charismatic movement and the prolific Muslim Sufi orders found throughout the world.

The mystic is at once loved and hated, respected and feared, condemned and accepted. To many, he is a person out of sync. To the mystic, it is the world that is out of sync. Otherworldly and full of faith, the mystic goes skipping through the by-lanes of life. The main highways of orthodox belief are too rigid and traditional. His quest is for the "event." His heart cries out for the spectacular, the refreshing, the renewing. The spirit, after all, is meant to be liberated. The spirit indeed is the perpetual bird poised at the door of the cage, waiting for the moment he is released in a flight that will take him into the vast space of the universe, where he can soar and be free.

The Christian and the Muslim mystic have much in common. It is my sincere hope that common ground will be explored. There is much in Christianity that will appeal to the earnest, God-seeking Muslim mystic. The Christian obligation is to present truth in the most attractive manner possible. This should lead evangelicals to a new consideration of the potentials of a power-encounter ministry that will show Muslims that our God is indeed alive.

THE CROSS AND THE CRESCENT

7

The Christ and the Prophet

Innumerable books have been written on the lives of Muhammad and Jesus. It is not my purpose to present an exhaustive survey of the two most renowned personages of history. Rather, I will focus on the spiritual aspects of their personal lives and ministries. It is in their role as spiritual guides that they have impacted half of the world's population.

Prophet Muhammad

Muslims acknowledge an integral link between Muhammad's personal integrity and his role as a channel of revelation of Allah in the Quran. In the Quran and Hadith the character of Muhammad is declared to be exemplary. "Verily in the messenger of Allah ye have a good example for him who looketh unto Allah and the Last Day, and remembereth Allah much . . . Allah and His messenger are true" (Sura 33:21-22). Here the Prophet is said to be an example for all believers, for he, after all, was the first Muslim. "I am the first of those who surrender [unto Him]" (Sura 6:164).

Muslims have deemed it important to elevate the position of the Prophet from his birth. One legend of Muhammad's birth states, "In the hour of his birth a brilliant light shone over the entire world from East to West. When Muhammad was born he fell to the ground, took a handful of earth, and gazed toward heaven. He was born clean and without a spot, as a lamb is born, circumcised, and with the navel-cord already cut" (Andrae 1960, 35).

Names given to Muhammad are innumerable. He has been called "the leader of the universe, the Nightingale of Love, the Sun of the world of monotheism, the Master of the Lovers, the Axis of the spheres of both worlds, the Rose of the meadows of prophethood" (Schimmel 1985, 113). Even after discounting hyperbolic rhetoric, one can still get a feel of the intensity of devotion Muslims have experienced for their beloved prophet.

Sufis, being mystics, take the adoration of Muhammad to the outer limit. Their nonconformist, mystical orientation to life allows them a great deal of latitude in dealing with the exaltation of the Prophet as is depicted in this poem:

> *O Prophet: thou art the messenger and the possessor*
> *of the three worlds;*
> *Thou art the Noumenon or Ultimate Reality*
> *assuming the form of the Lord.*
> *Thou art the beauty of the Sun and the Moon and*
> *thou art the Sky;*
> *Thou art the nine planets, air, sun and fire.*

*Thou art the world-purity, and art not born of the
    womb of a female;
Thou art a name hidden and manifest and thou art
    God of all gods.*

(Haq 1975, 410).

Orthodox Muslims will shudder when they read the assertion that Muhammad is God of all gods. But they will probably take no action of protest. They would reason that the heresy is at least headed in the right direction. The heart of the Muslim in his devotion toward Muhammad takes him further than his theological orthodoxy would normally allow him to go.

Husain ibn Mansur al-Hallaj (858-929) was one of the early mystic martyrs. His exaltation of the prophet soars into the realm of the heavenlies.

Who was more manifest, more visible, greater, more luminous, more powerful or more discerning than he? He is and was, and was known before created things and existences and beings. He was and still is remembered before "before" and after "after", and before substances and qualities. His substance is altogether light, his speech is prophecy, his knowledge heavenly, his form of expression Arabic, his tribe is "neither of the East or of the West" (Sura 24:35), his genealogy is from the patriarchs, his mission is conciliation and his title is "the unlettered one." (Mansur 1974, 21)

Another writer has assigned Muhammad the purity of Adam, the grief of Jacob, the endurance of Job, the weeping of David, and the soul riches of Solomon. "He was more exalted than the highest kings. He excels the prophets as the sun excels the moon or the ocean the drop" (Padwick 1961, 170-171).

The Quran does honor the Prophet, but not to the extent of the excesses of some of his followers. "Lo! Allah and His angels shower blessings on the Prophet" (Sura 33:56). Another verse places Muhammad in close proximity to God. "O ye who believe! Obey Allah and obey the messenger" (Sura 47:33). In yet another striking passage Allah gives instruction to Muhammad to relay a particular message to all the world. "Say, (O Muhammad, to mankind): If ye love Allah, follow me; Allah will love you and forgive you your sins. Allah is Forgiving, Merciful" (Sura 3:31). In the Hadith the prophet is reported to have said, "None of you will have faith till he loves me more than his father, his children and all mankind" (Bukhari [Vol. 1], 20).

The Pakistani poet Muhammad Iqbal (1877-1938) immortalized Muhammad in two of his more famous statements: "Love of the Prophet runs like blood in the veins of his community" (Schimmel 1985, 256). The second quote is startling: "You can deny God, but you cannot deny the Prophet" (Schimmel 1975, 227). Perhaps his point is that the historicity of Muhammad is indisputable. One can deny what one cannot see (Allah), but a man who fills history books is verifiable beyond any doubt.

Many of the qualities of Muhammad have been referred to in an ode to the Prophet written by Abdul Darim al-Jili in the late fourteenth century.

O Centre of the compass! O inmost ground of the truth!

O pivot of necessity and contingency!
O eye of the entire circle of existence! O point of
the Koran and the Furqan!
O perfect one, and perfecter of the most perfect,
who has been beautified by the majesty of God
the Merciful!
Thou art the Pole (qutb) of the most wondrous
things. The sphere of perfection in its solitude
turns on thee.
Thou art transcendent, nay thou art immanent, nay
thine is all that is known and unknown
everlasting and perishable.
Thine in reality is Being and not-being; nadir and
zenith are thy two garments.
Thou art both the light and its opposite, nay but
thou art only darkness to a gnostic that is dazed.
(Schimmel 1985, 137-138)

Sufi poets enjoyed employing the dynamics of nature in their writings. All creation is allowed to offer praise and glorify the Prophet.

The man in whose presence the trees did obeisance
The man at whose light the flowers opened
The man at whose blessing the fruits matured
The man at whose promise the trees moved
themselves from all directions
The man at whose light all other lights burst forth
The man to the skirts of whose robes wild creatures
clung when he
was travelling in
the most desert lands. (Padwick 1961, 147)

A devout Muslim invokes the blessings of Allah upon Muhammad at least forty times each day. This occurs during the five stated prayer times, plus the usage of the formula "Peace be upon him" each time Muhammad's name is mentioned in conversation or is written on paper. It is reinforcing to Muslims to realize that every moment of every day hundreds of thousands of Muslims are calling down the blessings of Allah upon their revered Prophet. One writer has asked, "Has there been in the history of man any other who has been so richly blessed?" (Khan 1980, 283).

Muslims, in their efforts to venerate the Prophet, have gone to excesses in regard to relics. One can discover the actual hair and teeth of Muhammad in many parts of the world. In Topkapi Palace in Istanbul I had my first close-up look at Muhammad's tooth and strand of hair. These relics are kept under tight security. The ornate Hazrat-bal Mosque was built in Srinagar, Kashmir, for the purpose of accommodating a strand of the prophet's hair. Some years ago there were devastating riots in Srinagar because of the theft of that precious hair. Such appreciation for Muhammad's hair got its initial boost from this narration found in the Hadith. "I said to Abida, 'I have some of the hair of the Prophet which I got from Anas or from his family.' Abida replied, 'No doubt if I had a single hair, it would have been dearer to me than the whole world and whatever is in it'" (Bukhari [Vol. 1], 119).

Muhammad's Night Journey

No event in the Prophet's life was more spectacular than his journey from Mecca to Jerusalem and up through the seven heavens. This all occurred in one night. The one quranic verse which refers to this happening states, "Glorified be He Who carried His servant by night from the Inviolable Place of Worship to the Far Distant Place of Worship, the neighborhood whereof We have blessed, that We might show him of Our tokens!" (Sura 17:1). This narration is restricted to the journey from Mecca to Jerusalem. It says nothing of Muhammad's trip into the seven heavens.

However, one Hadith tells of the commencement of the journey.

> *Allah's Apostle said, "While I was at Mecca the roof of my house was opened and Gabriel descended, opened my chest, and washed it with Zam-zam water Then he brought a golden tray full of wisdom and faith and having poured its contents into my chest, he closed it. Then he took my hand and ascended with me to the nearest heaven." (Bukhari [Vol. 1], 211)*

Another Hadith gives this portrait of heavenly inhabitants:

> *Allah's Apostle said, "On the night of my Ascension to Heaven, I saw (the Prophet) Moses who was a thin person with lank hair, looking like one of the men of the tribe of Shanu'a; and I saw Jesus who was of average height with red face as if he had just come out of a bathroom. And I resemble prophet Abraham more than any of his offspring does." (Bukhari [Vol. 4], 398)*

A great deal of attention has always focused on Buraq, the speedy white horse that carried Muhammad on his heavenly tour. It had a woman's head and a peacock's tail. I have seen this unique animal depicted on posters in marketplaces throughout the Muslim world.

The mystics have had a grand time speculating on the events of Muhammad's night journey. Persian mystic Fariduddin Attar, in his "Ilahinama," has written one of these lucid accounts:

At night came Gabriel, and filled with joy
He called: "Wake up, you leader of the world!
Get up, leave this dark place and travel now
To the eternal kingdom of the Lord!
Direct your foot to 'Where there is no place'
And knock there at the sanctuary's door.
The world is all excited for your sake,
The Cherubs are tonight your lowly slaves,
And messengers and prophets stand in rows
To see your beauty in this blessed night.
The gates of Paradise and skies are open -
To look at you, fills many hearts with joy!
You ask from Him tonight what you intend,
For without doubt you will behold the Lord!"
Buraq was now brought near as lightning swift;
God had created him from His pure light,
From head to toe enlivened by God's light,
And from the wind he learned swiftness and speed.
The Prophet mounted him in time and space; He
left this place for
  "Where there is no place."

There rose a tumult in the greatest Throne:
"Here comes the first, the full moon of the worlds!"
The angels stood with trays to scatter coins
For him, whom they all loved with heart and soul.
He saw the prophets on his road in line
To tell him of the mysteries divine. (Schimmel 1985,
166)

Was the Prophet's journey actual or imagined? How close did it relate to Paul's experience mentioned in 2 Corinthians 12:1-10? A majority of Muslims believe Muhammad really went into heaven. The event is remembered as "the night of the ascension" and is commemorated each year on the 27th of the Islamic month of Rajab. It is only the more liberal Muslims who regard the story as myth.

Here we find Muhammad at the spiritual apex of his earthly career. Allah favored his Prophet with a peek into the mysteries of the heavenlies. How exciting for earthbound Muslims to reflect on "the last and greatest of all prophets," yes, their Prophet sailing through the universe on a specially designed animal! He stops to have a chat along the way with many of the great seers of old. And then he is overwhelmingly privileged to have an actual audience with Allah, who is sitting majestically on His throne! How reinforcing this story is to the faith of myriads of Muslims who have locked their lives into Islam by saying, "And Muhammad is the Prophet of Allah."

Muhammad Is Alive!

This is a cornerstone of Muslim belief. The great spiritual leader of one billion people did die a physical death, but he presently is very active in the heavenly realm. "We are Allah's and lo! unto Him we are returning" (Sura 2:156). These few words constitute the most commonly spoken epitaph in the Muslim world. There is a real recognition of mortality, but also of immortality. This applies to the Prophet also.

"Muhammad is but a messenger, messengers (the like of whom) have passed away before him. Will it be that, when he dieth or is slain, ye will turn back on your heels?" (Sura 3:144). This revelation given in Muhammad's time seemed to be given as a preparation for the inevitable death of the Prophet. When Muhammad actually died, the scene was chaotic. There was hysterical weeping and screaming. In the midst of these emotional outbursts, Umar was standing, excitedly proclaiming that the Prophet had not died. He could not face the reality of Muhammad's departure from this earth.

Abu Bakr came into the room and demanded that everyone become quiet. His next words have been preserved in the Hadith. "If anyone amongst you used to worship Muhammad, then Muhammad is dead, but if (anyone of) you used to worship Allah, then Allah is Alive and shall never die" (Bukhari [Vol. 5], 524). Muhammad indeed was dead, but a universal Muslim belief is that he is presently alive in spirit and engaged actively in an intercessory role for Muslims. Allah is said to be predisposed to grant the desires and prayers that are uttered by His onetime spokesman on earth. Two Hadith support this belief.

The Prophet said, "The people will come to me, and I will Prostrate myself underneath Allah's Throne.

Then I will be addressed: 'O Muhammad! Raise your head: intercede, for your intercession will be accepted and ask (for anything), for you will be given (it).'" (Bukhari [Vol. 4], 151-152)

The Prophet said, "Some people will be taken out of the Fire through the intercession of Muhammad, they will enter Paradise and will be called al-Jahannamiyin [the (Hell) Fire people]." (Bukhari [Vol. 8], 371)

Thousands of poems have been written in honor of the Prophet performing this intensely spiritual act of intercession. Shakil Badayuni, an Indian Muslim poet, has written from a mind-set that indicates his desire to find favor with Muhammad after his death.

My wish is this, that when I die
I still may smile,
And while I go, Muhammad's name
be on my tongue. (Schimmel 1985, 87)

A Reflection on Muhammad's Spirituality

Muhammad was a sinner. "Then have patience (O Muhammad). Lo! The promise of Allah is true. And ask forgiveness of thy sin" (Sura 40:55). Two Hadith passages reinforce this quranic verse:

Narrated Umar: I heard the Prophet saying, "Do not exaggerate in praising me as the Christians praised the son of Mary, for I am only a Slave. So,

call me the Slave of Allah and His Apostle."
(Bukhari [Vol. 4], 435)

The Prophet prayed, "O Allah! Wash away my sins
with the water of snow and hail, and cleanse my
heart from the sins as a white garment is cleansed
of filth." (Bukhari [Vol. 8], 257)

How does one reconcile the Muslim's near deification
of Muhammad with these Islamic scriptures? My experience
is that the average Muslim chooses to ignore any hint of
fallibility in the Prophet, from whatever source. He may
admit Muhammad was a sinner prior to his call to
prophethood, but that after Allah's anointing came upon
him, he no longer committed any transgression. This type
of thinking gives credence to Muhammad's miracle-working
powers, his ability to soar through the heavens, and his
continuing enablement to make intercession to Allah on
behalf of needy Muslims.

What of Muhammad and his strong drive toward the
opposite sex? Most scholars agree that the Prophet married
twelve times. Is this in keeping with his position as one of
the greatest spiritual leaders of all time? Did Muhammad
have a clearly defined moral defect in regard to sex? Let us
look at the Hadith as a basis for historical facts as agreed
upon within Islam.

It is evident that beauty was at least one criterion for
wife selection.

Then we reached Khaibar; and when Allah enabled
him to conquer the form (of Khaibar), the beauty of

Safiya bint Huyai bin Akhtab was described to him. Her husband had been killed while she was a bride. So Allah's Apostle selected her for himself and took her along with him till we reached a place called Sad-As-Sahba, where her menses were over and he took her for his wife. (Bukhari [Vol. 4], 92)

One of the Prophet's most controversial marriages was to Zaynab, his adopted son's divorced wife. The Hadith indicate that Muhammad visited Zaynab while she was still married and was stricken with her beauty. Zeyd, the adopted son, understood this, divorced his wife, and gave full approval of her marriage to the Prophet. It is all given divine sanction by this startling quranic verse. These are believed to be the very words of Allah Himself:

So when Zeyd had performed the necessary formality (of divorce) from her, We gave her unto thee in marriage, so that (henceforth) there may be no sin for believers in respect of wives of their adopted sons, when the latter have performed the necessary formality (of release) from them. The commandment of Allah must be fulfilled. There is no reproach for the Prophet in that which Allah maketh his due. (Sura 33:37-38)

Westerners find the idea of a father marrying his adopted son's wife to be repugnant.

The next most criticized marriage of Muhammad was to Aisha, whom he married when he was is his mid-fifties. Many readers will find the following act of Muhammad to be shocking:

Khadija [Muhammad's first wife] died three years before the Prophet departed to Medina. He stayed there for two years or so and then he married Aisha when she was a girl of six years of age, and he consummated that marriage when she was nine years old. (Bukhari [Vol. 5], 153)

In another Hadith, Aisha is represented as being taken away from her dolls in order to go and live with Muhammad. From all indications the marriage developed well. "I came to the Prophet and said, 'Which person do you love most?' He replied, 'Aisha'" (Bukhari [Vol. 5], 453). Aisha is consistently represented as honoring Muhammad, though she was only eighteen years of age when he, at sixty-three, died.

One could fairly ask what the Prophet had in mind as he visited a married woman:

Allah's Apostle used to visit Um Haram bint Milhan and she was the wife of Ubada bin As-Samit. One day the Prophet visited her and she provided him with food and started looking for lice in his head. Then Allah's Apostle slept. (Bukhari [Vol. 9], 108)

The Apostle also used to give advice to his friends in regard to the advantage of marrying a much younger virgin as compared to marrying a "matron" who was most likely an older widow.

When I took the permission of Allah's Apostle, he asked me whether I had married a virgin or a matron

and I replied that I had married a matron. He said,
"Why hadn't you married a virgin who would have
played with you, and you would have played with
her?" (Bukhari [Vol. 4], 134)

According to a well-known saying among Muslims, the Prophet loved women, perfumes, and prayer, reportedly in that order. His frequency of marital relationships is even mentioned in the Hadith. "The Prophet used to visit all his wives in one night, and he had nine wives at that time" (Bukhari [Vol. 1], 172-173).

Muslims respond by saying all of the Prophet's activities were within the revealed will of Allah. He never committed adultery or fornication. Most of his wives were widows who were in need of a protective husband. And how can we condemn Muhammad as we compare him to other prophets of the Old Testament, particularly David and his adultery and arranged murder of Uriah? Muslims also point out that Solomon had seven hundred wives and three hundred concubines!

So where does all this lead us in our desire to evaluate Muhammad as a spiritual guide of the multitude? Do we emphasize his sex drive? What about his propensity toward violence and retribution? Do we do with Muhammad what the poet Dante did? He consigned the Prophet to the twenty-eighth sphere of the Inferno. In Dante's *Divine Comedy,* Muhammad is shown with his body split from head to waist. He is viciously tearing apart his mutilated breast with his own hands because of his sin of espousing a false religion. To the medieval mind, Muhammad's claim to divine revelation was an impious fraud that earned him the title of "chief among the damned souls." Later generations of Christians have taken a more lenient view of Muhammad, but many are still inclined to view him as a morally questionable man.

But were all our biblical heroes of the faith morally pure? With whom are we comparing Muhammad? Is his counterpart Noah as he laid drunk in his tent; or Moses as he stood over the Egyptian he had just killed; or David with multiple wives and concubines; or Solomon whose many foreign wives turned him from the true God; or even Peter who walked so long with Truth and then cursed and denied? Or are we to compare Muhammad with our Lord Jesus Christ? Unequivocally we can and do declare Mohammad to be a sinner with no claims to deity or saviorhood. He simply is not to be categorized with Christ. But let us remember that neither the Quran nor Muhammad made any such claims.

Was the Prophet a true prophet or a false prophet? Was he a sincere prophet without deceptive designs on his followers? Was he, at any time, consciously using his alleged "revelations" as a force to manipulate his disciples and accomplish his own ends? John Gilchrist has observed that "we can safely reject the view that Muhammad was a deliberate imposter" (Gilchrist 1986, 54).

We must bear in mind how much Muhammad suffered for his belief in the legitimacy of his mission, He was ridiculed, spit upon, and stoned. Two of his daughters were divorced by their husbands. His uncle Abu Talib sought to persuade Muhammad to stop propagating Islam. The prophet's reply has rung down through the centuries, "O Uncle, if they place the sun in my right hand and the moon in my left hand, I will not desist from preaching" (Qasimi 1987, 77).

There are indeed many complexities and mysteries surrounding the person of Muhammad – I personally cannot affirm him as a true prophet. If I did, I would be forced to accept his revelations as from God and therefore binding on all men. The Quran undercuts the biblical message in so many places. I cast my lot with the Bible as God's unique, final, and inerrant revelation. But I am not prepared to declare Muhammad a purposeful imposter and deceiver. He may have been. But I will leave it to God to judge his heart. Many sincere but very diverse religious leaders have walked through the landscape of world history. They will, each one, be required to stand before God. I have utmost confidence in God's competence as a judge.

Was Muhammad, then, a spiritual person? Certainly not in a classical New Testament sense. But was he a God-seeker, sincere and devoted, attempting to carry out what he truly believed to be the will and revelation of Allah? That is my tentative inclination, though held without rancor or ultimate dogmatism.

Savior Jesus

In his usual articulate manner of writing, Kenneth Cragg has made a masterful comparison between the Quran's Isa (Jesus) and the Christ of the New Testament.

Consider the Quranic Jesus alongside the New Testament. How sadly attenuated is this Christian prophet as Islam knows Him! Where are the stirring

*words, the deep insights, the gracious deeds, the
compelling qualities of Him Who was called the
Master? The mystery of His self-consciousness as
the Messiah is unsuspected: the tender, searching
intimacy of His relation to the disciples
undiscovered. Where is "the Way, the Truth and
the Life" in this abridgment? Where are the words
from the cross in a Jesus for whom Judas suffered?
Where is the triumph of the Resurrection from a
grave which was not occupied? We have in the
QurŸan neither Galilee, nor Gethsemane; neither
Nazareth nor Olivet. Even Bethlehem is unknown
by name, and the story of its greatest night is remote
and strange. Is the Sermon on the Mount to be left
to silence in the Muslim's world? Must the story of
the Good Samaritan never be told there; the simple,
human narrative of the prodigal son never mirror
there the essence of waywardness and forgiveness?
Is "Come unto Me all ye that are weary . . . and I
will give you rest" an invitation that need not be
heard, and is Jesus' taking bread and giving thanks
a negligible tale? Should not all mankind be initiated
into the meaning of the question: "Will ye also go
away?" (Cragg 1964, 261-262)*

Islam is distinctly uncomfortable with Jesus. On the one
hand Muslims desire to follow the traditional dictates of
Islam and honor Christ as one of the greatest prophets of
all time. On the other hand the alleged excesses of "Christ
worship" as found in Christendom have made Muslims more
than a little hesitant to attribute more than a passing word

of respect toward Jesus. To Muslims, Christ's deity and crucifixion present massive stumbling blocks.

It is impossible in a few short pages to overview all aspects of the intensely spiritual ministry of Jesus. Therefore, I have chosen to center on the cross – for Christians the most precious of all theological truths and for Muslims the most repugnant of all Christian beliefs. As has been rightfully observed, "The fundamental difference between Islam and Christianity is the absence in the former of the doctrine of the cross. The cross of Christ is the missing link in the Moslem's creed" (Zwemer 1920a, 75-76).

The Quran makes a frontal attack on the cross.

And because of their saying, We slew the Messiah Jesus son of Mary, Allah's messenger – they slew him not nor crucified, but it appeared so unto them; and lo! those who disagree concerning it are in doubt thereof; they have no knowledge thereof save pursuit of a conjecture; they slew him not for certain, but Allah took him up unto Himself. Allah was ever Mighty, Wise. (Sura 4:157-158)

Samuel Zwemer has sought to pull together Muslim rationale for their deep antipathy toward the cross.

1. It is opposed to reason.
2. It is opposed to theism. How can God who is omnipresent and everlasting degrade himself by dwelling in a virgin's womb?
3. It is opposed to God's knowledge; for the plan of salvation – if such it is – was an afterthought.

4. It is opposed to both the mercy and justice of God; to his mercy because He allowed Christ to suffer, being innocent, without delivering Him; and to his justice in allowing those who crucified Him to do it unpunished.
5. It leads to impiety, because if this is the way of salvation, then no matter how wicked a man is he finds deliverance through the cross, and will never be punished for his sins.
(Zwemer 1920a, 85)

The crucifixion occupies a dominant place in the New Testament. It is mentioned in all its books with the exception of three short epistles: Philemon, 2 John, and 3 John. The synoptic Gospels devote more space to the cross than any other aspect of Christ's life or teaching. Matthew focuses on the cross in 141 verses. Mark gives 119 verses, and Luke assigns two long chapters to the Passion Week. Most amazing is John's Gospel, over half of which is devoted to Christ's last few days on earth.

Many of the world's greatest paintings have centered on the cross. Magnificent musical works have drawn inspiration from the themes of the cross. Christ's death has been the rich subject of films and drama. In most of the art forms we have found the influence of the cross.

The most significant of all spiritual lessons to be derived from the crucifixion is that of selfless love.

See Christ here, on the cross! See His wounds, see His torn hands, see how the King of Glory is crowned with thorns! Do you know what Love is? Here is Love, here on this cross, here is Love, suffering these nails, these thorns, that scourge loaded with lead, smashed to pieces, bleeding to death because of your sins and bleeding to death because of people that will never know Him, and never think of Him and will never remember His Sacrifice. Learn from Him how to love God and how to love men! Learn of this cross, this Love, how to give your life away to Him. (Merton 1948, 323)

The cross has been a perpetual symbol of hope in times of deep despair. Alexander Solzhenitsyn has graphically chronicled one of his greatest discoveries that took place while he was a prisoner in the Soviet Gulag.

Solzhenitsyn worked long, arduous hours in the cruel climate of northern Russia. An overwhelming sense of hopelessness once so overpowered him that he threw his shovel down and sat on a crude workbench. He lowered his head waiting for the forceful blow of the guard's stick that would finally end his futile struggle with life.

As he sat waiting, he became aware of an old, wrinkled man sitting beside him. With a blank expression on his face, the man took a nearby stick and began to trace out the sign of the cross in the sand at Solzhenitsyn's feet. Solzhenitsyn was captivated by the message contained in those few grains of sand. How aware he was of his hopeless condition. How could one licked man make a difference? But he reflected on how Jesus on the cross began a process that turned the world upside down. With renewed strength, he pulled himself up, picked up his shovel and went back to work. At that moment he had no idea that his writings on truth and freedom would one day inflame the world (Colson 1983, 172).

Another moving experience of the power of the cross has been related by Catherine Marshall concerning a Lutheran pastor who had been a Nazi stormtrooper.

In December 1941 the trooper was with the German armies invading Russia. In the Crimea, in heavily wooded terrain, the battle began going against the Germans. As they had to fall back, the German found himself within the Russian lines, separated from his regiment. Alone he made his way through the forest, fearful at every minute of being captured. Suddenly, he saw a thin cloud of smoke coming from the chimney of a hut. Creeping up warily, gun in hand, he knocked on the door. It was answered by a tiny elderly Russian woman.

Shoving past her and searching the hut, he satisfied himself that the woman lived alone. Apparently, her menfolk were off fighting – perhaps had already been killed. To the German's surprise, the woman offered him food and drink. Neither spoke a word of the other's language, but in the end the Russian woman hid the soldier, feeding him and caring for him for three days and nights. The German grew increasingly baffled. Certainly, no worse enemy than he, a Nazi, could have come to the door here in Russia, where Germans murdered more civilians than the total number of Jews killed in all of Europe. The woods swarmed with Russian troops; surely she knew that if she were caught harboring a German she would be shot.

Out of his mounting desire to communicate, he managed through sign language and facial expressions to convey his question, "Why have you risked your life to hide and befriend me?"

The old woman looked at him for a long moment in silence, then turned and pointed to a crucifix on the wall above her bed.

Telling me the incident, the Lutheran pastor added, "After I escaped back to the German lines, try as I would I couldn't forget what had happened. I hadn't known love like that was possible. In the end, I was drawn irresistibly to the One who enabled the little Russian lady to prefer another to herself – even when that other was a cruel and deadly enemy. I wanted to know the power of the cross in my life too. That's why I'm a Christian today." (Marshall 1974, 240-241)

Millions have experienced life-changing transformations through applied faith in the cross of Christ. It is the focus point at which all of history converges. As important as the incarnation of God is, its truth is in competition with the incarnated deities of Greek and Hindu mythology. The Resurrection, though doctrinally of great importance, has similar parallels in religious legends found around the world. But the master plan of God, expressed through an incarnation of Himself leading to a substitutionary atonement on a cross, is unique in the annals of history. Christendom stands or falls on the cross.

Samuel Zwemer comments, "The cross is the pivot as well as the centre of New Testament thought. It is the exclusive mark of the Christian faith, the symbol of

Christianity and its cynosure" (Zwemer n.d.: preface). Spirituality, to the devout believer in Christ, is expressed most profoundly in the cross. It can never be intellectually dissected and analyzed. The only way to approach the cross is through reverent faith. H. B. Dehqani-Tafti, a Muslim convert to Christianity, has beautifully expressed this truth.

> *I can never understand how God Almighty came into the world and allowed the cross to happen to Him, but somehow deep down I can, a little bit, understand why He did that. I can never understand how the sin of man is forgiven on the cross; but when I look at Him on the cross and try to understand His love, His intentions, and His way of fulfilling His purpose, I cannot but fall down and cry bitterly: "O Lord, have mercy upon me, a miserable sinner." (Dehqani-Tafti 1959, 71)*

Dehqani-Tafti's response to the cross eloquently sums up the Christian position. Faith leads to humility, which leads to eternal life. This is the provision made for mankind by our Spiritual Guide. We can ask for no more.

8

Hell and Heaven

Belief in life after death is nearly universal. The heart of man refuses to believe that his last breath is really the end to existence. Rewards must be given to the righteous and punishment meted out to the evildoers. Death the great equalizer must also be death the pathway into bliss or torture. A Hitler cannot cohabit eternity with a Mother Teresa.

In both Christianity and Islam the doctrine of the future is extremely important. Both teach that this life is only a short prelude to an endless existence that will be spent in ultimate happiness or grotesque suffering.

Melted Skins

But as for those who disbelieve, garments of fire will be cut out for them; boiling fluid will be poured down on their heads. Whereby that which is in their bellies, and their skins too will be melted. (Sura 12:19-20)

THE CROSS AND THE CRESCENT

There are seventy-seven allusions to hell in the Quran. It is always referred to as a place of punishment. Persons are sent to hell for lying, engaging in corruption, scoffing at the Prophet's message, denying the coming Hour of Judgment, ignoring the needs of the poor, and inordinately fixating on the acquisition of wealth.

The Quran makes little mention of an intermediate state between death and the Great Judgment. It is generally held that the soul is in a state of suspension. But this is not clearly defined. The nearest biblical equivalent would be the shadowy *Sheol* of the Old Testament. This is borne out in a quranic passage that describes the trumpet on the Judgment Day bringing forth the dead from a place of sleep.

> *And the trumpet is blown and lo! from the graves they hie unto their Lord, Crying: "Woe upon us! Who hath raised us from our place of sleep? This is that which the Benificent did promise, and the messengers spoke truth, It is but one Shout, and behold them brought together before Us!" (Sura 36:50-52)*

The next important event on Allah's calendar following the resurrection of the human race is a test of faith and works. This event seems to be a judgment by the weighing of good and bad deeds on the scales of God. "And We set a just balance for the Day of Resurrection so that no soul is wronged in aught. Though it be of the weight of a grain of mustard seed, We bring it. And We suffice for reckoners" (Sura 21:47).

The other more commonly held judgment relates to a bridge over hell. This is rather obliquely referred to in Suras 36:66 and 37:23-24. Both the saved and condemned must pass over the bridge. Angels are stationed on the bridge to assist in the interrogation of those who are attempting to pass over it. Allah is there to help facilitate passage for the just and the pardoned. Professing Muslims who are judged guilty of sin will fall from the bridge into the fire, but their stay in hell will be of a limited duration.

Those who have neither faith nor good deeds will find that the bridge becomes narrower and sharper than a sword. The doomed are unable to proceed; they fall into the terrible fires of hell below. It appears from the Hadith that this will be the terrible fate of all Christians.

Then it will be said to the Christians, "What did you used to worship?" They will reply, "We used to worship Messiah, the son of Allah." It will be said, "You are liars, for Allah has neither a wife nor a son. What do you want now?" They will say, "We want you to provide us with water." It will be said to them, "Drink," and they will fall down in Hell (instead). (Bukhari [Vol. 9], 395)

The position of women on the Judgment Day seems to be somewhat perilous. On one hand the Quran gives hope. "And whoso doeth good works, whether of male or female, and he (or she) is a believer, such will enter paradise" (Sura 4:124). On the other hand, the Hadith presents a rather gloomy outlook for women. "Allah's Apostle said, 'A woman was tortured and was put in Hell because of a cat which she had kept locked till it died of hunger'" (Bukhari [Vol. 3], 323). That seems an extreme penalty.

A frequently quoted Hadith is great fuel for Muslim feminists:

Once Allah 's Apostle went out to the Musalla (to offer the prayer) of Id-al-Adha or al-Fitr prayer. Then he passed by the women and said, "O women! Give alms, as I have seen that the majority of the dwellers of Hell-fire were you (women)." They asked, "Why is it so, O Allah's Apostle?" He replied, "You curse frequently and are ungrateful to your husbands. I have not seen anyone more deficient in intelligence and religion than you. A cautious sensible man could be led astray by some of you." The women asked, "O Allah's Apostle! What is deficient in our intelligence and religion?" He said, "Is not the evidence of two women equal to the witness of one man?" They replied in the affirmative. He said, "This is the deficiency in your intelligence. Isn't it true that a woman can neither pray nor fast during her menses?" The women replied in the affirmative. He said, "This is the deficiency in your religion." (Bukhari [Vol. 1], 181-182)

Muslims are somewhat apprehensive concerning the possibility of their going to hell. They do not have absolute assurance of eternal life. "Only God knows" is the Muslim's response to a query concerning his future destination. But he has hope that Allah's mercy will finally prevail and that his sojourn in hell will be of short duration, as mentioned above. The Quran supports this view. "There is not one of you but shall approach it. That is a fixed ordinance of thy Lord. Then we shall rescue those who kept from evil and leave the evil-doers crouching there" (Sura 19:71-72).

A touching appeal was found woven into a Shia embroidery.

My God, wilt Thou burn with Thy fire my face which used to pray to Thee? My God, wilt Thou burn with fire my eyes which used to weep with fear of Thee? My God, wilt Thou burn with fire my tongue which used to recite the Quran? My God, wilt Thou burn with fire my body which was humbled before Thee? My God, wilt Thou burn with fire my limbs which used to bow and prostrate themselves before Thee? (Padwick 1961, 283)

Another interesting discourse with God is carried on by Yunus Emre, a fourteenth-century Anatolian mystic.

"O my God, if Thou shouldst interrogate me once I shall give this answer:

Though I may have sinned against myself, What have I done against Thee? ... Thou hast created the scales to weigh sin – Do you want to cast me into the Fire? Scales are fitting for a merchant, A goldsmith, a druggist, or a peddler needs them. But Thou art All-Knowing and know my state. Dost Thou really need scales to examine me?" (Schimmel 1979, 167-168)

This uncertainty of final destination makes the prospect of a sojourn in the raging fires of hell all the more frightening. There are stories told of Muslims dying of fear as they heard fiery preachers graphically describe the torments of hell. The Quran certainly reinforces Muslim anxiety about the terribleness of hell. Jane Smith and Yvonne Haddad have researched key quranic citations about the future abode of the wicked.

The Qur'an offers a number of rather specific indications of the tortures of the Fire: its flames crackle and roar (Sura 25:14); it has fierce, boiling waters (Sura 55:44), scorching wind, and black smoke (Sura 56:42-43); it roars and boils as if it would burst with rage (Sura 67:7-8). The people of the Fire are sighing and wailing, wretched (Sura 11:106), their scorched skins are constantly exchanged for new ones so that they can taste the torment anew (Sura 4:45), they drink festering water and though death appears on all sides they cannot die (Sura 14:16-17), people are linked together in chains of 70 cubits (Sura 69:30-32) wearing pitch for clothing and fire on their faces (Sura 14:50), boiling water will be poured over their heads, melting their insides as well as their skins, and hooks of iron will drag them back should they try to escape (Sura 22:19-21). (Smith and Haddad 1981, 85-86)

The Hadith are equally graphic.

I heard the Prophet saying, "The least punished person of the Hell Fire people on the Day of Resurrection will be a man under whose arch of the feet a smouldering ember will be placed so that his brain will boil because of it." (Bukhari [Vol. 8], 368)

Allah's Apostle said, "Anyone whom Allah has given wealth but does not pay his Zakat, then, on the Day of Resurrection, his wealth will be presented to him in the shape of a bald-headed poisonous male snake with two poisonous glands in its mouth and it will encircle itself round his neck and bite him over his cheeks and say, 'I am your wealth; I am your treasure.'" (Bukhari [Vol. 6], 69)

Has fear of hell caused Muslims to become demonstrably more spiritual? It is fair to say that many Muslims are affected by the fear of the wrath and justice of Allah. Others, however, continue on in their ungodly ways, quite unaffected by any concern for future judgment. Not altogether unlike Christianity!

The Lake of Fire

And I saw the dead, the great and the small, standing before the throne, and books were opened; and another book was opened, which is the book of life; and the dead were judged from the things which were written in the books, according to their deeds. And the sea gave up the dead which were in it, and death and Hades gave up the dead which were in them; and they were judged, every one of them according to their deeds. And death and Hades were thrown into the lake of fire. This is the second death, the lake of fire. And if anyone's name was not found written in the book of life he was thrown into the lake of fire. (Rev. 20:12-15)

These are harsh words. They are no less severe than the Islamic perspective on that great and awesome day of ultimate finality. Both religions present hell as a place of terrible torment and suffering. The New Testament speaks of hell in a variety of ways.

- It is a place of outer darkness where there will be weeping and gnashing of teeth (Matt. 8:12).
- The wicked will be cast into a furnace of fire (Matt. 13:50).
- The fire and punishment will be of everlasting duration (Matt. 25:41).
- Hell is a place where the worm does not die and the fire is never quenched (Mark 9:44).
- There is torment from the heat and water is desired for relief (Luke 16:24).
- A great gulf exists between heaven and hell (Luke 16:26).
- Within the furnace of hell there is a great deal of smoke (Rev. 9:2).
- Hell is a lake of fire and brimstone (Rev. 20:10).

Evangelical theology reflects the biblical understanding that all who have not placed their saving faith in Jesus as Savior are doomed to spend eternity in this state of torture. Of course, there have always been dissenting opinions among Christians. Some would say hell is not eternal but is of a shorter duration. A growing number refuse to consign to hell those who have never heard of Christ. Then there are some who are moving toward what they consider is a "biblical universalism." Neal Punt, author of *Unconditional Good News: Toward an Understanding of Biblical Universalism*, is one author who postulates such a view.

But mainline evangelicalism stands with C. S. Lewis:

Some will not be redeemed. There is no doctrine which I would more willingly remove from Christianity than this, if it lay in my power. But it has the full support of Scripture and, specially, of our Lord's own words; it has always been held by Christendom; and it has the support of reason. If a game is played, it must be possible to lose it. If the happiness of a creature lies in self-surrender, no one can make that surrender but himself (though many can help him to make it) and he may refuse. I would pay any price to be able to say truthfully "All will be saved." But my reason retorts, "Without their will, or with it?" If I say "Without their will" I at once perceive a contradiction; how can the supreme voluntary act of self-surrender be involuntary? If I say "With their will," my reason replies, "How if they will not give in?" (Lewis 1940, 106-107)

In my missionary questionnaire, the following interchange took place on the subject of hell:

Are all non-born-again people in the world going to hell when they die?

Yes: 357 No: 8

If your answer is yes, do you believe they deserve to go to hell?

Yes: 333 No: 10
(47 people opted not to answer this question)

If your answer is they are going to hell, does this bother you?

Yes: 332 No: 26

Hell has been a key evangelistic component in sermons like "Sinners in the Hands of an Angry God" or "Pay Day Someday." Preachers with great skills of rhetoric have figuratively dangled the lost in their congregations over the fire and brimstone of hell. As a result, not a few sinners have fled to Christ from the wrath to come.

To other Christians, hell is the key motivation to proclaim salvation in Christ to the uttermost parts of the earth. For me personally, I would not have given twenty-six years of my life to Muslim evangelism if I did not believe in the reality of hell and heaven. I am "compelled" by such biblical truths. Like C. S. Lewis, I wish such a doctrine was not around. But since it is an integral part of Scripture, I have no other choice but to proclaim it.

Think back to chapter 4 of this book. We, as sensitive Christians, are smitten with the question of why the righteous are allowed to suffer in this life. Even as I write this, a lovely missionary mother of three small children is being buried in a Filipino provincial town three hours from Manila. Four days ago Annie Stockton confronted a thief in her kitchen at three in the afternoon. She was brutally stabbed many times as she ran and then crawled toward the front gate. Three hours later she entered heaven – three hours later three lovely kids had no mom, a loving husband had no wife, and Overseas Missionary Fellowship had lost a very promising missionary.

When we think of Annie's last few moments on earth in deep physical pain, we are emotionally torn asunder. But what of the reality of those who will burn in the raging fires of eternal duration? How deeply smitten are we? How motivational is this biblical truth in our lives? Perhaps most of us give a sleepy nod of mental assent to the fiery preacher and then go on our own way doing what we always have done. Some Christians find it easy to crack jokes about hell. I have never understood that.

A tough subject! But hell is as biblical as heaven. We ignore its reality to our peril.

Rivers of Wine

A similitude of the Garden which those who keep their duty (to Allah) are promised: Therein are rivers of water unpolluted, and rivers of milk whereof the flavour changeth not, and rivers of wine delicious to the drinkers. (Sura 47:15)

It is rather startling to think of Muslims sitting around heaven throughout eternity having endless glasses of wine placed before them – in light of Islam's very strict prohibition against alcohol.

In a Hadith very close in content to Paul's writing, Muslims are told to joyfully anticipate future days of bliss.

The Prophet said, "Allah said, 'I have prepared for My pious worshippers such things as no eye has ever seen, no ear has ever heard of, and nobody has ever thought of. All that is reserved, besides which, all that you have seen, is nothing.'" (Bukhari [Vol. 4], 289)

Heaven is strictly for Muslims. "No one will enter Paradise but a Muslim soul" (Bukhari [Vol. 4], 190). It is a closed fraternity. All of the fleshly enjoyments of eternity are reserved for those who have faithfully followed the dictates of Islam.

Muhammad was assured by Allah that even Muslims who had engaged in major sins would be allowed to go to heaven. "Gabriel came and said to me, 'Whoever amongst your followers dies, worshipping none along with Allah will enter Paradise.' I said, 'Even if he did such-and-such things (i.e. even if he stole or committed illegal sexual intercourse)?' He said, 'Yes'" (Bukhari [Vol. 3], 337). This is true because of Islamic teaching on the mercy and forgiveness of Allah.

There is a special class of Muslims who are assured of direct access to heaven at the time of their demise. These are the martyrs who have died in an Islamic *jihad* (holy war). "And what though ye be slain in Allah's way or die therein? Surely pardon from Allah and mercy are better than all that they amass. What though ye be slain or die, when unto Allah ye are gathered?" (Sura 3:157-158).

This assurance fuels Islamic fanaticism and has caused Iranian boys to walk through Iraqi mine fields, full of confidence that being blown apart is a grand entree into heaven. Such was the frame of mind possessed by young Sanaa al-Muhaidli, who self-destructed by driving a car packed with explosives into an Israeli military convoy in southern Lebanon. She is considered a great patriot throughout the Muslim world.

The young girl left behind her legacy in moving words inscribed in her own blood:

> *My beloved ones! Life is only a stand of honour and self-respect. I am not dead. I am alive, and with you. O, how happy and joyful I am for this heroic martyrdom I have given....*
>
> *Do not cry for me for this courageous martyrdom. My flesh, scattered in pieces on the earth, will be once again, reunited, in heaven!*
>
> *Oh, mother! How happy I will be when my flesh leaves my bones, and when my blood surges into the soul of the South while I am exterminating those Zionist enemies. ("A Martyr's Last Statement" 1985, 19)*

This young lady's death wish has been fulfilled. Many other Muslims have followed her footsteps.

The Delights of Paradise

The Muslim Heaven is depicted as a place of massive dimensions. "The Prophet said, 'In Paradise there is a tree which is so big that a rider can travel in its shade for one hundred years without passing it'" (Bukhari [Vol. 6], 376). The garden is as wide as heaven and earth. Muslims wear ornate garments as they leisurely walk around paradise. On all sides are fountains, pavilions, and rivers. Luscious fruits are available in abundance.

The most exciting aspect of heaven that has captivated Muslim artists, poets, and laymen has nothing to do with any of the above. It has everything to do with beautiful young virgins available to those Muslims who have persevered faithfully in their commitment to Allah while alive on earth.

These *houris* (Arabic *hur*) are only directly mentioned four times in the Quran:

1. Muslims shall wed them (Sura 44:54).
2. They recline on couches and are fair in complexion with wide, lovely eyes (Sura 52:20).
3. They have never been touched by man or jinn (spiritual beings). They relax on green cushions and fair carpets. Their place of abode is in closely guarded pavilions (Sura 55:72-76).
4. They are like hidden pearls (Sura 56:23). Also, they are referred to as virgins created as a new creation (Sura 56:35-36).

Other indirect references to them are sensuous. They are said to be amorous and possess swelling breasts. They have been kept sexually pure and go about modestly with their eyes cast downward. These women are not the wives of their Muslim husbands on earth. They are a creation especially designed for the sexual enjoyment of faithful Muslims in heaven. Though Muslim women go to paradise, there is no clear indication of what they will do there or if any special men will entertain them throughout eternity. One gets the impression that the Islamic heaven is distinctly chauvinistic.

Descriptions of paradise in the Hadith are even more lucid than the Quran.

Allah's Apostle said, "The first batch (of people)

*who will enter Paradise will be (glittering) like a
full moon; and those who will enter next will be
(glittering) like the brightest star. Their hearts will
be as if the heart of a single man, for they will have
no enmity amongst themselves, and everyone of them
shall have two wives, each of whom will be so
beautiful, pure, and transparent that the marrow of
the bones of their legs will be seen through the flesh.
They will be glorifying Allah in the morning and
evening, and will never fall ill, and they will neither
blow their noses, nor spit. Their utensils will be of
gold and silver, and their combs will be of gold,
and the matter used in their censers will be aloes-
wood, and their sweat will smell like musk."
(Bukhari [Vol. 4], 307-308)*

It is easy to see cultural values in this description. The
utensils, combs, and censers were priority items in the time
of Muhammad. Bodily secretions were looked upon as
unclean, as this Hadith further elucidates.

*Allah's Apostle said, "They will not urinate, relieve
nature, spit, or have nasal secretions. Their combs
will be of gold, and their sweat will smell like musk.
The aloes-wood will be used in their censers. Their
wives will be houris. All of them will look alike and
will resemble their father Adam (in stature), sixty
cubits tall." (Bukhari [Vol. 4], 343)*

After reading this, it is no surprise to read the viewpoint
of one Arabian Muslim on the subject of the Islamic
paradise:

Today much effort is being spent to prove that Muhammad's paradise was only symbolic. Wise men explain away everything. But let me tell you this, I have lived my life faithful to God in this baking desert. I have avoided one earthly temptation after another in an effort to gain paradise. If I get there and find no cool rivers, no date trees and no beautiful girls ... to keep me company, I shall feel badly defrauded. (Waddy [1976] 1982, 129)

The Muslim heaven seems to me to be a terribly sensual place. And it is grossly unfair to faithful Muslim women who have also endured the "baking desert." I have never heard a Muslim woman protest the Islamic view of heaven. They simply resign themselves to the will of Allah. But to the men, such a paradise is a much anticipated reward for faithful allegiance to Allah.

Streets of Gold

The material of the wall was jasper; and the city was pure gold, like clear glass. The foundation stones of the city wall were adorned with every kind of precious stone. The first foundation stone was jasper; the second sapphire; the third chalcedony; the fourth, emerald; the fifth, sardonyx; the sixth, sardius; the seventh, chrysolite; the eighth, beryl; the ninth, topaz; the tenth, chrysophase; the eleventh, jacinth; the twelfth, amethyst. And the twelve gates were twelve pearls; each one of the

gates was a single pearl. And the street of the city
was pure gold, like transparent glass. (Rev. 21:18-
21)

In my more facetious moments, I have reflected on the
Muslim and the Christian views of heaven. The
contemplation of paradise led to a dream world for the
seventh-century Arabian desert-dweller. He was a captive
to the swirling dust and blazing heat. There was little water.
Prohibitions existed on sex and wine. But there in the future
is a world of fantasy sanctioned by God Himself. It is full
of legalized sex and booze that doesn't cause one to be dizzy
or have headaches. Pavilions and fountains abound. Beside
the rivers are beautiful shade trees with the most luscious
fruit imaginable. Paradise indeed!

And then there is heaven for the twentieth-century Wall
Street broker. For too long he, as a Christian, has fought
the battle of greed. The acquisition of stock, lands, and
properties has been a driving force in his life. But the
Carpenter of Galilee is always there standing in the shadows.
Our broker friend is tired of the conflict. But there in the
distance is a vision of better things to come. In fact, he has
been told that there are things in the Christian heaven which
he has not seen or even thought about. And these, then,
must be beyond the documented treasures of precious
stones, costly pearls, and pure gold streets. Truly a capitalistic
fantasy come alive.

Amusing speculations aside, the Christian most
assuredly has been told to look toward a day of release.
And though there are material rewards to be anticipated,
there is Someone our hearts long to see. He is the central

attraction of heaven.

And I saw the holy city, new Jerusalem, coming down out of heaven from God, made ready as a bride adorned for her husband. And I heard a loud voice from the throne, saying, "Behold, the tabernacle of God is among men, and He shall dwell among them, and they shall be His people, and God Himself shall be among them, and He shall wipe away every tear from their eyes; and there shall no longer be any death; there shall no longer be any mourning, or crying, or pain; the first things have passed away. And He who sits on the throne said, 'Behold, I am making all things new.' " (Rev. 21:2-5)

One of the high points of my missionary life was flying from the coastal town of Jayapura, Indonesia, into the very center of the huge island of Irian Jaya. As we flew over mountains and swamps, I looked down on the fires rising from many small settlements. In the 1950s a huge turning to Christ had begun there and continues up to the present. As our plane landed in a valley of fairyland beauty, we were immediately surrounded by seminude women and men wearing only genital gourds. These were precious people redeemed by the blood of the Lamb. Once headhunters, they were now farmers and herdsmen, accomplished by the grace of God and the sacrifice unto death by more than one missionary.

It was one of these nationals who wrote such a stirring and eloquent homily on heaven. Ototome Maiseni, superintendent of thirty churches in the Duqindoga Valley and one of the first believers in that area, shared these words to a group of believers who had just lost ninety members of their church due to a flu epidemic:

> *There are two kinds of happiness. One is found on this earth and the other is found in heaven.*
>
> *Consider first the happiness found now on this earth. People gather many possessions, many cowrie shells, many pigs, and much food. They want to become famous. They want their names heard on every mountaintop. They are happy gathering these things and becoming successful.*
>
> *In their earthly enthusiasm they do not bother to listen to a single word that God would say to them. They hate to hear from Him.*
>
> *"Why should I listen?" they ask. "Do I have need of something, that I should trouble myself to listen to God? What do I lack? Nothing!" And they dance about in a display of shallow happiness.*
>
> *Although they seem to have an abundance of earthly happiness they do not think about tomorrow, when God will cause the heavens and earth to pass away.*
>
> *Instead they prance with bow and arrows, pulling their bowstrings back. "We have killed many people in war," they boast. "The blood of many men is on our hands." Every night they sit about and sing to girls. They keep adding wives to their harems, and in adding wives they add gardens. More gardens mean more pigs. More pigs mean more shells to buy more wives. Because of this never-ending cycle they strut around and preen themselves like casuari*

birds.

"You are poor and foolish," they taunt us. "Why do you persist in serving your God? You don't have enough to eat. You don't even have a shirt on your back. Where are your wages? How stupid you are!"

Yes, the unbeliever drinks earthly joy to the full. But when Jesus comes his happiness will be terminated. In the end he will regret his evil deeds.

Those who follow the chief of this world will find their joy ceasing, their flowers fading, for their pleasures last but a moment. Do not be influenced by the jeering unbeliever. He sings for one hour and cries for an eternity.

Now consider those of us who live in sorrow on this earth. Who are we? We are those who have received Jesus in our hearts. We are men who hunger. We are the ones who go out and cut down brush, build fences and dig in the dirt to plant a garden.

Our backs ache, our muddy, calloused hands wipe the sweat from our brows. We split rocks. We fell trees. We labor from dawn to sunset, day after day.

"What a crazy way to live!" taunts the man who has no hunger. "Working and sweating! What good does it do you? Even while you work you starve!"

Yes, we cry and are hungry. We grow weary as we serve Jesus. Doing God's work is not a little task. Many times sadness comes to our hearts. Sickness comes. The pressures of the work crush us.

"The Christian life is too hard for us," some of our number complain, and they leave the trail and

turn from God.

That is a wrong decision. We are on this earth only one little hour. Our real home is in heaven. Our citizenship is there. Happiness is for then. At that time we will receive great joy.

Glory will be ours then. Those who grieve in this short hour will be the recipients of never-ending happiness. Those who laugh today will end in inexpressible sorrow tomorrow. But we who are hungry today will in the tomorrow of tomorrows know only joy that lasts and lasts – like eternal life lasts, forever and ever and ever.

We will live with God where there is no hunger, no sorrow, no pain. We who believe, we who are victorious over sin, we will receive the great gift of eternal joy at God's right hand. (Scott 1980, 79-81)

A more touching tribute to the anticipated reality of heaven has seldom been made.

There are those who accuse Christians of being escapists. We cannot, they say, handle the pressures of contemporary society. We keep pressing on by living on a fantasy. The initial response to such an attack simply points to Scripture. We have committed our lives to belief in the integrity of God's Word. Repeatedly we are warned in Scripture of the transitory nature of our short moments in this life. We are not to settle down as permanent dwellers with no consideration for eternal concerns.

But let us respond to the "heavenly cop-out" charge in another way. To respond to God in faith and obedience in this life brings its own rewards, quite apart from a promise of future benefits. None could say it better than E. Stanley

Jones, who penned these words just two months before his death in India:

> *If at the end when I get out there and find there is no heaven, I will say, "Well, universe, you let me down. You had the feeling of the eternal and the real, but I see there is no heaven, nothing but a cipher, emptiness. But I am not sorry I was a Christian. Give me back my choices to make over and I would say, 'Heaven or no heaven, I'm a Christian by conviction and choice.' It doesn't take heaven to make me glad of that." (Jones 1975, 148)*

To that, the devout Christian, who pushes ever on by faith, can only add a hearty affirmation.

9

The Quest for Truth

T he word *truth* has such a positive sound about it. It seems to embody all that is noble, uplifting, and pure. Yet throughout history, sincere and courageous people have engaged in the most barbaric acts imaginable as they sought to impose their particular view of what truth is. Both Muslims and Christians have been guilty.

To me, there is no other issue so urgent as defining and acting upon conceptual and practical truth. I close this book with a short personal reflection on where I have ended up in my pursuit of spiritual truth.

Pursuit of Truth

Muslims are wholeheartedly convinced they have found the truth. This strong, immovable conviction rode off the deserts of Arabia on camels and horses in the mid-seventh century. It traversed mountains, crossed rivers, and pressed through the sand dunes of the Sahara. From the beginning Muslims believed that truth received must be truth shared.

Islam took its great commission seriously. Muslims lived and died for their faith. Ultimate truth demands no less.

The Quran forcefully makes its claim to absolute truth. "And lo! We know that some among you will deny (it). And lo! it is indeed an anguish for the disbelievers. And lo! it is absolute truth. So glorify the name of the Tremendous Lord" (Sura 69:49-52). In light of such a dogmatic assertion, it is understandable why Muslims have generally closed their minds to other views of truth. Any investigation of alternative claims seems to them to be a breach of trust in the clear, unequivocal pronouncement of Allah. Christians, at least in contemporary times, have been greatly influenced by the spirit of inquiry. "Sure, Jesus said He was truth and the path to God, but why did He say that? What was the context? What was His real meaning? Do His words have universal or only local application? Are they timeless or time-bound?" And on and on goes our seemingly boundless capacity for critique.

The Muslim sits back and smiles. "You Christians are only self-destructing," he says as he picks up a copy of *The Myth of God Incarnate*, written by supposedly Christian scholars who question Jesus' divinity and the authority of the Bible. The Muslim will allow no such questioning of his faith. Attacks on the veracity of Muhammad have led to executions. The purity of Islam must be maintained. An attack on the Quran is an attack on Allah. Salman Rushdie experienced this worldwide outpouring of Islamic wrath following the publication of his *The Satanic Verses*.

Muslims are distressed that the world has not yet converted to Islam. To them it is so obvious where truth is to be found. In fact, they believe all persons were born

Muslims. (That is, every newborn human being is a Muslim by birthright, but the person is then "sidetracked" by his parents.) But many have strayed and now need to return to the true faith. The Hadith states, "Allah's Apostle said, 'Every child is born with a true faith of Islam (i.e., to worship none but Allah alone) but his parents convert him to Judaism, [or] Christianity'" (Bukhari II:247).

Seyyed Hossein Nasr articulates his devotion to Islamic truth as few can:

The aspect of serenity, which also characterizes all true expressions of Islam, is essentially the love of truth. It is to put the Truth before everything else. It is to be impartial, to be logical on the level of discourse, not to let one's emotions colour and prejudice one's intellectual judgment. It is not to be a rationalist, but to see the truth of things and to love the Truth above all else. To love the Truth is to love God who is the Truth, one of His Names being the Truth (al Haqq). (Nasr 1966, 75)

I find it a bit difficult to understand how Dr. Nasr can make such high claims for Islam. Most Muslims I have met are not impartial, logical, unemotional, unprejudiced, and rational. But, to be fair, Islam is made up of many different kinds of people, and as Dr. Nasr himself represents the best of Islam, he perhaps evaluates the entire religion from his perspective.

Dr. Maurice Bucaille, the French surgeon who converted to Islam, has declared himself one who has discovered ultimate truth. He states that the Quran meets the criteria for truth and can be easily understood by all unbiased minds. He lists the proofs of truth as:

1. the rational teaching of the Quran;
2. the absolute perfection of the Quran, "free from mistakes, omissions, interpolations, and multiplicity of versions";
3. absence of myths and superstitions in God's Word;
4. the scientific nature of the Quran;
5. truth of the prophecy found in the Quran. He then ends with these words, "May we all see the eternal truth" (Bucaille n.d., 20-21).

Here is a European trained in higher science. Yet he has made objective statements about the Quran that simply cannot withstand critical analysis. Perhaps the most "spiritual" answer from a Christian perspective is to relegate this to the deceptive influence of Satan. But that is exactly what Muslims say of Christians who believe in an authoritative Bible and in a unity that is expressed in a Trinity. And so the standoff on "absolute truth" remains, and the debate continues unabated.

Can truth ever be evaluated from an unbiased point of view? A Muslim imam friend who says he prays for me each evening that I might convert to the True Path has commented on the problem of objectivity. He is convinced that all Christians would become Muslims if they could only set aside parental and cultural influences. In frustration he said, "I guess the only way we could prove truth is to have men from Mars land on earth, evaluate the two religions, and choose one as truth. Everyone else is laden with presuppositions that make an objective assessment nearly impossible." I can sympathize with his statement as I seek to draw out the kind of nonprejudiced thinking from Muslims that he wants to receive from Christians.

Philosopher David Hume and theologian Ernst Troeltsch worked with the doctrine of analogy. This refers to the mental process of recognizing things by comparing them to our experiences and categories of understanding. There is always linkage between our past and what we are presently experiencing. This is all summed up in the word *presuppositions*. We bring influences from the past to bear on any new situation. I concur with the commonly held view that it is impossible to be *completely* objective. The only hope for objectivity for anyone is a recognition of this and a concerted effort to minimize bias. It is my belief that Christians generally do a better job of this than Muslims, but perhaps my belief is one more example of my presuppositions at work!

At Harvard University, *Veritas* (Latin for truth) is everywhere. The university seal, which has *Veritas* written on it, is found impressed on chairs, woven into clothes, and printed on stationery. Here is an academic community intellectually committed to pursuing absolute truth in every discipline. I would often listen to a brilliant professor postulate an opinion directly opposed to my own view. Then I would look to the Harvard seal hanging on the classroom wall behind him. Both of us were committed to *Veritas*. Yet how different our opinions were.

Religio, from which we get our English word *religion*, means "to bind." It is extended to mean "to bind to the truth." But how amazingly prolific have been religious interpretations of truth down through the ages. Mohandas

K. Gandhi, working from a Hindu perspective, shared his thoughts on holding on to relative truth while seeking absolute truth.

I worship God as Truth only. I have not yet found Him, but I am seeking after Him. I am prepared to sacrifice the things dearest to me in pursuit of this quest. Even if the sacrifice demanded be my very life, I hope I may be prepared to give it. But as long as I have not realized this Absolute Truth, so long must I hold by the relative truth as I have conceived it. That relative truth must, meanwhile, be my beacon, my shield and buckler. Though this path is strait and narrow and sharp as the razor's edge, for me it has been the quickest and easiest. (Gandhi 1957, xiv)

Recently I visited Midsayap, a remote town in the southern island of Mindanao in the Philippines. As I drove through the town, on the main road I observed one mosque and the following churches: Four Square Gospel, Church of the Latter-day Saints, Roman Catholic, United Church of the Philippines, Southern Baptist, Church of the Deliverance, and Christian and Missionary Alliance. Each of these churches holds to a belief in an authoritative Bible. Yet I could not help but ponder the confusion a Muslim would feel in that town if he wanted to go to church and hear the true message of Christianity. Many Muslim Filipinos have spoken to me of this problem of a proliferation of Christian denominations. It is very difficult to give a simple yet adequate response.

Pursuit of truth – as we struggle with the concept, can we not at least understand these words by Kenneth Cragg as he explores the option of live-and-let-live?

"For Christians": why not leave it there, living and letting live? Why be concerned that the impact – better, the imprint – of Jesus, as the New Testament knew it, should be felt and received by the world of Islam? Are not the obstacles too massive, the deterrents too formidable? Is zeal in the matter ill-judged, or misplaced? Is evangelism somehow a partisan pursuit - an enthusiasm which has not taken the real measure of the world? Is there not something plainly God-meant in the pluralism of religions and all the psychic, cultural, language diversity of the world, and the seeming irreconcilability of faiths within societies? (Cragg 1985, 295)

But Cragg cannot leave it there. Neither can I. Something compels us to believe we Christians have the truth. That leads us to the next section.

Christ as Truth

The Muslim listens to the Christian evangelist proclaim that there is salvation in no other name than that of Jesus, the Son of God. He hears only blasphemy in the message. His emotions rise. Allah has been attacked in a most profane manner.

One Muslim set forth his response in a 1985 publication in Singapore.

*I must confess I am absolutely incapable of believing
and placing my trust in a God . . .*
*–Whose best attributes found their manifestation on
the cross,*
*–Who sacrificed His only son to save me from the
consequence of my evil deeds,*
*–Who created me with the taint of sin inherent in
my nature, and then sat in judgment on me for the
consequence of the evil nature which is not of my
own making, but His own gift,*
*–Who miraculously changes my ugly nature into
something beautiful, not through my actions but
through my belief in some of His so-called
manifestations. . . .*
*–Who created man unfit by nature to keep the law,
and Whose saving power reaches only those who
believe in one dogma or another.*
("Four Cardinal Attributes" 1985, 13-14)

Though these words reveal some misunderstandings,
still there are a number of Christian areas of mystery
addressed concerning which our best theologians can only
await a future day for fuller enlightenment. Like Peter, we
at times wrestle with things hard to understand. But if
Christianity stood only on unquestionable and totally
verifiable propositions, what need would there be for a
humble faith linkage between the created and the Creator?
God, from the outset, desired a relationship with His children
that would be sustained by faith rather than by sight.
Anything less, it seems to me, is robotic in nature and lacks
the dynamic of love.

I am nine inches taller than my wife and fifty-five pounds heavier. There are many things I could force my wife to do. My strength could simply overwhelm her. But there is one thing I can never coerce Julie to do. And that is the very thing that is her most precious gift to me. Only by her free will can she, from her heart, say, "Phil, I love you." I could force those words from her lips, but they would be worthless and totally devoid of meaning.

God could have created a very different human race. But He chose to give us a will that can say, "I love you" or "I reject you." God receives a tremendous joy from seeing His created child, out of a free will, kneel and say, "Father, because of all You have done for me in Christ, I just want to tell You, I love You with all my heart."

Assuredly, this simple statement embodies a massive volume of faith. It goes back to the garden and takes into account a terrible cleavage between man and God. It affirms the Old Testament's record of alienation and self-will. But even more mind-stretching is the manger – and then the miracles – and the Cross and the Resurrection. To top it off is the amazing sight of myself – proud, arrogant, and stiff-necked – bowing down with millions who preceded me in an act of faith in the atoning work of Christ, which alone unites me to God for all eternity.

Lesslie Newbigin, for many years an Anglican missionary in India, has summed up his faith with these words: "I am – in Pascal's phrase – wagering my life on the faith that Jesus is the ultimate authority. My answer is a confession: I believe" (Newbigin 1978, 17).

Christ – the ultimate and only full expression of embodied truth. We live for truth and we are willing to die for it. We closet it in our hearts, and we shout it from the rooftops. Truth! How compelling and how all-embracing. G. H. Jansen, a journalist, has asked whether the emotional gulf created between Christians and Muslims through preaching has been worth the result of a few thousand conversions (Jansen 1979, 61). While decrying polarization and alienation, I am still forced to answer Jansen with an affirmation. A full commitment to Christ as unique truth will prevent evangelicals from breaking off their attempts to bring Muslims to the foot of the cross.

In 1986 I had the privilege of visiting the Tuareg nomadic tribal people in the country of Niger. As we drove in a Land Rover out into the southern belt of the Sahara Desert, I was totally amazed that American missionaries could live and witness in such a hostile climate. In the midst of dust that "penetrates behind the eyeballs," I saw love in action.

The road stopped in the middle of barrenness. A Tuareg dressed in a full-length blue robe with a veil over his face pointed the way to the village we were to visit. The Land Rover groaned as it went up over the sand dunes, seemingly being directed by instinct. Soon we arrived at a small settlement of Tuaregs. What a joy to squeeze through the two-foot-high opening of the tent and sit with one of the few Tuareg believers in all of Niger. We sipped strong tea together, which mystically seemed more like the juice of Communion. Here was a precious member of the body of Christ in one of the most remote and backward places on earth.

After some time, the Muslim Tuareg chief arrived. He escorted us to his home, which was constructed of adobe bricks. We sat together, drank tea, and talked over many issues of life. Over to one side some of the family were going through the prayer ritual. I reflected on how little life had changed among Muslims of the desert in the past 1,300 years.

We expressed our profound thanks for the homemade wallets given to us as gifts by the chief. We drove back to the airstrip and piled into the mission plane for our flight back to Niamey, the capital city. As we circled over the desert, my thoughts went to the sacrifice that the missionaries had poured into that work for twenty-five years. Results? Just a few dozen Tuaregs in Niger are presently professing Christ in an open manner. What a price to pay for negligible results. The world scoffs and says, "What a waste!" But for the Christian who is committed to the biblical Christ, it is all part of a master plan of obedience to ultimate truth.

Spirituality

This has been a difficult book for me to write. My emotions have been stretched as I have reflected on some terribly sad areas of life, particularly the relationship between spirituality and suffering. I am writing this on the day after Christmas. For many in the Philippines it has been a tragic holiday season. The world's worst peacetime sea disaster took place a few days ago when an overloaded ferry boat with up to two thousand Filipino passengers collided with an oil tanker and sank in a fireball of flames with only a few survivors. Each day the papers show grisly pictures of the burned and shark-eaten bodies being pulled out of the sea.

In five days I will be flying to the U.S. to bring closure to a very precious relationship. My mother is dying of cancer of the lung and liver. Mom has epitomized sacrificial love to me for fifty years. It will be a tough good-bye. And so, to all the excruciating issues of life, what should be our spiritual response?

The Greeks used to enjoy a "torch race" that would captivate the crowds. The goal of the race was not to just outrun the other competitors and be the first to cross the finish line. The object was to be the first person to complete the race with a lit torch. If the flame was extinguished, the runner was disqualified.

Many Christians are able to make it to the finish line, but their torch is all too often only a flicker instead of a brightly burning flame. There is adherence to a set of cognitive doctrines and perhaps even regular attendance at church. But the real challenge in Christianity is to make it to the last breath of life with a burning heart full of spiritual zeal and reality.

Sitting in the guesthouse of the Southern Baptists in Dhaka, Bangladesh, a few years ago, I looked out the window and pensively studied the scene. It was borsha kal (monsoon season) and the rice fields were flooded. It seemed we were an island in the midst of a beautiful lake.

The boatmen knew where the deeper channels were within the fields, so there were two antlike columns of boats sailing in opposite directions. One line was going with the wind. No sweat. The boatman relaxed and puffed on his waterpipe as he delicately steered his craft toward the desired haven. The wind was his friend. He was in sync with the elements. Life was literally a breeze.

The other line of boats was going against the wind. The tattered sails had been lowered. Two men on each boat were straining with the oars to make their craft inch forward. The elements were no friend of theirs. Yet, they were a determined group. Their bodies were covered with sweat and faces contorted with pain. But, for sure, they would make it to home port.

I could not help but analogize boatmen and Christians. We have the option of flowing with the mainstream of life in the world. No harrassments for our faith. No ridicule, no price to pay for morality and honesty. But do we have that option?

No, not really. The Christian is in the world, but not of the world. He is told by Jesus Christ that he will suffer persecution and tribulation for his faith and witness. We are the boatmen going upstream against the tide. There will be struggle and pain. But through it all, let us keep pressing on . . . and on . . . and on! By God's grace we, too, will reach our desired haven.

But whatever things were gain to me, those things I have counted as loss for the sake of Christ. More than that, I count all things to be loss in view of the surpassing value of knowing Christ Jesus my Lord, for whom I have suffered the loss of all things, and count them but rubbish in order that I may gain Christ, and may be found in Him, not having a righteousness of my own derived from the Law, but that which is through faith in Christ, the righteousness which comes from God on the basis of faith, that I may know Him, and the power of His resurrection and the fellowship of His sufferings, being conformed to His death; in order that I may attain to the resurrection from the dead. (Phil. 3:7-11)

THE CROSS AND THE CRESCENT

Questionnaire on Missionary Spirituality

This is the questionnaire I sent out to missionaries across the globe. Three hundred and ninety missionaries in thirty-two countries responded.

Question	Always	Frequently	Infrequently	Never
Does your mind wander when you pray?	___	___	___	___
Is Bible reading a joy?	___	___	___	___
Is your Bible reading New Testament oriented?	___	___	___	___
Do you use a commentary as you read the Bible?	___	___	___	___
If married, do you have family devotions together?	___	___	___	___
Do you question God regarding evil and suffering?	___	___	___	___
Do you have absolute assurance of eternal life with Christ?	___	___	___	___
Are you afraid to die?	___	___	___	___
Is Christ's return a dynamic reality to you?	___	___	___	___
Do you ever feel you would like to be something other than a missionary?	___	___	___	___

Are you happy with the policies of your mission board?	___	___	___	___
Do you ever wish you had more academic degrees?	___	___	___	___
Do you enjoy deputation?	___	___	___	___
Do you have intellectual doubts about Christianity?	___	___	___	___
Do you ever feel you are preaching a message you don't fully believe?	___	___	___	___
Are you ever discouraged about life?	___	___	___	___
Is frustration a part of your life?	___	___	___	___
Are you ever emotionally tense?	___	___	___	___
Is anger a problem to you?	___	___	___	___
Is pride a problem to you?	___	___	___	___
Do you love your missionary colleagues?	___	___	___	___
Can you forgive missionaries who have hurt you?	___	___	___	___
Do you love national Christians on the mission field?	___	___	___	___
Do you have sexual fantasies of lust?	___	___	___	___
Do you read sexually stimulating literature?	___	___	___	___
Do you attend R-rated movies?	___	___	___	___
Do you attend X-rated movies?	___	___	___	___
On an average, how much time do you spend in prayer each day?	___	___	___	___
On an average, how much time do you spend reading the Bible each day?	___	___	___	___
What is your greatest spiritual struggle in life?	___	___	___	___
What magazines do you read regularly?	___	___	___	___

How many secular books do
  you read each month?   ___   ___   ___   ___

How many Christian-type books
  do you read each month?   ___   ___   ___   ___

Do you understand the
  doctrine of inerrancy?   ___   ___   ___   ___

Do you fully subscribe to
  inerrancy?   ___   ___   ___   ___

If you subscribe to inerrancy and
  came to doubt it, would you
  inform your mission leadership
  and colleagues?   ___   ___   ___   ___

Have you taken tranquilizers since
  becoming a missionary?   ___   ___   ___   ___

Do you drink alcoholic
  beverages?   ___   ___   ___   ___

Have you remained sexually
  moral since becoming
  a missionary?   ___   ___   ___   ___

Have you had a charismatic-
  type experience?   ___   ___   ___   ___

Have you ever spoken
  in tongues?   ___   ___   ___   ___

Do you feel post-salvation
  sanctification experiences
  can be biblically valid? ___   ___   ___   ___

THE CROSS AND THE CRESCENT

Glossary of Terms

Ablutions: Ritual washing for Muslims prior to prayer.

Ahl al-Kitab: "People of the Book," the name Muslims use for Christians and Jews.

Al-Hamdu-li-llah: "Praise to God."

Al-ilah or Allah: The God.

Alhaji: A Muslim who has made the pilgrimage (*Hajj*) to Mecca.

Baraka: Blessing.

Dervish: Muslim mystic given to frenzied (yet orderly) dance, trances, and recitation of the names of Allah.

Dhikr: Ceremony that centers around the recitation of the names and attributes of God.

Faqir: Muslim holy man who solicits alms.

Five Pillars: The five duties binding on all Muslims. See *Hajj, Ramadan, Salat, Shahadah, Zakat.*

Hadith: The traditions of Muhammad's words and actions, supplementing the more authoritative Quran.

Hajj: The pilgrimage to Mecca in Arabia, obligatory for all Muslims.

Houris: Women in heaven, prepared by God for the enjoyment of Muslim men.

Imam: The prayer leader in the mosque, trained in interpreting the Quran.

In-shallah: "If God wills."

Injil: The Gospels of the New Testament.

Isa: The Muslim name for Jesus.

Jihad: Islamic religious war – that is, promoting the message of Islam by force of arms.

Jinn: Minor spiritual beings, made of smokeless flame and capable, like humans, of salvation or damnation.

Koran: See *Quran.*

Mantra: A word or phrase that has spiritual significance for an individual mystic.

Muhammad Rasul al-lah: The confession "Muhammad is the messenger of God."

Muta: Temporary marriage; found especially among the Shia sect of Islam.

Night Journey: The journey of Muhammad from Mecca to the temple of Jerusalem and on to Paradise, made on a winged horse.

Night of Power: The night in the Muslim calendar month of Ramadan when Muhammad first began to receive Quranic revelations.

Popular Islam: Islam as it is practiced by adherents on the grassroots level of society, usually with a mystical emphasis.

Quran: Literally, "recitation" - the holy book of Islam. Often seen spelled quran *Koran.*

Ramadan: The Islamic month of fasting.

Salat: Prescribed Muslim ritual of prayer five times a day, facing toward Mecca and using ritual movements.

Shahadah: The central confession of Islam: "There is no God but God, and Mohammad is his messenger [or prophet]." It is the first and most indispensable of the Five Pillars of Islam.

Sufism: A mystically oriented school of thought within Islam. An individual Muslim mystic is a Sufi. Sufis claim direct experiences of Allah.

Sura: A chapter of the Quran.

Tanzil: Revelation of God's word to Muhammad.

Tasbih: Use of rosary beads as an aid to worship.

Tawrat: The Old Testament Law.

Ummah: The Muslim community, that is, those who have received Allah's revelation through Muhammad and submit to it.

Wajd: Ecstasy.

Zabur: The Old Testament Psalms.

Zakat: Literally, "purification" - one of the Five Pillars of Islam; it mandates that Muslims give 2.5 percent of their income to Islamic causes.

THE CROSS AND THE CRESCENT

Bibliography

The entries preceded by an asterisk are those which I highly recommend for reading.

"A Martyr's Last Statement." *Arabia* June 1985.

Ajijola, Alhaj A. D. *The Myth of the Cross*. Lahore, Pakistan: Islamic Publications, 1975.

Ali, Syed Nawab. *Some Moral and Religious Teachings of al-Ghazzali*. Lahore, Pakistan: Sh. Muhammad Ashraf, 1920.

Anderson, Norman. *Christianity and World Religions*. Downers Grove, Ill.: InterVarsity, 1984.

Andrae, Tor. *Mohammed, The Man and His Faith*. Translated by Theophil Menzel. New York: Harper & Row, 1960.

Ansari, F. R. *Islam and Christianity in the Modem World*. Karachi, Pakistan: World Federation of Islamic Missions, 1944.

Archer, Gleason L. *Encyclopedia of Bible Difficulties*. Grand Rapids: Zondervan, 1982.

Arsalan, Amir Shakib. *Our Decline and Its Causes*. Translated by M. A. Shakoor. Lahore, Pakistan: Sh. Muhammad Ashraf, 1944.

Badr, Camilia. "I Wonder." *Friday Times* (Manila) 1 (1985):1.

Bahay, Maria. "Birthday Offering to the Blessed Mother." *Panorama* (Manila), 18 August 1985.

Bell, Richard, and W. Montgomery Watt. *Introduction to the Quran*. Edinburgh: University Press, 1970.

Benoist, Ali Selman. Testimony in *Islam Our Choice*. Singapore: Muslim Converts' Association, n.d.

Bucaille, Maurice. *The Bible, The Quran and Science*. Translated by Alastair D. Pannell and the author. Indianapolis: North American Trust Publication, 1979.

_____. *The Quran and Modern Science*. Singapore: Muslim Converts' Association of Singapore, n.d.

*al-Bukhari. *The Translation of the Meanings of Sahih al-Bukhari*. Translated by Muhammad Muhsin Khan. Vols. 1-9. Beirut: Dar Al Arabia, n.d.

Chase, J. Richard. "The Campaign for Wheaton and AIDS." *InForm* (bulletin of Wheaton College). Vol. 64, no. 3 (1987).

Chittick, William C. *The Sufi Path of Love*. Albany: State University of New York Press, 1983.

Clayton, Thomas Muhammad. Testimony in *Islam Our Choice*. Edited by Ebrahim Ahmed Bawany. Karachi, Pakistan: Begum Aisha Bawany Wakf, 1976.

*Colson, Charles W. *Loving God*. Basingstoke, England: Marshall Morgan & Scott, 1983.

Cornford, F. M. *Poems from the Russian*. Translated by E. P. Salaman. London:1943.

Cragg, Kenneth. *The Call of the Minaret*. New York: Oxford University Press, 1964.

*_____. *Jesus and the Muslim*. London: George Allen & Unwin, 1985.

*_____. *Muhammad and the Christian*. Maryknoll, New York: Orbis, 1984.

*_____. *The Wisdom of the Sufis*. New York: New Directions, 1976.

Deedat, Ahmed. *Is the Bible God's Word?* Ann Arbor: Crescent Imports and Publications, n.d.

Dehqani-Tafti, H. B. *Design of My World*. London: Lutterworth, 1959.

*_____. *The Hard Awakening*. London: SPCK, 1981.

Donaldson, Bess Allen. "The Koran as Magic." *Moslem World* 27(1937):254-266.

Donovan, Vincent J. *Christianity Rediscovered*. Maryknoll: Orbis, 1978.

Doyo, Ceres R "The Dairy of Fr. Peter Geremia." *Panorama* (Manila), 18 August 1985.

Durrell, Lawrence. *Mountolive*. London: Faber and Faber, 1958.

*Elliot, Elisabeth. *These Strange Ashes*. New York: Harper & Row, 1975.

Esther, Gulshan, and Thelma Sangster. *The Torn Veil*. Basingstoke, England: Marshalls Paperbacks, 1984.

Falaturi, Abdoldjavad. "How Can a Muslim Experience God, Given Islam's Radical Monotheism?" In *We Believe in One God.* Edited by Annemarie Schimmel and Abdoldjavad Falaturi. New York: Seabury, 1979.

Feinberg, P. D. "Inerrancy and Infallibility of the Bible." In *Evangelical Dictionary of Theology.* Edited by Walter A. Elwell. Grand Rapids: Baker, 1984.

*Ford, Leighton. *Sandy, A Heart For God.* Homebush West, Australia: Anzea, 1985.

*Foster, Richard J. *Celebration of Discipline: The Path to Spiritual Growth.* San Francisco: Harper & Row, 1978.

*_____. *Money, Sex and Power.* San Francisco: Harper & Row, 1985.

"The Four Cardinal Attributes of God." In *The Muslim Reader* Singapore: Muslim Converts Association. June 1985.

Gandhi, Mohandas K. *An Autobiography: The Story of My Experiments with Truth.* Translated by Mahadev Desai. Boston: Beacon, 1957.

Germanus, Abdul Karim. Testimony in *Islam Our Choice.* Edited by Ebrahim Ahmed Bawany. Karachi, Pakistan: Begum Aisha Bawany Wakf, 1976.

al-Ghazali, Abu Hamid. *Inner Dimensions of Islamic Worship.* Translated by Muhtar Holland. Leicester, England: The Islamic Foundation, 1983.

*Gilchrist, John. *Muhammad and the Religion of Islam.* Benoni, South Africa: Jesus to the Muslims, 1986.

Glubb, John Bagot. *The Life and Times of Muhammad.* New York: Stein and Day Publishers, 1971.

*Goforth, Rosalind. *Goforth of China.* Minneapolis: Dimension, 1937.

Gramlich, Richard. "Mystical Dimensions of Islamic Monotheism." In *We Believe in One God.* Edited by Annemarie Schimmel and Abdoldjavad Falaturi. New York: Seabury, 1979.

Gustafson, Kim. "Middle East Paradigm." Unpublished paper. April 1985.

Guyon, Jeanne (Madame). *Spiritual Torrents.* Augusta, Maine: Christian Books, 1984.

Hannah, Mark. *The True Path.* Colorado Springs: International Doorways, 1975.

Haq, Muhammad Enamul. *A History of Sufi-ism in Bengal.* Dacca Bangladesh: Asiatic Society of Bangladesh, 1975.

Harkness, Georgia. *Mysticism: Its Meaning and Message.* Nashville: Abingdon, 1973.

Henry, Marie. *The Secret Life of Hannah Whitall Smith.* Grand Rapids: Chosen, 1984.

*Hession, Roy and Revel. *The Calvary Road.* Fort Washington, Pa.: Christian Literature Crusade, 1950.

Hick, John. *The Myth of God Incarnate*. Philadelphia: Westminster, 1977.

Holmes, Urban T, III. *A History of Christian Spirituality*. New York: Seabury, 1981.

Honey, Ayesha Bridget. Testimony in *Islam Our Choice*. Singapore: Muslim Converts' Association, n.d.

Houston, J. M. "Spirituality." In *Evangelical Dictionary of Theology*, edited by Walter A. Elwell. Grand Rapids: Baker, 1984.

al-Hujwiri, Ali Bin Uthman. *The Kashf al-Mahjub*. Translated by Reynold A. Nicholson. New Delhi, India: Taj, 1982.

Islam Our Choice. Singapore: The Muslim Converts' Association, n.d.

Ismail, Ustaz Iljas. *Islamic Ethics and Morality*. Manila: Convislam, 1980.

Jansen, G. H. *Militant Islam*. New York: Harper & Row, 1979.

Joaquin, Francoise. "Is This Being Christian?" *Mr. & Ms.* (Manila), 5-11 July 1985.

Jolly, Mavis B. Testimony in *Islam Our Choice*. Singapore: Muslim Converts' Association, n.d.

*Jones, E. Stanley. *Christ and Human Suffering*. New York: Abingdon, 1933.

*_____. *The Divine Yes*. Nashville: Abingdon, 1975.

*Kateregga, Badru D., and David W. Shenk. *Islam and Christianity*. Nairobi, Kenya: Uzima, 1980.

Kelen, Betty. *Muhammad the Messenger of God*. Nashville: Thomas Nelson, 1975.

*Kelsey, Morton. *Healing and Christianity*. New York: Harper & Row, 1973.

*_____. *The Other Side of Silence*. London: SPCK, 1976.

Kempis, Thomas à. *The Imitation of Christ*. New York: Grosset and Dunlap, n.d.

Khan, Muhammad Zafrulla. Muhammad: *Seal of the Prophets*. London: Routledge & Kegan Paul, 1980.

Khomeini, Ayatollah. *Sayings of the Ayatollah Khomeini*. Translated by Harold J. Salemson. New York: Bantam, 1979.

The Kneeling Christian. Grand Rapids: Zondervan, 1971.

Kushner, Harold S. *When Bad Things Happen to Good People*. New York: Avon, 1981.

Laubach, Frank C. *Thirty Years with the Silent Billion*. Westwood, N.J.: Revell, 1960.

*Lewis, C. S. *The Problem of Pain*. London: Centenary, 1940.

MacDonald, Duncan Black. *The Religious Attitude and Life in Islam*. 1909; reprint. New York: AMS, 1970.

McDowell, Josh, and John Gilchrist. *The Islam Debate*. San Bernardino, Cal.: Here's Life, 1983.

*McKinley, Jim. *Death to Life: Bangladesh.* Louisville: Highview Baptist Church, 1978.

*McQuilkin, J. Robertson. *Understanding and Applying the Bible.* Chicago: Moody, 1983.

*Mahmoody, Betty. *Not Without My Daughter.* New York: St. Martin's, 1987.

Mansur, Husain Ibn. *Tawasin.* Translated by Aisha Abd al-Rahman al-Tarjumana. London: 1974.

Marshall, Catherine. *Something More.* New York: McGraw-Hill, 1974.

*Merton, Thomas. *The Seven Storey Mountain.* New York: Harcourt-Brace, 1948.

*Miller. Calvin. *The Table of Inwardness.* Downers Grove, Ill.: InterVarsity, 1984. Mr. & Ms. (Manila), 24 August 1984.

*_____. *A Thirst for Meaning.* Grand Rapids: Zondervan, 1973.

Muck, Terry C. "Ten Questions about the Devotional Life." *Leadership* 3 (1982): 30-39.

Myra, Harold L. "A Message from the Publisher." *Christianity Today* 9 August 1985.

*Nasr, Seyyed Hossein. *Ideals and Realities of Islam.* Boston: Beacon, 1966.

_____. *Islamic Spirituality.* Vol. 19 of *World Spirituality.* New York: Crossroad, 1987.

_____. *Living Sufism.* London: Mandala, 1972.

*Nehls, Gerhard. *Christians Ask Muslims.* Capetown, South Africa: Life Challenge, n.d.

Neill, Stephen. *Christian Faith and Other Faiths.* London: Oxford University Press, 1970.

_____. *Crises of Belief.* London: Hodder and Stoughton, 1984.

Newbigin, Lesslie. *The Open Secret.* London: SPCK, 1978.

_____. *Studies in Islamic Mysticism.* Delhi, India: Idarah-i Adabiyat-i Delli, 1921.

Nicholson, Reynold Alleyne. *The Mystics of Islam.* London: Routledge and Kegan Paul, 1975.

"Nigerian Religionists Rethink," *Mission News,* no. 4. Ilorin, Nigeria: Missions Nigeria Limited, 1985.

Nurbakhsh, Javad. *In the Tavern of Ruin.* New York: Khaniqahi-Nimatullahi, 1978.

*Packer, J. I. *Beyond the Battle for the Bible.* Westchester, Ill.: Cornerstone, 1980.

Padwick, Constance E. *Muslim Devotions.* London: SPCK, 1961.

Parrinder, Geoffrey. *Mysticism in the World's Religions.* London: Sheldon, 1976.

Parshall, Phil. *Beyond the Mosque.* Grand Rapids: Baker, 1985.

_____. *Bridges to Islam.* Grand Rapids: Baker, 1983.

_____. *New Paths in Muslim Evangelism.* Grand Rapids: Baker, 1980.

*Phillips, J. B. *The Price of Success.* Wheaton, Ill.: Harold Shaw, 1984.

*_____. *Ring of Truth.* London: Hodder and Stoughton, 1967.

*Pickthall, Mohammed Marmaduke. *The Meaning of the Glorious Quran.* New York: New American Library, 1953.

Pinnock, Clark H. *Biblical Revelation: The Foundation of Christian Theology.* Chicago: Moody, 1971.

_____. *The Scripture Principle.* San Francisco: Harper & Row, 1984.

Punt, Neal. *Unconditional Good News.* Grand Rapids: Eerdmans, 1980.

Qasimi, Ja'far. "The Life of the Prophet." In *Islamic Spirituality.* Edited by Seyyed H. Nasr. Vol. 19 of *World Spirituality.* New York: Crossroad, 1987.

Rahman, Afzalur. *Muhammad, Blessing for Mankind.* London: The Muslim Schools Trust, 1979a.

_____. *Prayer: Its Significance and Benefits.* London: The Muslim Schools Trust, 1979b.

Rahman, Fazlur. *Islam.* Chicago: University of Chicago Press, 1966.

_____. *Islam and Modernity.* Chicago: University of Chicago Press, 1982.

*Randi, James. *The Faith Healers.* Buffalo: Prometheus, 1987.

Rogers, Jack, ed. *Biblical Authority.* Waco: Word, 1977.

Roman, Isidro M. "Mecca Pilgrimage Smuggle Coverup?" *Bulletin Today* (Manila), 7 October 1985:1.

Rosenblatt, Roger. "The Atomic Age." *Time*, 29 July 1985a.

_____. "A Christmas Story." *Time*, 30 December 1985c.

*_____. "The Quality of Mercy Killing." *Time*, 26 August 1985b.

Russell, Bertrand. *The Autobiography of Bertrand Russell.* 1951; reprint. New York: Bantam, 1967.

Ryle, J. C. *Holiness.* 1883; reprint. Grand Rapids: Baker, 1979.

*Schaeffer, Francis A. *True Spirituality.* Wheaton, Ill.: Tyndale, 1971.

Schilling, S. Paul. *God and Human Anguish.* Nashville: Abingdon, 1977.

*Schimmel, Annemarie. *As Through a Veil.* New York: Columbia University Press, 1982.

*_____. *And Muhammad Is His Messenger.* Chapel Hill: The University of North Carolina Press, 1985.

*_____. "Creation and Judgment in the Koran and in Mystico-Poetical Interpretation." In *We Believe in One God.* Edited by Annemarie Schimmel and Abdoldjavad Falaturi. New York: Seabury, 1979,149-177.

*_____. *Mystical Dimensions of Islam.* Chapel Hill: University of North Carolina Press, 1975.

Schimmel, Annemarie, and Abdoldjavad Falaturi, eds. *We Believe in One God.* New York: Seabury, 1979.

Schuon, Frithjof. "The Spiritual Significance of the Substance of the Prophet." In *Islamic Spirituality.* Edited by Seyyed H. Nasr Vol. 19 of *World Spirituality.* New York: Crossroad, 1987, 48-63.

Scott, Waldron. *Bring Forth Justice.* Grand Rapids: Eerdmans, 1980.

*Sheikh, Bilquis. *I Dared to Call Him Father.* Eastbourne, England: Kingsway, 1978.

Skilton, John H. "The Transmission of the Scriptures." In *The Infallible Word.* Edited by N. B. Stonehouse and Paul Wooley. Philadelphia: Presbyterian and Reformed, 1946.

*Smedes, Lewis B. *Forgive and Forget.* San Francisco: Harper & Row, 1984.

_____. *Sex for Christians.* Grand Rapids: Eerdmans, 1976.

Smith, Jane Idleman, and Yvonne Yazbeck Haddad. *The Islamic Understanding of Death and Resurrection.* Albany: State University of New York, 1981.

Smith, Margaret. *An Introduction to Mysticism.* London: Sheldon, 1931.

_____. *Readings from the Mystics of Islam.* London: Sheldon, 1950.

*_____. *The Way of the Mystics.* London: Sheldon, 1976.

*Solzhenitsyn, Alexander. *One Day in the Life of Ivan Denisovich.* Translated by Ralph Parker. New York: New American Library, 1963.

*_____. *A World Split Apart.* New York: Harper & Row, 1978.

Sproul, R. C. "Hath God Said?" In *Can We Trust the Bible?* Edited by Earl D. Radmacher. Wheaton, Ill.: Tyndale, 1979.

Stafford, Tim. "Great Sex: Reclaiming a Christian Sexual Ethic." *Christianity Today* 2 October 1987.

Stott, John R. W. "God on the Gallows." *Christianity Today* 27 January 1987.

*Stowell, Joseph M. *Through the Fire.* Wheaton, Ill.: Victor, 1985.

Subhan, John A. *How a Sufi Found His Lord.* 3rd ed. Lucknow, India: Lucknow Publishing House, 1950.

Swindoll, Charles. "The Temptation of Ministry: Improving Your Reserve." *Leadership* 3 (1985):16-27.

Syrjanen, Seppo. *In Search of Meaning and Identity.* Helsinki, Finland: The Finnish Society for Missiology and Ecumenics, 1984.

Tari, Mel, as told to Cliff Dudley. *Like a Mighty Wind.* Carol Stream, Ill.: Creation House, 1971.

Tippett, Alan R. "Probing Missionary Inadequacies at the Popular Level." *International Review of Missions*, October 1960.

*Tozer, A. W. *The Pursuit of God.* Harrisburg, Pa.: Christian Publications, n.d.

Trimingham, J. Spencer. *The Sufi Orders in Islam.* London: Oxford
University Press, 1971.

Valiuddin, Mir. *Contemplative Disciplines in Sufism.* London: East-West,
1980.

Van Dooren, L. A. T. *Prayer: The Christian's Vital Breath.* Carnforth,
England: Caperwray Hall, n.d.

*Vanauken, Sheldon. *A Severe Mercy.* New York: Bantam, 1977.

_____. *Under the Mercy.* Nashville: Nelson, 1985.

Villiers, Alan. *Sons of Sinbad.* New York: Scribner's, 1940.

Waddy, Charis. *The Muslim Mind.* London: Longman, 1976, (second
edition, 1982).

"The War Within: An Anatomy of Lust." *Leadership* 3 (1985):30-48.

*Watson, David. *Fear No Evil.* Wheaton, Ill.: Harold Shaw, 1984.

Watt, W. Montgomery. *Muhammad, Prophet and Statesman.* London:
Oxford University Press, 1961.

Webber, Robert E. *Worship Is a Verb.* Waco: Word, 1985.

*Wiesel, Elie. *Night.* New York: Avon, 1958.

*_____. *One Generation After.* New York: Avon, 1970.

Williamson, Benedict. *Supernatural Mysticism.* London: Kegan Paul,
Trench, Trubner, 1921.

*Wimber, John, with Kevin Springer. *Power Evangelism.* San Francisco:
Harper & Row, 1986.

Woodbridge, John D. "Why Did Thomas Howard Become a Roman
Catholic: Interview with Thomas Howard." *Christianity Today* 17 May
1985.

*Yancey, Philip. *Disappointment with God.* Grand Rapids: Zondervan, 1988.

*_____. *Where Is God When It Hurts?* Grand Rapids: Zondervan, 1977.

Zwemer, Samuel M. *Christianity the Final Religion.* Grand Rapids:
Eerdmans, 1920a.

_____. *The Glory of the Cross.* London: Marshall, Morgan and Scott, n.d.

*_____. *The Influence of Animism on Islam.* New York: Macmillan, 1920c.

_____. *Islam, A Challenge to Faith.* New York: Student Volunteer
Movement for Foreign Missions, 1907.

_____. *The Moslem Doctrine of God.* New York: American Tract Society,
1905.

*_____. *A Moslem Seeker after God.* New York: Revell, 1920b.

Other fantastic titles available from Gabriel Publishing!

Gabriel
Publishing

Contact us for details on any of these books -
PO Box 1047, 129 Mobilization Dr., Waynesboro, GA 30830
Tel.: (706) 554-1594   Fax: (706) 554-7444
E-mail: gabriel@omlit.om.org

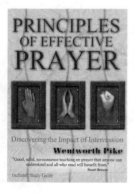

Principles of Effective Prayer
Wentworth Pike
ISBN: 1-884543-65-0

What is prayer? Why pray? Created as a devotional study for individuals or a textbook for groups, *Principles of Effective Prayer* answers these questions and many others. Developed as a class taught at Prairie Bible Institute (Canada), this book will lead you into a life and ministry of effective, God-glorifying prayer!

Also available are great Bibles for personal study or to share the Gospel with a friend! We have large print or compact in different formats and translations! Contact us for information.

101 Ways to Change Your World
Geoff Tunnicliffe
ISBN: 1-884543-47-2

Geoff Tunnicliffe has compiled an invaluable collection of ways to change the world in his newly revised *101 Ways to Change Your World*. In addition to 101 practical ways to put faith into action, Tunnicliffe has also included statistics and resources for individuals desiring to make a difference in God's World.

Street Boy
Fletch Brown
ISBN: 1-884543-64-2

Jaime Jorka, a street boy in the Philippines, lays a challenge before the missionary whose wallet he has stolen - and discovers for himself what Jesus can do. This true-to-life story reveals the plight of street children worldwide and shows that they too can be won to Christ. "The lot of the street children of the world is a guilty secret that needs to be exposed and addressed. This book does it admirably." - Stuart Briscoe

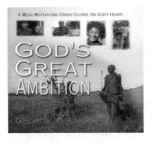

God's Great Ambition
Dan & Dave Davidson
George Verwer
ISBN: 1-884543-69-3

This unique collection of quotes and Scriptures has been designed to motivate thousands of people into action in world missions. George Verwer and the Davidsons are well-known for their ministries of mission mobilization as speakers and writers. Prepare to be blasted out of your comfort zone by this spiritual dynamite!

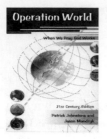

Operation World
21st Century Edition
Patrick Johnstone & Jason Mandryk
ISBN: 1-85078-357-8

The definitive prayer handbook for the church is now available in its 21st Century Edition containing 80% new material! Packed with informative and inspiring fuel for prayer about every country in the world, *Operation World* is essential reading for anyone who wants to make a difference! Over 2,000,000 in print!

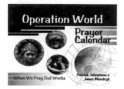

Operation World Prayer Calendar
ISBN: 1-884543-59-6
Spiral-bound desktop perpetual format

Containing clear graphics and useful geographic, cultural, economic and political statistics on 122 countries of the world, the *Operation World Prayer Calendar* is a fantastic tool to help you pray intelligently for the world. Pray for each country for three days and see how God works!

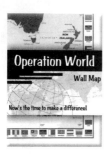

Operation World Wall Map
Laminated or Folded

This beautiful, full-color wall map is a great way to locate the countries each day that you are praying for and build a global picture. Not only an excellent resource for schools, churches and offices but a valuable tool for the home.

Youth & Missions
Leading the Way
Paul Borthwick
ISBN: 1-884543-49-9
1-884543-37-5

In *Youth and Missions*, noted author and missions professor Paul Borthwick has created a practical handbook filled with principles, guidelines and examples of how to help young people grow in their understanding of the world and their role in it. He effectively addresses the great need for younger men and women to rise to the challenge of leadership in the growing leadership vacuum in his book *Leading the Way*.

Dr. Thomas Hale's Tales of Nepal

Living Stones of the Himalayas
(1-884543-35-9)
Don't Let the Goats Eat the Loquat Trees
(1-884543-36-7)
On the Far Side of Liglig Mountain
(1-884543-34-0)

These fascinating accounts of the true-life stories of doctors Tom and Cynthia Hale share everyday and incredible experiences of life with the beguiling character and personalities of the Nepalese people. In sharing these experiences the reader is truly transported to a most enchanting land.